The Illustrated Story of

COPYRIGHT

EDWARD SAMUELS

THOMAS DUNNE BOOKS

ST. MARTIN'S PRESS  NEW YORK

D1272608

This book is designed to provide you with accurate and authoritative information about the history of copyright. However, Professor Samuels is not currently engaged in the practice of law, and this publication is not a substitute for the advice of an attorney. If you require legal or other expert advice, you should seek the services of a competent attorney or other professional.

THOMAS DUNNE BOOKS.
An imprint of St. Martin's Press.

THE ILLUSTRATED STORY OF COPYRIGHT. Copyright © 2000 by Edward Samuels. All rights reserved. Printed in the United States of America. No part of this book may be used or reproduced in any manner whatsoever without written permission except in the case of brief quotations embodied in critical articles or reviews. For information, address St. Martin's Press, 175 Fifth Avenue, New York, N.Y. 10010.

Designed by Michael Mendelsohn at MM Design 2000, Inc.

Production Editor: David Stanford Burr

Library of Congress Cataloging-in-Publication Data

Samuels, Edward B.
    The illustrated story of copyright / Edward Samuels.
        p. cm.
    Includes bibliographical references and index.
    ISBN 0-312-26176-4
        1. Copyright—United States—History. I. Title.

KF2994 .S26 2000
346.7304'82—dc21

First Edition: December 2000

10 9 8 7 6 5 4 3 2 1

Contents

ACKNOWLEDGMENTS

... or, How to Write a Book on Copyright

When I started this book, I assumed that I would write it the same way I've written law review articles. I'd do some research, and then hunker down in my office to create my work in a fairly solitary endeavor, occasionally calling for help from my library liaison or my research assistant. I would send the manuscript to various publishers the same way I send articles out to law reviews, and one of them would agree to publish it.

But that's not the way it works. People started asking questions like "Exactly *who* is the intended audience?" or "A book on law? That's a hard sell." They only wanted to see the two-page synopsis. "Does it matter whether the book is well written or not?" I'd ask, and people would shrug and say, "It's all in the concept."

So, how do you write and publish a book on copyright for a general audience? First, you have to teach at a law school (like New York Law School) that supports scholarship, and that funds your research and expenses with summer research grants. (Thank you, Dean Harry Wellington, Associate Dean Ellen Ryerson, and everyone else.) You have to have creative and diligent research assistants over several years. (Mine were Gila Garber during the research and early writing, Roy Evans during the bulk of the writing, and Susan Harper during the elaborate permissions phase.) You need a library director (in my case, Joyce Saltalamachia) and a professional library liaison (Grace Lee) who get what you need, and sometimes even anticipate your needs, an eager audiovisual magician (Bob Ward), someone to shepherd all the permission checks through the administrative process (Barbara Barnes), and a diligent assistant who happily gets the work done when you need it (Joan Argento). You need faculty colleagues who are sometimes critical, but more often supportive even when they don't have to be. (I have too many helpful colleagues to list them all here, but if you look at the list of faculty at the Web site, www.nyls.edu, just about all of them listed there are the supportive ones.) And you need adjunct professors and lawyers in your field who are willing to read portions of your work and give you meaningful feedback (like Paul Adler, Herbert Jacoby, and Kenneth Norwick, adjuncts at New York Law School; and Eleanor Appelwhaite, Richard Dannay, and Roy Mersky).

Now here comes the crucial part. You must have the good fortune to have once had a student in your evening class who retired as vice president of a major publishing company, and after law school went on to practice copyright at one of the major copyright firms in the country and to teach publishing law as an adjunct at your law school. Get him or her to take you under their wing, in the belief that this book really ought to see the light of day. (My benefactor was Martin Levin.) He'll introduce you to a literary agency that is actually run by copyright lawyers who, when you submit your proposal, ask for the sample chapters you offered, and then ask for more, and then ask to read the whole book before agreeing to represent you. (The agency is McIntosh & Otis, Inc., and the lawyer/agents are Eugene Winick and Sam Pinkus.) Then the agents will find the best publisher, combining the personal support of an editor who takes good care of his authors (Thomas Dunne) and the business of a major publishing house (St. Martin's Press). The editor's assistant (Emily Hopkins—thank you) will chart your book through the vagaries of publication, and a sharp copy editor (Ann Adelman) will improve it.

Getting all of the permissions to use the materials in your book will itself be a full-time job. You had better arrange for a special "half-sabbatical" (a full year teaching half a normal load, and serving on only half the regular number of committees) to clear the time to accomplish the task. While getting all the permissions is a monumental chore, you'll meet (at least over the phone or through mail or e-mail) some of the most interesting people in the world. Because many of them work in copyright-related businesses, they'll be very interested in your project. And many of them, such as the attorneys and plaintiffs in lawsuits, will be able to give you a unique insight into their cases in particular and the vagaries of the law in general. There are too many to name them all here, but I particularly valued my conversations with cartoonists Dan O'Neill, Bion Smalley, and Fred Laswell (check out his Web site at www.uncle-fred.com); photographers Howard Altman, Jon Brenneis, Johan Elbers, John Duke Kisch, Art Rogers, and Felice Frankel (check out her Web site at web.mit.edu/edgerton/felice/felice.html, or track down a copy of her book with George Whitesides, *On the Surface of Things: Images of the Extraordinary in Science,* 1997); and photographer's representative David Vena. Thanks also to Clarence Thorne, with whom I went on several interesting photographic expeditions, and Anita Costello, who created two of the illustrations for this book.

The individuals who administer the various museums, photographic collections, and corporate archives are a special breed of patient collaborators. I cannot name them all, but I particularly valued the assistance of Nancy Adams, Heather Ahlstrom, Whitney Bagnall, Ronald Brashear, Lydia Cisaruk, Vicki Cwiok, Richard Gelbke, Steven Lubar, Ron Mandelbaum, William Massa, Ann Neal, Allen Reuben, Kelly Souder, Kathleen Stocking, Douglas Tarr, Nicole Wells, Justin White, and Ed Whitley.

And to the following people at various corporations and law firms who helped me with various requests for material, thank you. This is not a complete list, and I apologize to any who are left out: Teri Bishop, Jim Cooper, Michelle Evans, Colleen Floyd, Edward Goodman, Tom Harlin, Bernard Helfat, Christopher Holme, Josh Kastorf, Sheila Keady, Peter Nolan, Del Smith Penny, Marybeth Peters, Janet Peterson, Richard Petrocelli, Jeff Pollack, Barbara Rich, Alexander Rogers, Jerry Rosenthal, Scholle Sawyer, Bob Shapiro, Jamie Silverberg, Judith Singer, and all the folks at Wolf/Westside Camera.

Thanks also to Ebay (ebay.com) for allowing me to find many items I couldn't even have imagined finding otherwise—and particularly to the ebay sellers who sold me some of the items pictured in the book: bill, billysgirl2, blue-devil, densha2@aol.com, ihousemom, jfkelly@myhost.com, and walrus 9.

And first, now, and always, to my family for their insights and inspirations: thank you, Marcia, Richard, and Claire.

THE ILLUSTRATED STORY OF COPYRIGHT

Thomas Jefferson Never Saw Anything like This

With every new technology that facilitates the copying or dissemination of creative works—photocopiers, tape recorders, video recorders, and computers—there are people who have predicted the death of copyright. Some of today's cyber-prophets claim that the Internet represents the end of copyright as we know it. You can't regulate the Internet, we're told. The Internet was designed to withstand nuclear attack, we're told. The Internet treats censorship or regulation as a malfunction, or damage to the system, and simply routes around it. There are no boundaries in cyberspace, and no government or entity can possibly enforce property rights there. Two-hundred-year-old systems of copyright and the interests they protect are obsolete.

Well, that assumes that copyright has been standing still for the last two hundred years. Yet hardly anything could be further from the truth. In the past century, copyright has changed dramatically in response to repeated technological revolutions in the way we create and replicate our literary and artistic works.

We'll eventually get to a discussion of the Internet. But first, we'll take a look at how copyright, throughout the twentieth century, has in fact been adapting to the new technologies. In Part One of this book, "Copyright and Technology," we'll focus upon five different technologies, and see what effect each of them has had upon the preexisting law. We'll study (1) the book publishing industry and photocopying, (2) the music and sound recording and radio industries, (3) the movie and television industries, and (4) the computer and computer software industries; only

The machine in the parlor, circa 1890.

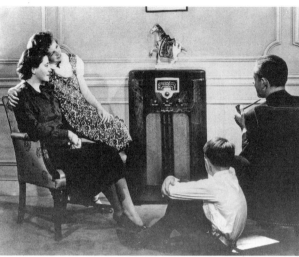

The machine in the parlor, circa 1930.

in the fifth chapter will we be ready to deal with (5) some of the interesting challenges raised by multimedia and the Internet.

Each of these industries to some extent has followed a similar birth and growth pattern: a new technology radically alters the economics of an existing industry, while giving birth to a whole new industry. In the case of books, it was the photocopying machine. In the case of music, it was the invention of the phonograph, and later the development of radio and the inexpensive home tape recorder. In the case of drama, it was the invention of the motion picture, and later television. In the case of computers and computer programs, the new industry altered the economics of a wide range of creative works, from books and paintings to music and video. The explosive growth of the Internet likewise promises (or threatens) to alter every aspect in the creation and distribution of a wide range of works.

In each of these contexts, the law has had a range of responses to the new technologies. In some cases, the new industries have adapted pretty well on their own, without much need for judicial or legislative intervention. In other cases, it was up to the courts to resolve the basic issues by applying or adapting existing copyright principles. In some cases, Congress has had to amend the law to make the old principles fit the

The machine in the parlor, circa 1950.

The machine in the parlor, circa 1990.
Below is my home "entertainment center," which I assume to be typical. On the left are the television with cable box, two VCRs, and some tapes. On the right are a record turntable (remember those?), a receiver, a tape deck, a CD player, and vinyl records. In addition to the 114 records you see here, we have 63 elsewhere, as well as 149 music CDs, 23 prerecorded music tapes, 74 recorded cassettes, 75 prerecorded videotapes, 163 videotapes (originally blank, now full), and 3 portable CD-player/audio tape recorders in other rooms. The two video recorders can be set up to record one program while we watch another, or to tape from one video recorder to another. The audio tape recorder is only a "single-deck" recorder, but one of the portable units has a dual tape deck specifically designed to record from one tape to another.

new technology. Whatever the vehicle for change, the result is that copyright law doesn't look at all as it did 210 years ago, when Congress passed the first copyright act. As we look at the copyright industries today, it's obvious that Thomas Jefferson never saw anything like this!

As we'll see in Part Two, "Copyright Basics," copyright has been constantly changing in other ways as well. In chapter 6, we'll see how copyright has expanded to include not only the new technologies highlighted in Part One but also maps and charts, paintings and sculpture, photographs, architectural works, and even boat hull designs. In chapter 7, we'll see how the general rights of copyright have also been extended over the years, so that today copyright includes not only the right to print maps, charts, and books, but also the right to make derivative works, such as movie adaptations and translations, and to publicly perform or display the ever-expanding range of copyrighted works.

The machine in the parlor, circa 1998.
My computer and accessories of a few years ago, which I assume to be more elaborate than average. The computer is a Power Macintosh, but with an IBM-compatible card installed so that I can run IBM programs as well. Input devices include the keyboard, the mouse, the CD-ROM drive, the miniature video camera (on top of the monitor), the scanner, and an internal card that allows input from TV, video recorder, or video camera. Output devices include the monitor and the two printers. The modem allows communication over the phone lines with any computer connected to the Internet. (All of this is located in a small room previously identified as "the maid's room," now "the computer room.") The associated disks, books, and other computer paraphernalia take up the better part of ten three-foot shelves, and various "retired" paraphernalia take up several boxes stored in just about every spare space.

In chapter 8, we'll explore some of the significant limiting principles of copyright that help to preserve the careful balance between copyright owners and copyright users, including the principle of fair use. Chapter 9 considers some fundamental questions that have not been completely dealt with in the prior chapters: How long does copyright last? What does it take to get a copyright? Who owns the copyright? And what about other legal theories of protection?

What we'll discover is that copyright is more important today than it's ever been. There are several reasons I reach this conclusion. I begin with the initial premise that the fundamental principles of copyright are still sound. We still want to encourage creativity, and we still have no better way of subsidizing it than by giving economic rewards, in the form of property rights, to those who produce the works that we value. If others want to provide entertainment and information for free, or without obtaining exclusive rights in their creations, that's all well and good; but I don't think we want to be limited to the entertainment and information that can be supplied either by kindhearted donors or by nonprofit organizations.

I'm bolstered in my belief by the fact that many of the industries protected by copyright are in fact more successful today than at any other time in U.S. history. The publishing industry has had its ups and downs, but has managed to adapt reasonably well to the new technological environment. The record and movie industries, despite complaints of sales lost to piracy, have generally thrived. The computer software business hardly existed twenty years ago, and now represents a substantial portion of the gross national product. These copyright-based businesses are hardly the ones we would expect to thrive if copyright were in fact obsolete.

Instead of obsolescence, copyright in the United States would seem to be in something of a renascence. Congress and the administration seem to be more sensitive to copyright interests than ever. In part, this is because of our recent realization that the United States is a net exporter of creative works, and that it's in our best interests not only to recognize and promote copyright laws and principles, but to encourage other countries to do likewise. And copyright has become a hot international topic as well. In chapter 10, we'll look at the U.S. law in the broader context of international copyright, and see how in recent years the international agenda has come to dominate the national agenda.

HOW TO READ THIS BOOK

There are several different ways to read this book. If you're going to read it cover to cover, I recommend that you just start with chapter 1 and read away. That way, you'll first get into the technological issues, which are probably the most exciting aspects of copyright today. If you're a traditionalist who likes to "lay the foundation" before getting into some of the more difficult issues, you could choose to read Part Two before Part One. The book is written so that it will make sense whichever part you read first.

I've included lots of cross-references within the book that serve as "hyperlinks" to the parts of the book that discuss other materials. For example, where basic principles are raised in the technology chapters of Part One, you are referred to the appropriate discussion in Part Two. For example, where new technologies are mentioned in or are relevant to the section on Copyright Basics, you are referred to the appropriate discus-

Check out my Web site.

For corrections, updates, and reviews of this book, as well as sound samples, general discussions of interest, and links to other copyright sites, check out my Web site at www.nyls.edu/samuels/copyright.

sion in Part One. So, if you're a younger reader who has been raised on interactive media, you are welcome to read the book like a "Choose Your Own Adventure" story, following the cross-references wherever they take you throughout the book.

No matter how you put it together, I hope you'll come away with an appreciation of what copyright is and how it works. Whether you're involved in the industries or just a consumer of music and disks and radio, motion pictures and television, computers and the Internet, or books and visual art and the performing arts generally, I think you'll find that copyright is a remarkable system that has so far served these industries well.

PART ONE

Copyright and Technology

Printing presses.
A sixteenth-century engraving of a print shop. The pressman at right might be able to "pull the bar" three thousand times in a twelve-hour day.

The first American printing press.
This press was brought to the American colonies and set up at Harvard in 1640 by Stephen Day.

A nineteenth-century rotary printer could print tens of thousands of impressions an hour.

CHAPTER ONE

Books and Other Literary Works

THE PRINTING PRESS—THE FIRST COPYRIGHT TECHNOLOGY

For most of Part One, we're going to be focusing upon twentieth-century technologies. But in order to understand their impact on copyright, we must go back over five hundred years to the first copyright technology, the printing press. The movable type printing press was developed by Johann Gutenberg in Germany around 1440, and introduced to England by William Caxton in the last quarter of the fifteenth century. Prior to that time, it wasn't all that important to think about the rights of authors in books because it was so expensive and time-consuming to produce books that few were in fact duplicated. With the printing press, however, it became possible to reproduce books in multiple copies, by the hundreds or even the thousands.

The Statute of Anne, 1710

In the 1550s, the Stationers' Company was chartered by royal decree, and effectively controlled the printing and dissemination of books throughout England. This arrangement not only served the interest of the crown in regulating the content of books; it also protected the investment of the first company to publish a given book

The early production of books.

In the heyday of the Greek and Roman civilizations, books were generally reproduced for wealthy patrons by scribes or slaves. Atticus, the Roman literary patron, went into the book publishing business, and with his slaves, it is said, he could produce one thousand copies of a small volume in a single day. From about A.D. 500 through 1500, the primary keeper and reproducer of books was the church, using the labor of thousands of monks who were supported primarily by their farms. In the twelfth and thirteenth centuries, universities started getting into the business of producing books, using paid scribes. Around 1440, Gutenberg introduced the movable type printing press to the Western world, an invention that for the first time allowed the efficient mass production of books.

The age of authorship . . .

Prior to the printing press, the concept or appreciation of "authorship" was not well developed. Instead, it was the *owners* of the copies who were more likely to be compensated for the right to reproduce the books.

> Wandering clerics and pious travelers entrusted their manuscript treasures to the monastic and cathedral libraries, which vied for the best-collated versions of sacred texts and received substantial fees for the right to copy them. . . . The age of "authorship" had not yet arrived. When reading a sacred *text,* medieval scholars were quite indifferent to the identity of the author.
>
> —Daniel J. Boorstin

Magic was everywhere . . .

The revolution of the printing press was celebrated by Carl Sagan in his remarkable television series and book *Cosmos:*

> For thousands of years, writing was chiseled into clay and stone, scratched onto wax or bark or leather; painted on bamboo or papyrus or silk—but always one copy at a time and, except for the inscriptions on monuments, always for a tiny readership. Then in China between the second and sixth centuries, paper, ink and printing with carved wooden blocks were all invented, permitting many copies of a work to be made and distributed. It took a thousand years for the idea to catch on in remote and backward Europe. Then, suddenly, books were being printed all over the world. Just before the invention of movable type, around 1450, there were

by effectively eliminating piracy. In addition, as in other countries throughout Europe, authors would petition the crown for the exclusive right to print their books within the country for a set number of years.

In the late seventeenth century, the sentiment against specialized "monopolies" grew, and in 1694, Parliament allowed the old Stationers' Licensing Acts to expire. The publishers argued that they had a "common law" right of exclusivity in the works they published, but such a right was no longer supported by statute. At the beginning of the eighteenth century, they lobbied Parliament to renew the old licensing acts, but Parliament refused. Instead, in 1710, Parliament passed a remarkable statute that for the first time protected the rights of authors rather than publishers of books. It was entitled "An Act for the Encouragement of Learning, by Vesting the Copies of Printed Books in the Authors or Purchasers of such Copies, during the Times therein mentioned."

The new statute represented a careful balancing of interests. On the one hand, the authors' rights were quite extensive, and the remedies for violation of the statute were severe. On the other hand, there were some considerable limitations on the authors' new rights. For one thing, the rights created under the statute lasted no more than twenty-eight years. In addition, the authors had to publicly register their claims of authorship, in order to protect the "many Persons" who "through Ignorance" might otherwise "offend against this Act." Another requirement was that authors registering under the statute had to deliver nine copies of each book to the warehouse keeper designated in the statute, to be made available "for the Use of the Royal Library, the Libraries of the Universities of Oxford and Cambridge, the Libraries of the four Universities in Scotland, the Library of Sion College in London, and the Library commonly called the Library belonging to the Faculty of

Advocates at Edinburgh." Failure to deliver such copies could result in a forfeiture of the value of the printed copies of the books, plus £5 for every copy not so delivered. Quite a public works statute! If authors wanted the rights granted by Parliament, they had to donate books to all the major libraries.

The U.S. Constitution, 1787

Over two hundred years ago, elected representatives gathered at a constitutional convention in Philadelphia to establish a new American government. There were many concerns on the agenda, including the desires "to form a more perfect Union, establish Justice, insure domestic Tranquillity, provide for the common defence, promote the general Welfare, and secure the Blessings of Liberty to ourselves and our Posterity," according to the Preamble to the U.S. Constitution (1787). These framers of our constitution also established a system that was specifically designed "to promote the Progress of Science and useful Arts," by giving Congress the power to grant "to Authors and Inventors the exclusive Right to their respective Writings and Discoveries."

What did these people mean by "the exclusive Right" of "Authors" in their "Writings"?* They were referring to the copyright law they knew from the British system. The premise is amazingly simple, and yet profound. In exchange for the works contributed to society by creative people, as an inducement to get them to create, we grant them special rights in what they create. Basically, we recognize a property right in creative works, and give that right initially to the authors of those works. What the framers of the Constitution envisioned was a system in which we don't have to pay all authors in advance in order to get them to create their works. Instead, we pay them in rights—rights in the very works that they create.

no more than a few tens of thousands of books in all of Europe, all handwritten; about as many as in China in 100 B.C., and a tenth as many as in the Great Library of Alexandria. Fifty years later, around 1500, there were ten million printed books. Learning had become available to anyone who could read. Magic was everywhere.

Statute of Anne, 8 Anne C. 19 (1710).
The date on the statute indicates that it was passed in March 1709. At that time, March 25 was considered the first day of the calendar year. Beginning in 1752, the formal new year was moved back to January 1; dates in the early months of prior years were by convention identified as if they fell under the new calendar. So March 1709 became March 1710.

*Exclusive rights, see p. 166.

Early grants of monopoly.

Many authors received specific grants of monopoly prior to the development of copyright. Many, however, were unable to adequately protect their rights. Cervantes, for example, was able to sell the publishing rights in some of his books for a substantial price. But pirated editions of *Don Quixote* abounded, because Cervantes's publisher only secured the official printing privilege for limited areas. One bold pirate wrote an entire fake sequel.

The "right" in "copy."

Shortly after William Caxton introduced the printing press to England in the fifteenth century, there were more books than there were educated people to read them. Such an imbalance between the supply of and demand for books led to economic disaster for many printers, and pressure to regulate and protect the publishing business. The charter of the Stationers' Company in 1556 granted its members (the leading publishers in London) an officially state-sanctioned monopoly over the printing of books, and provided for the burning of prohibited books and the imprisonment of anyone printing unauthorized books.

Toward the end of the seventeenth century, members of Stationers Hall recognized among themselves the rights in "copy," and agreed that, once one of their members published a particular book, other members would not print copies of the same book. This practice was supported by a series of special licensing acts. However, in 1694, the last of these licensing acts expired, and independent printing businesses began springing up all over England.

Today, these rights include, among other things, the exclusive rights to make and distribute copies of the works—and by "exclusive" right, we mean the right to prevent others from copying and distributing copies—with many limitations that we'll discuss later. If other people come to value an author's work, then they'll be willing to pay the author (or the author's publisher) for copies. Thus, the grant of exclusive rights can represent a source of income to the author, who can sell individual copies of the work; or—and this is important—the author can sell to someone else, such as a publisher, the exclusive right to make and distribute further copies of the work. What we've done is create a property right that the successful author can either exploit directly, or sell to someone else. Just as important, if it turns out that nobody particularly values the author's work, then no one has to pay a dime for it.

In *The Federalist Papers,* James Madison gave pretty much the only official explanation we have of the purpose of this constitutional provision: "The utility of this power will scarcely be questioned. The copyright of authors has been solemnly adjudged, in Great Britain. . . . The public good fully coincides . . . with the claims of individuals."

The First U.S. Copyright Law, 1790

President George Washington addressed a joint session of the First Congress in January 1790. In his speech, he urged the new Congress that "there is nothing which can better deserve your patronage than the promotion of science and literature." He went on: "Whether this desirable object [knowledge] will be best promoted by affording aids to seminaries of learning already established, by the institution of a national university, or by any other expedients, will be well worthy of a place in the deliberations of the legislature."

Congress responded with an address to the president: "We concur with you in the sentiment that . . . the promotion of science and literature will contribute to the security of a free Government; in the progress of our deliberations we shall not lose sight of objects so worthy of our regard."

At the same time, the First Congress had received petitions from several authors asking for the grant of exclusive rights to print their books, and had considered a bill that would generally grant exclusive rights to authors. In response, the House ordered "That a committee be appointed to prepare and bring in a bill or bills, making a general provision for securing to authors and inventors the exclusive right to their respective writings and discoveries." The appointed committee reported back such a bill, and the House and Senate, pursuant to the power granted them under the Constitution, adopted it.

On May 31, 1790, the president signed the first U.S. national copyright law, "An Act for the encouragement of learning." Following the basic structure of its English predecessor, it granted to the authors of "maps, charts,* and books" the exclusive right to "print, reprint, publish or vend" their works for a period of up to twenty-eight years. The penalty for violating such rights was that

> such offender . . . shall forfeit all and every copy . . . of such map, chart, book, or books, and all and every sheet . . . being part of the same . . . to the author or proprietor . . . who shall forthwith destroy the same: And every such offender and offenders shall also forfeit and pay the sum of fifty cents for every sheet which shall be found in his or their possession . . . contrary to the true intent and meaning of this act. . . .

The father of American copyright.
Noah Webster crusaded to obtain copyright protection not only for his successful spelling books and dictionaries, but generally for all authors. Under the Articles of Confederation, he personally traveled around the country to lobby each legislature to pass a copyright statute. He also maintained an active correspondence with many of the drafters of the Constitution, and early members of Congress and the administration, some of whom were authors themselves—including James Madison, George Washington, Thomas Jefferson, and Alexander Hamilton. This engraving is from a Samuel F. B. Morse portrait of Webster. Webster's lobbying efforts continued through 1831, when he successfully argued for an extension of the period of copyright protection. The extension bill was introduced and supported by his son-in-law, William W. Ellsworth, in the House, and his cousin, Daniel Webster, in the Senate.

Webster's *American Spelling Book* of 1783, which eventually sold over 30 million copies, and his *American Dictionary of the English Language*, published in 1838 when he was in his seventies, were instrumental in developing a standard form of English for the new country.

 *Maps and charts, see p. 131.

No man but a blockhead.

No man but a blockhead ever wrote, except for money.

–Samuel Johnson

Freedom of speech.

The First Amendment, passed by Congress in 1789 and ratified by the requisite three-fourths of the states in 1791, provides that "Congress shall make no law . . . abridging the freedom of speech, or of the press."

The embarrassing precursor to the statute.

Some modern critics of the expansion of copyright delight in emphasizing the embarrassing precursor to the Statute of Anne, suggesting that copyright has been forever tainted by the fact that it evolved from what were essentially censorship laws. However, there was a critical gap in protection, from 1694 through 1710, and the new Statute of Anne was not simply an extension of the previous law. Parliament seems not to have been guided by the complaints of the publishers, who in 1709 had lobbied for a return to the old licensing acts. Instead, they were obviously influenced by the pleas of several famous authors for the recognition of rights not of printers, but of authors. (It has been suggested that Joseph Addison and Jonathan Swift were responsible for the 1709 draft of

There were other similarities to the English Statute of Anne, including the requirement that one copy of the work be deposited with the clerk of the local district court, and one copy be delivered to the secretary of state—at the time, Thomas Jefferson—"to be preserved in his office." What a way to build a library! Jefferson must have loved it.

One might have argued that our society would be best served by allowing the printers to print away, whatever they wanted, since obviously democracy required uncensored discourse. Indeed, the First Amendment, almost contemporaneous with the U.S. Constitution and the first copyright act, specifically affirmed freedom of speech and of the press as basic tenets of the new government. And yet, the same lawmakers also saw that freedom of speech didn't mean freedom to "steal" someone else's speech. If we didn't grant some level of protection to authors, then the authors might decide to stop writing, and we would kill the goose that lays the proverbial golden egg.

The granting of property rights in creative works isn't the only way to foster creativity. We could decide not to grant special rights to our writers, and trust that the good ones will be able to get enough money from public or private sources to continue their good work, either by grants or through tangentially related jobs (like playing the organ or waiting on tables). But the primary solution our society has adopted, following the model of England and of the rest of the world, is to support the arts indirectly by creating economic incentives for people to create the works.

It's not a perfect system. There are probably many deserving works that for one reason or another aren't going to succeed in the marketplace. But how many starving artists would toil away at their trade if it weren't for the prospect, however remote, that if they make it big, they will be handsomely rewarded? Since the odds against any creative person's actually succeeding are rather small, we have to make the payoff, if they're successful, sufficiently large to tempt them.

I call it the lottery incentive theory. If you make the jackpot big enough, a lot of people will wait in line to buy tickets, even if the odds against winning are astronomically high. And it's a relatively cheap system, because you don't have to pay off very many of the participants to keep them playing.

THE PHOTOCOPYING MACHINE

Early printing presses were quite laborious to use, allowing a printer to press pages only one sheet at a time. Over the years, the process was mechanized, so that paper was fed automatically on fast rotary presses. Yet the general principles remained remarkably unchanged for about five hundred years. Most printing presses through much of the twentieth century still required the setting of type; the creation of a plate, usually made of metal; and the transfer of ink to paper by pressing the paper against the plate.

the law, but that account has since been discredited.)

One way of putting the Stationers' Licensing Acts into perspective is to realize that they were not the spiritual precursors to copyright at all. However, because the crown and the publishers had found a way to protect the rights of publishers, and the publishers were accordingly willing to pay authors for their creations, a satisfactory solution had been worked out that eased the pressure for a more direct copyright law to protect authors. Once the stopgap measure was removed, the need for the protection of authors' rights came to the fore.

Federal Hall.
The first American federal copyright law was passed by Congress at Federal Hall in New York, the federal capital at the time. This 1798 watercolor by Archibald Robertson shows Federal Hall, with Trinity Church in the background. The House met on the first floor (the "lower chamber") and the Senate on the second floor (the "upper chamber").

State copyright laws under the Articles of Confederation.

Prior to 1789, the United States was governed by the Articles of Confederation. Since those Articles didn't give sufficient power to the central government, Congress had in 1783 passed a resolution recommending that each of the thirteen states adopt a copyright law. All states but Delaware passed such a law.

The preambles in some of the state statutes passed under the Articles of Confederation were even more effusive than their later federal counterpart. For example, in Connecticut's 1783 statute, the preamble stated that

> it is perfectly agreeable to the principles of natural equity and justice, that every author should be secured in receiving the profits that may arise from the sale of his works, and such security may encourage men of learning and genius to publish their writings; which may do honor to their country, and service to mankind.

The Massachusetts statute of the same year served also as a model for New Hampshire and Rhode Island:

> [T]he improvement of knowledge, the progress of civilization, the public weal of the community, and the advancement of human happiness, greatly depend on the efforts of learned and ingenious persons in the various arts and sciences: As the principal encouragement such persons can have to make great and beneficial exertions of this nature, must exist in the legal security of the fruits of their study and industry to themselves; and as such security is one of the natural rights of all men, there being no property more peculiarly a man's own than that which is produced by the labour of his mind.

A new printing process was invented by Chester F. Carlson in 1938. The process, dubbed *xerography* (from *xeros,* the Greek work for "dry," and *graphein,* "to write"), used an electrostatic dry-printing process. The dark parts of a picture are negatively charged with electricity, and the light parts have their charge reduced by exposure to light. A positively charged toner powder sticks to the darker portions, but not the lighter portions; a heater seals the toner on the page. As recently as the 1950s, the process was thought of primarily as an alternative printing process. But in the 1960s, the Xerox Corporation began marketing the machine as a copier. For the first time in history, it became possible cheaply and efficiently to make copies of any type of document—including words and images—without having to go through the laborious process of making a new plate.

The new technology proved to be revolutionary. Businesses adopted it with a vengeance. But what if people used the new technology not only to copy business documents that they had produced but also works created by others, and in which others traditionally owned the exclusive right to make copies? What would happen to copyright in an era of free and easy access to the means of making multiple copies of copyrighted works?

Curiously enough, as it turns out, the photocopying threat to copyright has not been unmanageable for traditional entertainment works. Although books, magazines, and newspapers can be photocopied, the cost and labor of making copies are still great enough that photocopying has not replaced these industries. Although people may occasionally copy passages of their favorite books, poems, or artwork, the result is still a photocopy that is not as convenient to use, frequently not as pleasing to view, and often not much cheaper than buying the original. So, while it might be a technical copyright infringement for people to make copies

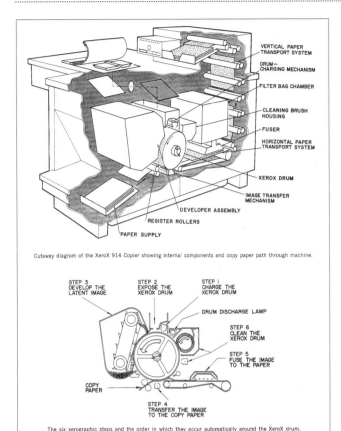

Cutaway diagram of the XeroX 914 Copier showing internal components and copy paper path through machine.

VERTICAL PAPER TRANSPORT SYSTEM
DRUM—CHARGING MECHANISM
FILTER BAG CHAMBER
CLEANING BRUSH HOUSING
FUSER
HORIZONTAL PAPER TRANSPORT SYSTEM
XEROX DRUM
IMAGE TRANSFER MECHANISM
DEVELOPER ASSEMBLY
REGISTER ROLLERS
PAPER SUPPLY

STEP 3 DEVELOP THE LATENT IMAGE
STEP 2 EXPOSE THE XEROX DRUM
STEP I CHARGE THE XEROX DRUM
DRUM DISCHARGE LAMP
STEP 6 CLEAN THE XEROX DRUM
STEP 5 FUSE THE IMAGE TO THE PAPER
COPY PAPER
STEP 4 TRANSFER THE IMAGE TO THE COPY PAPER

The six xerographic steps and the order in which they occur automatically around the XeroX drum.

Photocopiers and document reproduction.

The photocopiers commonly found in offices and classrooms use electric charges to transfer the image of an original document to a plain piece of paper. The document to be copied is placed face down on the platen and illuminated by a lamp. Its image is directed to a negatively charged (electrostatic) metal drum by a series of mirrors. Where light strikes the drum, the charge disappears, so that dark areas remain charged. Next, positively charged particles of toner powder are brushed onto the drum. These stick only to the charged areas. (The first—and second—erase lamps remove the charge on the drum between different copying tasks.) The image on the drum is then transferred to a piece of paper that has been given a negative charge by the transfer charger. A heater is used to seal the toner to the paper, which is why copies are warm when they emerge.

—Microsoft Encarta

Chester Carlson.

While a student at New York Law School in 1938, Chester Carlson, a physicist and former engineer at Bell Labs, invented xerography, the process that revolutionized office work. . . . Carlson, who used his legal training to patent each step of his invention as he developed it, became a wealthy philanthropist and gave away much of the $150 million he earned from his invention.

—Text from lobby display at New York Law School

of these works, the inability of the copyright owners to control photo-copying at the fringes of their markets has not significantly undercut these markets.

The greatest impact of the photocopier has been in the scholarly or research use of works, primarily nonfiction works. Libraries, educators, and businesses have felt a need to reproduce copyrighted works for their serious scholarly and research purposes, and such photocopying has indeed threatened the market in many of these works. The legal frame-work for dealing with these arguably beneficial uses of copyrighted works has been the concept known as "fair use."* The issue, in each of these contexts, is whether a certain amount of photocopying of copyrighted works is a fair use (and therefore not a copyright infringement) or is not a fair use (and therefore an infringement of copyright). As we shall see, the answer, and the method of finding the answer, are very different in the different contexts—library, education, and business uses.

Library Photocopying

Williams & Wilkins Company is a publisher of medical and scientific journals, such as *Journal of Immunology, Medicine,* and *Gastroenterology.* In 1968, the company sued the National Library of Medicine and the National Institutes of Health for copyright infringement of its journals. The Library and the Institutes, U.S. government organizations, did not simply make photocopies of single pages from the medical journals: instead, they had a sophisticated photocopying operation, sometimes referred to as a "factory type of photocopying," that supplied bound pho-tocopies of articles from any of the journals in their collection to doc-tors and researchers throughout the country.

The case pitted two worthy causes against each other. On the side of the publisher, Williams & Wilkins argued that such massive photo-copying clearly violated its copyright, which granted it the exclusive right to make copies of its works. Such massive photocopying also threatened to undercut subscriptions to its journals. Most of its journals had rela-tively limited subscription bases of only a few thousand doctors, researchers, and libraries throughout the country, and so the cost of each subscription had to be fairly high in order to cover the costs of publica-tion. If doctors figured out that they didn't have to subscribe to the jour-

*Fair use, see p. 190.

The National Institutes of Health.
The NIH is not exactly a small operation. This aerial photo shows the sprawling NIH complex in Bethesda, Maryland. The arrow points to a square building, the National Library of Medicine.

nals, but could get copies of desired articles from the government practically for free, then they might balk at continuing their expensive subscriptions. To allow massive photocopying in the name of science was not only unfair; it could have the effect of putting the publishers out of business.

On the other side, the government argued that it was absolutely essential to the scientific and medical communities that vital information be available to researchers in their fields, and that photocopying of individual articles was necessary to fulfilling the missions of the Library and the Institutes. They claimed that their actions were protected by the fair use doctrine. Indeed, in 1935, library and publishing representatives had entered into an informal understanding that "single photographic reproductions" of copyrighted works for scholars "in lieu of loan of such publication or in place of manual transcription and solely for purposes of research," and without any profit to the library, was allowed. Of course, that was before the advent of the modern photocopying machine. Yet the Library and Institutes insisted that they had internal guidelines that limited photocopying to individual requests for scholarly and research purposes, and that protected against abuse of the privilege. Indeed, most of the journals in their collections were published by nonprofit medical

The cautious court opinion.

First, plaintiff has not in our view shown, and there is inadequate reason to believe, that it is being or will be harmed substantially by these specific practices of NIH and NLM; second, we are convinced that medicine and medical research will be injured by holding these particular practices to be an infringement; and, third, since the problem of accommodating the interests of science with those of the publishers (and authors) calls fundamentally for legislative solution or guidance, which has not yet been given, we should not, during the period before congressional action is forthcoming, place such a risk of harm upon science and medicine.

– *Williams & Wilkins Co. v. U.S.,*
opinion of the Court of Claims

societies (as opposed to Williams & Wilkins, one of the few private publishers for profit), or the individual authors had contributed their articles to the journals on a nonprofit basis.

At the time of the case, "fair use" was a judge-made doctrine that provided something of an escape valve to what might otherwise be a harsh application of the copyright standards. In certain circumstances, a technical violation of copyright could be excused on public policy grounds. The government argued that social policy favored open access to information, and that the publishers could not in fact show that they were actually harmed by the photocopying, or demonstrate that subscriptions were being canceled because of the Library and Institutes' photocopying practices.

In response, Williams & Wilkins claimed that it was not trying to stop scientific research, but only to obtain a fair return for its contribution. It offered to authorize the government to make photocopies at the nominal cost of 2 cents per photocopied page, a modest fee compared to the other costs of photocopiers, supplies, and labor. The government, however, refused the offer. Other libraries, through the Association of Research Libraries and the American Library Association, voted to support the National Library of Medicine and the Institutes. It was clear that this was not simply a lawsuit against two government entities, but the test case that would help to define photocopying practices throughout the library community.

The case was brought in the Court of Claims, the exclusive court for claims against the United States, and assigned for trial to Commissioner James Davis. At the trial, Davis found in favor of Williams & Wilkins. On appeal, the case was reversed by the Court of Claims in a 4–3 vote. The majority held that the photocopying qualified for fair use, and the dissent characterized that decision as the "Dred Scott decision of copyright law." On appeal from that decision, the U.S. Supreme Court split evenly 4 to 4, with one justice not participating. The effect of the Supreme Court split was to affirm the Court of Claims decision in favor of fair use. So, while all of the judges who participated in the decision of the case had split 8 to 8, the decision was a squeaker in favor of fair use.

The case was not the last word on the subject. Even the Court of Claims decision had pointed out that Congress was already considering the matter in its long-term revision of the Copyright Act. Their awareness of the issue heightened by the suit, the libraries lobbied vigorously for a broad library exemption to copyright to allow for photocopying of works in their collections. Although librarians did not get the blanket exemption they had hoped for, they did get a specific though complicated section that, at least in limited contexts, allowed for photocopying by public libraries and archives.

The new provision, section 108 of the Copyright Act of 1976, has several main features. First, it limits the exception to libraries and archives that make their collections open to the public. Next, it limits copying to relatively small portions of works, or to copies that are made "solely for purposes of preservation or security," or "solely for the purpose of replacement of a copy . . . that is damaged, deteriorating, lost, or stolen," or for copies that are made for researchers "if the library or archives has

Cartoons by Bion Smalley.

"It's the new Copyright Compliance Center. We used to call it a library."

first determined, on the basis of a reasonable investigation, that a copy . . . of the copyrighted work cannot be obtained at a fair price." The section also allows a library to provide photocopying machines for the unsupervised use of its patrons, so long as the "equipment displays a notice that the making of a copy may be subject to the copyright law."

The balance that was struck allows for "the isolated and unrelated reproduction" of single copies, but, in the language of the statute, does not extend to "the related or concerted reproduction or distribution of multiple copies or phonorecords of the same material, whether made on one occasion or over a period of time, and whether intended for aggregate use by one or more individuals or for separate use by the individual members of a group." Thus, a library isn't supposed to fulfill copy requests by a patron for chapter one one day, chapter two the next day, and so on, with the effect that the patron copies more than is otherwise allowed under the statute. Similarly, a library isn't supposed to fulfill the requests of, let's say, twenty students, each of whom was instructed by a professor to have a copy made.

The debate in Congress centered upon the relationship between copyright and the emerging interlibrary loan system, which Congress wanted to foster. In response to fears that copyright might inhibit development of that system, Congress added the proviso that "nothing in this clause prevents a library or archives from participating in interlibrary arrangements that do not have, as their purpose or effect, that the library or archives receiving such copies or phonorecords for distribution does so in such aggregate quantities as to substitute for a subscription to or purchase of such works." This language was not very helpful, since it really didn't tell the librarians when an interlibrary loan system had the "purpose" or "effect" of substituting for a subscription.

Congress delegated the issue to a specially created National Commission on New Technological Uses of Copyrighted Works (CONTU), which came up with the suggestion that requests within any calendar year for six or more copies of articles from the same periodical or book constituted a "substitute" for a subscription to the periodical or purchase of the book, so that libraries requesting six or more copies through an interlibrary loan system should purchase their own subscription or book. These guidelines represented a rare attempt to provide a "bright line" rule that everyone could understand and apply. However, the guidelines came too late to include them in the 1976 Act. Instead, the conference committee simply cited them approvingly, stating that they considered the guidelines "to be a workable and fair interpretation of the intent" of the statute.

So, are the guidelines law or not? They're not part of the statute, but buried in the legislative history. What we have here is a commendable attempt to draw a bright line, though maybe not as brightly drawn as the parties may have desired.

In any event, we now have a legislative resolution of the library photocopying issue, and one that the parties have apparently learned to live with. The solution has not been left to the vagaries of case law development, but instead has been dictated by Congress in the statute itself. In the recent Digital Millennium Copyright Act* of 1998, Congress approved a few minor changes in the library photocopying section, thus indicating that, by and large, the section has worked well. The act, for example, was amended to allow the making of up to three copies of a work to replace a damaged, deteriorating, lost, or stolen copy; and an additional exception was added, allowing such copies "if the existing format in which the work is stored has become obsolete." In the digital age, a work that is stored in a digital or other form that can only be read by obsolete equipment is as good as lost or stolen.

Scholarly and Classroom Educational Photocopying

Another photocopying scenario that raised copyright concerns was the fairly rampant photocopying of copyrighted works for classroom distribution in schools and institutions of higher learning. In this context, Congress in 1976 chose not to pass a specific exemption, as in the case of library photocopying, but instead to rely upon the general principle of fair use.† Rather than leaving the doctrine entirely to judicial development, however, Congress for the first time codified the doctrine in section 107 of the new statute.

The one specific reference to the educational environment was the addition, fairly late in the legislative process, of the parenthetical language "allowing fair use for teaching (including multiple copies for classroom use)." The House Report explaining section 107 stated that the codification of fair use was "intended to restate the present judicial doctrine of fair use, not to change, narrow, or enlarge it in any way." Yet the new

*Digital Millennium Copyright Act, see p. 112.
†Fair use, see p. 190.

A process of accretion.

The specific working of section 107 as it now stands is the result of a process of accretion, resulting from the long controversy over the related problems of fair use and the reproduction (mostly by photocopying) of copyrighted material for educational and scholarly purposes. For example, the reference to fair use "by reproduction in copies or phonorecords or by any other means" is mainly intended to make clear that the doctrine has as much application to photocopying and taping as to older forms of use; it is not intended to give these kinds of reproduction any special status under the fair use provision or to sanction any reproduction beyond the normal and reasonable limits of fair use. Similarly, the newly-added reference to "multiple copies for classroom use" is a recognition that, under the proper circumstances of fairness, the doctrine can be applied to reproduction of multiple copies for the members of a class.

— House Report to the 1976
    Copyright Act

language, making clear what was not clear before, certainly had the effect of enlarging fair use to include things that were not obviously included before.

At the urging of Congressman Robert Kastenmeier and other members of the Judiciary subcommittee, several concerned organizations conducted talks in 1975 to develop "guidelines" on the use of classroom copying in not-for-profit educational institutions. These organizations came up with a set of guidelines for determining the "minimum standards of educational fair use." The guidelines allowed teachers to make copies of works for their own research purposes, at least up to a chapter from a book or an article from a magazine. The proposed scope of fair use for multiple copying for classroom use, however, was hemmed in by several key concepts. Multiple copies for classroom use were allowed if they met the tests of "brevity" (never more than twenty-five hundred words, and frequently no more than one thousand words), "spontaneity" (copying not to be repeated from term to term), and "cumulative effect" (generally no more than nine instances of multiple copying per course per term, with further limits on the number of works by any particular author).

Much as it had in the case of the guidelines for library photocopying discussed above, the House committee reported that it believed "the guidelines are a reasonable interpretation of the minimum standards of fair use." The committee endorsement did not, however, have the status of law. Several organizations representing higher education, including the American Association of University Professors, denounced the guidelines, complaining that the "minimum" amount of allowed copying would become the norm, and thus hamper the educational process. So, yet again, what started out as an attempt to provide "bright line" rules that could be easily followed ended up merely complicating the issue. Were the guidelines applicable or weren't they?

A test case was brought against New York University and several of its professors; and many of us in the teaching profession hoped that the result in that case would help to clarify the scope of fair use in the educational context. Alan Latman, who had represented Williams & Wilkins in its suit against the government and was the author of a major study on fair use for Congress, taught at the NYU School of Law (affiliated with New York University, not to be confused with New York Law School, founded in 1891, where I teach), and many of us thought that his involvement would assure a meaningful airing of the issues and a model for the rest of us to follow. Instead, the university settled the case in 1983 by essentially agreeing to instruct its professors to either follow the guidelines or obtain permission from copyright owners. Any professor who exceeded the guidelines and nonetheless wanted to make photocopies would have to get a determination by the university's legal counsel that the copying was permitted under copyright. In the absence of such a determination, "no defense or indemnification by the University shall be provided to a faculty member whose photocopying gives rise to a claim of copyright infringement."

This was arguably a brilliant move by the university. With the settlement, they got off the hook on copyright liability, and left the primary risk upon the individual professors. The net result, at least at NYU, was that guidelines that were specifically designed to be the minimum had effectively become the maximum. The settlement was not binding on teachers at other institutions, but it was also not exactly a victory for the educational community. If NYU wouldn't stand by the copying of its professors, were other universities likely to do so?

To this day, there has not been a definitive resolution of the issue in the educational setting, beyond the vague standards embodied in section 107 and the guidelines. Such a broadly drafted law, however, leaves most of the hard decision making to the courts as they decide individual cases, or to the teachers who must decide on their own just how much photocopying they think is appropriate under the circumstances.

Photocopying in the Commercial Setting

Test cases were also brought against some of the "copy shops" around universities. In 1991, a federal court in New York held that Kinko's Graphics Corporation was liable for systematically copying works for classroom use by students, including excerpts constituting as much as 25

The Copyright Clearance Center.
The working of the Copyright Clearance Center is described in the district court opinion in the Texaco case as follows:

The CCC is a nonprofit, central clearing-house established in 1977 by publishers, authors and photocopy users which, as agent for publishers, grants blanket advance permission for a fee to photocopy copyrighted material registered with CCC, and forwards the fees collected to copyright owners, net of service charge. . . . As of 1990, approximately 8,000 domestic and foreign publishers had registered approximately 1.5 million publications with CCC.

Currently, CCC offers two principal services for obtaining advance permission to photocopy copyrighted material that publishers have registered with the CCC. The first method, inaugurated in 1978, is called the Transactional Reporting Service ("TRS"). TRS provides photocopy users with blanket permission to photocopy from any CCC-registered publication, provided the user subsequently reports the making of the photocopy and pays the fees required by the copyright owner. The fee is printed on the first page of each article. The fee for each copy of an article in Catalysis [for example] has been $2 from 1978 through 1982 and $3 thereafter. . . .

Some major corporate users objected to the administrative costs of training personnel and setting up record-keeping necessary for full compliance with TRS. . . . In response, in 1983, CCC inaugurated a second service for obtaining advance permission to photocopy that eliminated the TRS's reporting require-

percent or more of the copyrighted works. In 1996, a federal appeals court reached a similar result in a suit against Michigan Document Services, Inc., for systematically making copies for use by University of Michigan students—including copies that represented up to 30 percent of copyrighted books. As a result of such cases, companies like Kinko's now offer an additional service to university professors and their students: they offer to obtain permissions for copies used in "course packs" prepared for the students.

Another specific target for copyright liability has been the large corporations that account for a sizable amount of the photocopying taking place across the country. In 1977, partly in response to congressional suggestions in the 1976 legislative process, publishers, authors, and photocopy users formed the Copyright Clearance Center (the CCC), an organization that, for a fee, grants blanket permission to copy works published by participating publishers (generally scientific and other scholarly journals). Payments are made in one of several ways: participants may simply agree to keep track of the photocopying they do, and send the CCC the fees printed in the journals (usually a few dollars). Alternatively, users can choose the Annual Authorization Service, by which they pay a blanket license fee based upon a survey of the amount of copying they do. Or users can pay a lump sum for access to all of the works in the CCC repertoire, the fee determined by a formula based upon the type and size of the business.

Over nine thousand licensed users participate in the CCC, including major corporations, government agencies, law firms, libraries, academic institutions, copy shops, and bookstores. Fees collected by the CCC are distributed among hundreds of thousands of authors, represented by over ninety-six hundred publishers, with over 1.75 million works. Illustrating how the Internet[*]

*Internet, see p. 101.

can promote as well as threaten copyright interests, the CCC maintains a Web site, and services its subscribers on-line through the Internet (at http://www.copyright.com).

Copyright enforcement requires a stick to accompany the carrot. One of the major corporations that resisted the licensing policies of the Copyright Clearance Center was Texaco, Inc. All other major oil companies participated in the system, but Texaco claimed that its use of photocopied materials was fair use, and refused to pay the fees. Texaco's argument was rejected by the courts, in large part precisely because their claims would undercut the CCC's ability to get the cooperation of users of copyrighted works. After losing in the courts, Texaco ultimately settled by agreeing to pay "a seven-figure amount" in damages, and to subscribe to the CCC.

ments. This was the Annual Authorization Service ("AAS"). . . . Under the AAS, the corporate user is granted a blanket annual license to make photocopies for internal use of any copyrighted material contained in any of the journals and books registered with the CCC. The annual license fee is determined on the basis of a limited photocopying survey, factored by the licensee's employee population and the copyright fees for the journals regularly copied by that user. . . .

The case was affirmed by the appellate court, on similar reasoning.

Casual Photocopying

What we have not addressed here is the proper fair use outcome in the millions of cases where individuals "casually" or "privately" photocopy works in their own homes, or by using commercially available photocopying machines or services for their own private purposes. Some commentators have observed that no court of law has ever held such casual or private photocopying to be an infringement of copyright, and so argue that there is, in effect, a "home" use or "private" use exemption to copyright. However, Congress and the courts generally have been more circumspect in their analysis, and have avoided stating that such home or private photocopying automatically qualifies for fair use. In adopting the language of the 1976 amendment that considers "whether such use is of a commercial nature or is for non-profit educational purposes," Congress made the commercial or noncommercial nature of the copying one factor—but not the only factor—in determining fair use. And while casual or private copying may not be commercial, it is also not always for "educational" purposes.

The most that can be said is that courts have simply not addressed the issue of whether casual or private or home photocopying is gener-

Cooperative ingenuity.

Again, quoting from the district court opinion in the Texaco case:

> [P]rivate cooperative ingenuity has found practical solutions to what had seemed unsurmountable problems. Texaco can no longer make the same claims as were successfully advanced by the NIH to the Court of Claims in 1973. A finding that such unauthorized copying is an infringement would no longer impede the progress of science. Texaco could conveniently, and without undue administrative burden, retain the benefits of photocopying at will, simply by complying with one of the CCC's licensing systems.
>
> The availability of a TRS or AAS license from the CCC renders moot the argument that so influenced *Williams & Wilkins* that a finding of infringement would harm science. The acceptance and use of CCC services by large research-oriented business corporations, including eleven major petroleum companies, undermines Texaco's reliance on the contention that unauthorized photocopying is customary and reasonable in private industrial research laboratories.

ally within the fair use exception to copyright. The reason they have not done so is that copyright owners generally don't sue for private photocopying because they simply never hear about it, or because they realize it would be pointless to sue individuals for such private copying. So when people ask me whether it is okay for them to make private photocopies of copyrighted works, I tell them that it is technically an infringement of copyright to make an unauthorized copy of a copyrighted work, but that there is at least a plausible fair use argument in most contexts, and their risk of being sued for such activity is minimal.

In the following chapters, we'll come back to the issue of "home" copying in other contexts—particularly audio and video taping.*

CONCLUSION

So, what happens when the technology of the fifteenth century meets the technology of the twentieth century? We don't have to just throw up our hands and say, "It can't work!" Instead, we've seen a full range of responses for dealing with the problem. Make major corporate users of the copyrighted works liable, and private arrangements can be set up to license the uses at a reasonable fee. Provide broad exemptions for particularly worthwhile uses, such as library photocopying, but keep such exemptions within bounds. And allow for some uses, such as scholarly and educational ones, by a broad application of fair use that is sensitive to the nuances of individual settings. In some contexts, such as home photocopying, the answer may remain ambiguous. But for the most part, it appears, solutions can be worked out, at least in the important contexts.

*Home audio taping, see p. 49; home video taping, p. 66.

CHAPTER TWO

Music and Sound Recordings

THE MUSIC BUSINESS

The first U.S. copyright law was passed in the very first Congress in 1790. But that law protected only "maps, charts, and books." It included books,* because that's what copyright law traditionally covered, and that's what the politicians were most familiar with; and it included maps and charts,† because it was important to a young, largely uncharted country to encourage the likes of Lewis and Clark in recording their expeditions of discovery.

But the new law said nothing about music. Maybe this omission wasn't all that surprising, considering that there wasn't a lot of original American music at the time. There were religious songs, but they were largely imported; and there were Revolutionary War songs, but as often as not they consisted of colonial lyrics patched onto English melodies, like "God Save the Thirteen Colonies" sung to the tune of "God Save the King," or "Free America" sung to the tune of "The British Grenadiers." Even "The Star-Spangled Banner" was Francis Scott Key's 1814 poem set to the tune of "To Anacreon in Heaven," an old English drinking song.

In 1831, Congress finally added music to the types of works eligible for federal copyright. But composers

The special nature of music.

The music publishers of the 19th century worked in a society that used and regarded music in a very special way. . . . To identify the special nature of music in that society, we can begin by recognizing that in order to have any music at all a century ago, either of two conditions had to be met: either people had to make it themselves, or they had to come within earshot of others making it. In this respect, the people of the 19th century differed in no way from their ancestors of the 18th, 16th, or 14th centuries, or indeed of any other period of historical time. They differ only from us.

This society whose members had to make music in order to have it at all, needed and used the sets of directions for making music that the publishers provided. The 19th-century publishers were primarily printers, printers of multiple copies of musical scores, sets of directions for making music set down by composers, engraved, printed, and sold by publishers.

–Richard French

*Books, see p. 11.
†Maps, see p. 131.

Foster's poverty.

It's probably unfair to suggest that Foster's poverty was caused by any "especial malignancy" on the part of others or of the law. After his early successes, he was able to make contracts to receive as much as two cents for each copy of his sheet music sold.

> If he found it difficult to make a bare living in his later years, one cause was the fact that out of his last hundred songs only one . . . was a hit. His average yearly income, during his comparatively prosperous years, was about seventeen hundred dollars. Today, as a double-A member of A.S.C.A.P. (which, of course, he would be), he would receive something more than ten times that sum. But that is idle speculation. We are talking of 1860, not 1946.
>
> —Deems Taylor

still weren't given the right to prevent others from *performing* their works, either for profit or otherwise. Throughout the nineteenth century, the composer's rights basically covered only the publication of sheet music. Many composers of the day were simply unable to cash in on the popularity of songs that were sung by practically everyone across the country. Stephen Foster, who wrote works "so essentially American that they are regarded as folk music," died virtually penniless in 1864.

By the 1890s, the publishing of sheet music finally came into its own. Some of the largest music publishers of the twentieth century, many of them setting up shop on "Tin Pan Alley" in New York, were formed by riding the coattails of popular composers of the day. The most successful work of the 1890s, "After the Ball," by Charles Harris, was popularized at the Chicago World's Fair, and sold over 2 million sheet music copies. In 1907, "School Days," by Gus Edwards, sold over 3 million copies.

But this method of doing business was doomed as a result of a technological development that had taken place back in 1877. Thomas Edison instructed his assis-

Tin Pan Alley, circa 1914.

Charles K. Harris's hit (1892), published by the music company he founded.

tant, John Kreusi, to work on a new invention, the phonograph machine. By the end of that year, Edison spoke his first immortal words to be mechanically recorded: "Mary Had a Little Lamb." Edison demonstrated his new machine for the editors of *Scientific American* magazine, and the world marveled.

With hindsight, the invention seems remarkably simple. The user spoke into a small horn, which collected the sound wave, while turning a crank to rotate a cylindrical tinfoil phonograph. A vibrating stylus etched a pattern onto the foil. When a needle, attached to a large amplification horn, was later pulled through the groove of the tinfoil by turning the crank of the phonograph, the vibrations reproduced the sounds originally spoken into the device.

Because of the crude nature of the technology, early recording favored "vocal bellowers and booming brass." The process was totally mechanical—there was no electricity involved. It took many years and many refinements, primarily electronic, before the phonograph developed into a machine capable of faithfully reproducing sound. But the world of music would never be the same.

Piano Rolls and Records:
A Congressional Compromise

How did the law respond to this new invention? Curiously, the case that presented the legal issues did not directly involve the phonograph. Instead, the test case involved the use of paper rolls to record and reproduce piano music. The player piano was invented by Henri Fourneaux of France, and publicly exhibited at the Philadelphia Centennial Exposition in 1876. It allowed for the recording of piano music by accomplished pianists, whose performances were recorded as holes punched into rolls of paper, which could then

A banner day for Edison.
April 18, 1878, was a banner day for Edison. In Washington, D.C., to address a meeting of the Academy of Sciences, Edison was first whisked off to the studio of Mathew Brady for this photograph (above), which shows him demonstrating his phonograph with his host, Uriah Painter (correspondent for the *Philadelphia Inquirer*), and his assistant/collaborator, Charles Batchelor. Edison then visited Joseph Henry, president of the Academy (see p. 98), and attended the Academy meeting, where Edison and Batchelor showed off the new invention. As Neil Baldwin explained, later that evening Edison and Batchelor visited President Rutherford B. Hayes for "a private phonograph session. They ended up staying past three in the morning, because the President, in his enthusiasm, awakened his wife so that she, too, could experience this marvelous machine."

How do you make a piano roll?

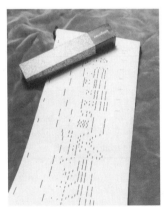

An Aeolian piano roll:
"Eastside, Westside."

be played back in player pianos to reproduce the original performances. In their day, they actually sounded a lot better than phonographs, because the music they reproduced was performed right on the piano, with all the tonal quality of a live performance. By 1902, there were about seventy-five thousand player pianos in the United States, and over one million piano rolls were sold.

Here's how the case ultimately came before the U.S. Supreme Court. In 1897, a man by the name of Adam Geibel wrote two songs—"Little Cotton Dolly" and "Kentucky Babe." Geibel sold the copyright in his songs to the White-Smith Music Company, which published the original sheet music.

The Apollo Company was in the business of manufacturing player piano rolls. When Apollo made perforated music rolls that would play "Little Cotton Dolly" and "Kentucky Babe," it did so without White-Smith's permission or the payment of any royalties. Not surprisingly, the White-Smith Company sued Apollo for copyright infringement. The case was ultimately appealed to the U.S. Supreme Court, which in 1908 rendered a rather incredible interpretation of the existing law.

The Supreme Court decided that Apollo's piano rolls did not infringe White-Smith's copyright in the two musical works. The decision had immediate impact upon music composers and the infant phonograph industry. By 1908, when the Supreme Court rendered its decision, the Columbia Graphophone Co. and the Victor Talking Machine Co. had begun building up considerable repertoires of phonograph recordings by such great artists as Enrico Caruso and other Metropolitan Opera stars. Under the White-Smith holding, the record producers didn't have to pay anything for their use of the music that was copyrighted by others!

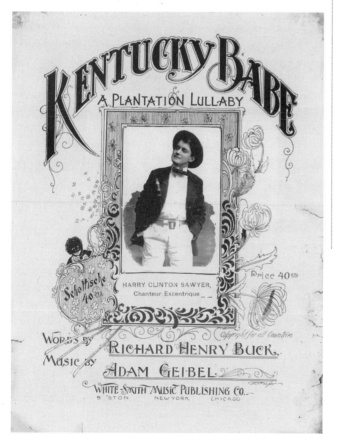

Player pianos.

George Gershwin, for example, made marvelously rich-sounding piano rolls that still represent the authoritative version of many of his works. Indeed, Gershwin learned to play the piano as a child by following the keys on a player piano. The liner notes to *Gershwin Plays Gershwin: The Piano Rolls* (1993) explain:

> The player piano was a central force in American musical life between 1900 and 1930. Referred to variously as automatic pianos, pianolas and reproducing pianos, players of all types were found not only in penny arcades, but in homes, concert halls, restaurants, saloons, stores—virtually anywhere music was heard. Player pianos are normal acoustic pianos except that an internal piano-playing mechanism works as a computer using air pressure instead of electrical energy. The paper piano rolls are the "software" used to activate the notes to play. A punched hole in a paper piano roll causes a corresponding note to play as it goes across a "reader"; a five-note chord has five perforations, and so on. Air pressure in player pianos is established by foot-pumping the bellows to exhaust the air. In later models, the bellows were motor-driven.

"Kentucky Babe."

The song is an example of a popular style of songs stereotyping African Americans that, by today's standards, is embarrassing.

The Sears, Roebuck catalogue of 1908—the very year the White-Smith case was decided. The top half of the page shows the Columbia P style records, along with the "talking machine" of the Edison design that played the cylinders shown. The bottom half shows the F H Harvard machine, based upon the Berliner design that played flat records. On the right, the advertisement announces that Sears has contracted to purchase over 1 million records, fifty thousand per month, to make the "standard size wax cylinder records" available in unprecedented numbers and at unprecedented low prices.

"Singing into the horn."

In less than a score of years Caruso established the financial security of the Victor company and the Metropolitan. He gave respectability to recording. Before his time the artists were a little sheepish about singing into the horn [right], somewhat as the "legitimate" actors were at baring their emotions before the primitive movie cameras.

—Francis Robinson.

The drawing is a self-portrait by Caruso, showing him recording in the days before microphones.

CARICATURE OF CARUSO MAKING A RECORD
Drawn by himself

The response by Congress was swift. For several years, Congress had been considering a major revision of copyright. A 1906 bill would have granted to music composers the very right that the Supreme Court said was not already there—the exclusive right to make "any mechanical device by which music may be reproduced to the ear." However, there were some embarrassing complications that were raised by the White-Smith case. The legal expenses of the plaintiff copyright owner were paid by the Aeolian Company, itself a "pioneer" in the piano roll business.

Now, why would a piano roll company sponsor a lawsuit to establish the rights of copyright owners against piano roll companies? Aeolian was just beginning to make a substantial capital investment in its manufacturing plants, and, as a prudent company, the one thing it didn't want was uncertainty about its rights to make piano rolls. The company wanted a definitive ruling on the subject, and so it agreed to pay for the litigation. In exchange, Aeolian was able to make an advantageous bargain with many of the music publishers of the day. The music publishers formed a new organization, known as the Music Publishers' Association, and the Association agreed that, if the copyright owners won the White-Smith case, they would grant to Aeolian, and only to Aeolian, the right to make mechanical reproductions of their music. So, in effect, Aeolian would win either way. If the copyright owners won, Aeolian would get by contract the exclusive right to create mechanical reproductions, edging out all its competitors. As it turned out, the copyright owners lost, and so Aeolian got the right, although not an exclusive right, to make its mechanical reproductions for free.

This sounded to the congressional committee like collusion, or an attempted monopoly, which was not desirable. In the hearings, committee members were relentless in their questioning of attorney Nathan Burkan, who had represented the Music Publishers' Association, about the possibility that a company like Aeolian might obtain a monopoly in the manufacture of piano rolls or records by buying up the composers' exclusive rights.

What's a copy?

"What is meant by a copy?" the Supreme Court asked in the *White-Smith v. Apollo* case. "Piano rolls are parts of a machine which, when duly applied and properly operated in connection with the mechanism to which they are adapted, produce musical tones in harmonious combination. But we cannot think that they are copies within the meaning of the copyright act." The Court emphasized that

> even those skilled in the making of these rolls are unable to read them as musical compositions, as those in staff notations are read by the performer.
>
> . . . [T]hey are not intended to be read as an ordinary piece of sheet music, which, to those skilled in the art, conveys, by reading, in playing or singing, definite impressions of the melody.

This analysis has since been totally overturned by Congress.

Types of records we can get with the compulsory license. Above, the Manchesters singing some Beatles hits, along with other classics like "Shortening Bread" and "My Bonnie Lies over the Ocean."

"Beattle" Mash?
The notes on the back of the album introduce "The Liverpool Moptops—these four young men, who with a group of excellent musicians, have adopted the style of BEAT-LING, the hottest craze in show business on either side of the Atlantic." Under American copyright law, the Beatles could not prevent such a record, which contains some Lennon-McCartney hits along with other works presumably written for the Liverpool Kids, so long as the group paid their compulsory licensing fees. Apple has objected strongly, however, to the unauthorized use of the word "Beatles" (or any variation) to sell such records.

The Ripoffs? Enough said.

The novel compromise ultimately adopted by Congress in 1909 was a special system of compensation that has come to be known as a *compulsory license.* On the one hand, the White-Smith case was overruled by Congress, and composers were granted the exclusive right to make mechanical reproductions of their music. On the other hand, this exclusive right was severely limited. Under the new law, composers could choose whether or not to allow recordings to be made of their works, and could charge whatever the market would bear for the first such recording. But thereafter, any other record companies would be allowed to make their own recordings of the song by paying a fixed rate, set in the statute at 2 cents per copy. So, if I wrote a song, I could license Eddie Cantor to record it for whatever I could get him to pay. But after that first recording, if Ethel Merman or Frank Sinatra or Bette Midler wanted to record their own renditions, perhaps updated versions for new generations, I couldn't stop them, so long as they paid me 2 cents per recording. What this assured was that performers, who might otherwise not be able to afford licenses to record songs, could buy the rights to virtually any song at the legally prescribed rate.

To be sure, composers in this way are treated differently from other copyright owners, in that they lose control over who can record their works. Nonetheless, the composers are at least better off than if they received nothing for recordings of their works, as would have been the case under the White-Smith decision.

The compromise was one that all parties pretty much learned to live with. When the copyright law was revised in 1976, there was plenty of discussion about whether to retain or abandon the compulsory license. The music copyright owners argued that they should be free to sell their works for whatever the market would bear, and to negotiate the fees, just like all other copyright owners. The recording companies, on the other hand, argued that the compulsory license was reasonable, and should be retained. After considerable debate, the consensus seemed to be that the compulsory license worked fairly well, and the remaining controversy centered upon what the statutory rate should be. The composers argued that the rate should be adjusted considerably upward from 2 cents per copy to allow for inflation over the sixty-plus intervening years since the compulsory license was first adopted. The recording companies argued that increases in the number of records sold more than offset the per record amount lost to inflation.

Ultimately, the 1976 response was to adjust the fees slightly upward to either 2.75 cents per work, or 0.5 cents per minute of playing time, whichever was greater. The new act also incorporated a mechanism for making periodic adjustments to these rates. The rates are currently scheduled to increase from 7.55 cents per song or 1.45 cents per minute of playing time as of 2000, up to 9.1 cents per song or 1.75 cents per minute of playing time in 2006. Thus, if someone makes a record singing ten songs written by others, the total statutory fees amount to over 75 cents per record.

So there we have the legislative response to the first technological challenge to copyright in the twentieth century. What we see is that Congress was ultimately able to meet the challenge, adopting a compromise position that most of the parties were willing, or at least able, to live with.

Radio and Performing Rights: A Little Self-Help

There was another technological development that occurred during the next two decades that threatened to undermine the 1909 victory of composers. In 1907, Lee De Forest, an engineer for Western Electric, developed the "Audion" vacuum tube, which could amplify radio

The compulsory license also brings us different styles of Beatles.
Here are "pseudo-classical" Beatles (left), percussion Beatles (center), and various stars who played Lennon-McCartney music (right).

A trap for the unsophisticated.
The compulsory license can have a devastating impact upon performers who over-rely upon it for their recorded materials. Under most recording contracts, all or a portion of the compulsory licensing fees are deducted from the artist's profits on any recording. If an artist incurs too many compulsory licensing fees, such charges can swallow up just about all of the artist's potential profit from the album. The compulsory license can thus be something of a trap for the unsophisticated recording artist.

"Our record just dropped right back off the charts."

The compulsory license is usually viewed as a benefit to new performers, allowing them access to a vast repertoire of successful songs which might otherwise be tied up by the large music companies. However, it's dangerous to generalize about who benefits from the compulsory license.

The television documentary series *Rock and Roll* highlighted the point that the British invasion of music in the early 1960s, spearheaded by the Beatles, cut off the rising popularity of black music among white audiences in the United States. In the following excerpts, to "cover" a song means to make a recording of someone else's song, usually using the compulsory license rather than a separately negotiated fee. (The Shirelles were quite successful, the first female group to sell more than 1 million records. They continued to perform publicly until the death of Doris Jackson in early 2000.)

Announcer: The ensuing British invasion brought hard times to America's rich tradition of black pop. Many black artists were squeezed off the pop charts as British bands began to cover their songs.

Doris Jackson (of The Shirelles): So actually they were smart, in the fact that they took our songs. And I mean, when I say our songs, I'm basically speaking about everybody across the board, and began to rerecord them and had an awful lot of success with them, so that of course did cut into our business.

Shirley Reeves (of The Shirelles): As a matter of fact, I remember Manfred Mann covering, we had a record that just started to make it across the country on the charts, called Sha-La-La, and Manfred Mann, a group from England, covered us and they immediately stopped playing

waves. In that same year, he began broadcasting recorded music from New York City. All of a sudden, records were not the only source of recorded music. And what's more, after the initial cost of purchasing or assembling a radio receiver, a listener could hear radio music virtually for free.

Some entrepreneurs saw in radio a remarkable new vehicle for advertising and promoting their acts. But by the 1920s, *Billboard* magazine and others in the profession were warning that free music or other acts on radio undercut opportunities to make money from live or recorded performances. "Radiophone Cuts Into Show Business," *Billboard* announced in a 1922 article. "Vaudeville Exchanges First To Realize Artists Hurt Their Value by Wireless Appearances." In that same year, the Actors Equity Association adopted a resolution advising its members to refuse radio appearances without pay. Some managers, such as Florenz Ziegfeld, prohibited their artists from appearing on radio while they were under contract to him. And in 1923, claiming that radio playing was beginning to cut into record sales, the young American Society of Composers, Authors and Publishers (ASCAP) asked broadcasting stations to refrain from playing music without compensating the composers of the songs.

The composers' fears were apparently justified. In part because of the Great Depression, but in part because radio provided "free" music to the public, record sales took a dramatic nosedive. While radio penetrated to 2 out of 5 homes by 1931, and to over 4 out of 5 homes by 1938, record sales plummeted from about $75 million in 1929 to a low of $5 million in 1933, and made only a partial recovery to $26 million by 1938. It wouldn't be much of a victory to get a portion of the profits from record sales if there were no record sales!

But was there anything the copyright owners could do to either prevent radio playing of their works or at least get a piece of the new action? As it turns out, there was something they could do. And it didn't require going to Congress: the solution was already in the existing copyright law.

All the way back in 1897, Congress finally had seen fit to grant composers the exclusive right, with limitations, to publicly perform their songs. That right was continued in the 1909 statute, but it was subject to an important limitation. A composer's rights only extended to "public" performances "for profit." But was the new radio industry really for profit? Listeners didn't have to pay directly to receive radio broadcasts—the revolution of radio was that it was free to anyone who had a receiver. And in the 1920s, radio stations were just beginning to figure out how to make money by selling advertising.

By the twenties, it had already been established by the courts that "for profit" wasn't limited to *direct* profits. The cases that were to be critical in clarifying the rights of composers in the context of radio were those that had been brought by ASCAP, in the teens and twenties.

Victor Herbert had been appalled to hear "Sweethearts," his hit song from the operetta of the same name, being played at the popular Shanley's Restaurant in Times Square just up the street from where the opera was playing on Broadway. While Herbert got his royalties from the theatrical presentation, he was getting not a penny from the orchestra playing his music in the restaurant. So, to test the strength of his new performing rights organization, he brought a lawsuit against the restaurant. The restaurant's defense was that the performance was not "for profit," since there was no separate charge for the music. The case was appealed to the Supreme Court, and in a colorful opinion by Justice Oliver Wendell Holmes, the Court found that the performance was indeed for profit. Another leading case held that the playing of piano music to accompany an otherwise

ours and started to play theirs, so our record just dropped right back off the charts.

Announcer: The same month as the Beatles' conquest of America, Lieber and Stoller released Go Now, by Betsy Banks, a return to their first love, R & B. In a sign of the times, the song never reached a white audience until it became the first American hit of one of the new British bands, The Moody Blues.

This is not to suggest that the compulsory license was responsible for the British invasion of American music. But it did add insult to injury when the British artists were able to make hits of the very songs that had been introduced by American artists.

"The Father of Radio."
Lee de Forest, in Manhattan in 1907, speaking into a microphone (taken from a telephone) on a makeshift stand. In the foreground is part of the record player, for musical entertainment.

Shanley's Restaurant,
at Broadway and 43rd Street,
circa 1914.

Off to see the Congress.
At front (left) is Victor Herbert,
plaintiff in the lawsuit against
Shanley's Restaurant. With him
(front row) are John Philip
Sousa, Irving Berlin, Harry von
Tilzer, and William Jerome.
Peering from the back row,
between Tilzer and Jerome, is
Nathan Burkan, the attorney
who helped to found ASCAP.

The entourage is shown at
Pennslvania Station in New
York in 1924, on their way to
testify against the Dill radio
bill that would have allowed
radio stations to play music
without compensation to
copyright owners. The bill was
defeated, and ASCAP's victories in the courts established
the rights of composers to
receive royalties for the playing
of their works on radio.

silent motion picture was a performance "for profit," even though the playing of the music was "incidental" to the viewing of the motion picture.* The theater had to obtain an ASCAP license.

So, given the statute and these earlier cases, was the playing of music on radio a public performance "for profit"? The test case was brought against the Bamberger Department Store in Newark, New Jersey, which in 1922 had begun broadcasting music and other entertainment programming from its store on a new radio station known as WOR. Although no money was paid or received for commercials in those early days of radio, the federal district court in New Jersey, analogizing to the earlier cases, had no difficulty in finding that Bamberger's motives were sufficiently commercial. The store announced at the beginning of its programs that the broadcast was from "L. Bamberger and Co., One of America's Great Stores, Newark, New Jersey." It also incidentally sold radio receivers, from which it of course expected to make a profit.

With the victory against WOR in 1923, ASCAP was able to begin collecting licensing fees from radio stations that played ASCAP music. Although that first license was a modest $250 per year for the privilege of playing all ASCAP music, the fees for larger radio stations soon went as high as $5,000. Today, radio and TV licensing represents the single greatest source of revenue for ASCAP and its composers. Together with BMI and SESAC, the other two major music-licensing organizations, total U.S. revenues for performing rights are almost $1 billion That may sound like a lot of money, but remember that it's divided by all of the composers to compensate them for all the nondramatic public performances of their works. An average member of ASCAP gets about $150–$200 per work per year, or about $5,000–$6,000 for all of a member's compositions. And of course, that average reflects high payments

---

"If it pays . . ."

If the rights under the copyright are infringed only by a performance where money is taken at the door, they are very imperfectly protected. . . . The defendants' performances are not eleemosynary [charitable]. They are part of a total for which the public pays, and the fact that the price of the whole is attributed to a particular item which those present are expected to order, is not important. It is true that the music is not the sole object, but neither is the food, which probably could be got cheaper elsewhere. . . . If music did not pay it would be given up. If it pays, it pays out of the public's pocket. Whether it pays or not, the purpose of employing it is profit, and that is enough.

– Justice Oliver Wendell Holmes,
Herbert v. Shanley (1917)

One of America's great stores.

A department store is conducted for profit, which leads us to the very significant fact that the cost of the broadcasting was charged against the general expenses of the business. . . . While the defendant does not broadcast the sales prices of its wares, or refer specifically thereto, it does broadcast a slogan which appears in all of the defendant's printed advertisements. . . . If the development or enlargement of the business of the department store was completely out of the minds of the promoters of this broadcasting enterprise, is it reasonable to believe that the slogan, "L. Bamberger and Co., One of America's Great Stores, Newark, N.J.," would be announced to all listeners one, two, three, four, five, or six times a day?

– District Judge Charles Lynch,
District Court of New Jersey (1923)

---

*Music accompaniment, see p. 181.

ASCAP.

ASCAP was founded in 1914 by Victor Herbert and other composers, together with their attorney, Nathan Burkan, who had represented their interests in the White-Smith case. The purpose of the organization is to collectively enforce copyrights of all its members against not only dance halls and restaurants, but also other organizations that publicly play their songs, such as radio, television, and cable stations, and, most recently, sites on the Internet. ASCAP licenses only for the so-called nondramatic performances. Composers still directly license users for "dramatic" presentations of their works, such as on the stage. The typical license is a so-called blanket license; for the payment of one annual fee, the subscriber is entitled to play an unlimited number of works from the vast repertoire of all ASCAP's songs. ASCAP distributes its proceeds among its members, based upon various criteria, including the results of elaborate polls to determine what songs are generally being performed. ASCAP gets its licensees to pay their fees with a carrot and a stick: the carrot is the relative bargain of having access to hundreds of thousands of musical works for one low fee. The stick is the threat of a lawsuit, and the likelihood that the user will have to pay more in litigation expenses and damages than it would have cost simply to pay the license fee in the first place.

for a few very successful composers, and small payments for the vast majority of composers.

In any event, the existing copyright law—together with some aggressive self-help by the composers and publishers themselves—was enough to take care of the radio revolution.

SOUND RECORDINGS: THE NEW INDUSTRY

The Protection of Sound Recordings

What we've been talking about until now are the rights composers have in their *music.* Although such rights include the right to *make* recordings of the music, until 1972 there were no separate federal rights in the sound recordings themselves. That is, the producers and performers who made recordings had no federal rights in their records, tapes, or CDs. For the rest of this chapter, we'll be talking about various ways in which copyright has been extended to protect such sound recordings directly.

Although the record companies had lobbied for protection of recordings as early as the 1906 hearings, for various reasons Congress did not act. The technological advance that reintroduced the issue with some

**Sources of Revenue
For Composers**

Use of copyrighted work	How payments made
Sheet music	Directly to publisher (which presumably has contractual arrangements with the composer).
Records, tapes, CD's, etc.	Directly to publisher for first authorized recording. Thereafter, at the compulsory licensing rate, frequently through Harry Fox Agency.
Motion pictures, television, home video	Synchronization or other fees usually paid through an agency like Harry Fox Agency.
Live performances and non-dramatic performances on television, radio, etc.	Performance fees usually collected through performance rights organizations - ASCAP, BMI, or SESAC

urgency was the development of the relatively inexpensive and efficient tape recorder. Record and tape piracy reached epidemic proportions in the 1960s and 1970s. The record companies went to Washington, and this time convinced Congress that record and tape piracy was enough of a "bad thing" that they ought to pass a law preventing it. Not only did record piracy hurt the record companies, but it also hurt consumers: if other companies "pirate" records without paying their fair share, then the original record companies have to charge more to make a profit, and we all end up paying in the form of higher prices for legitimate records and tapes. In 1971, Congress responded by passing a special amendment making sound recordings separately copyrightable under the federal statute, effective for records made after February 15, 1972.

As a result of the amendment, most records, tapes, and CDs since 1972 involve two separate copyrights. The copyright in the music (usually identified on the album by the symbol ©) belongs to the composer, and extends to the making, distribution, or public performance of the song. The copyright in the sound recording (usually identified on the album by the symbol Ⓟ, for "phonorecord") belongs to the record company (and sometimes partly to the performers), and extends only to the making or distribution of that particular recording of the song. (There's usually also a separate copyright in the cover art of the record or CD.)

So Congress wasn't exactly prompt in addressing the issue of record piracy—from 1909 to 1972 is a pretty long time even by congressional standards—but it did finally get around to the problem. And when it did, it did so by bringing sound recordings more or less into the existing framework that governed copyrights generally. With some fine-tuning, it was felt that the basic purpose of copyright—promoting the progress of art and science by creating exclusive rights in the works of authors—was served by extending federal copyright protection to sound recordings.

The New Revolution: Digitized Sound

Until the 1970s, sound recordings were stored only in analog form. The music was "stored" on records as a wavy groove etched into the disk; and on audiotape as a continuous magnetic signal that corresponded to the analog vibrations. Engineers tweaked the technology to produce ever higher fidelity stereo and long-playing records, magnetic tape recordings,

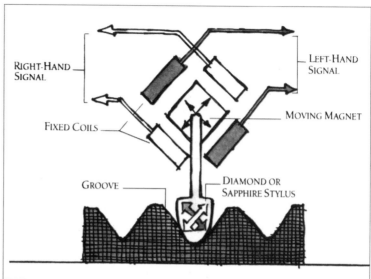

RIGHT-HAND SIGNAL

LEFT-HAND SIGNAL

MOVING MAGNET

FIXED COILS

GROOVE

DIAMOND OR SAPPHIRE STYLUS

Phonograph record, magnified about two hundred times.

How the stylus picks up stereo sound, vibrating in two distinct directions from the patterns etched on either side of the record groove.

and movie soundtracks. But the basic concept of storing an analog vibration, or an electronic or optical signal capable of reproducing an analog vibration, remained relatively unchanged in the century since Edison invented the phonograph.

Then, during the seventies, engineers perfected the technology that allowed sound to be "sampled" electronically, and converted into a series of numbers that could be stored and reproduced by computers. The first compact disk, or CD, was introduced in 1979, and within a decade the vinyl record was practically obsolete.

Like other major technologies, the development of digitized sound had both positive and negative effects on the industry. On the positive side, the sound quality, durability, and versatility of CDs was considered by many to be superior to that of records. Consumers were willing to pay a premium to buy their music in the new format. Many music collectors, dissatisfied with their worn vinyl records, went out and bought new copies of works they already owned. This was a record company's dream, to resell albums to people who already had them!

But there was also a downside to the new format, which became apparent in several distinct ways. While Congress might be criticized for having taken so long to protect sound recordings in the first place, it has been right at the forefront in amending copyright to deal with these

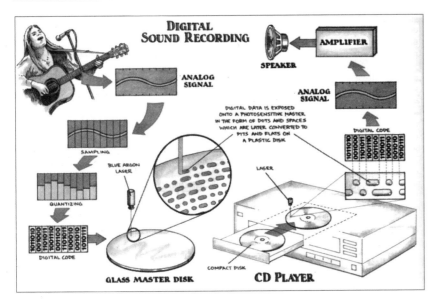

How an analog sound wave is converted to binary code and then recorded on a CD.

Digital sound recording is fundamentally different from analog sound recording. Instead of the pattern of the sound waves being reproduced in the grooves of a record or the patterns of magnetism on a tape, *information* about those sound waves is stored in the form of digital signals. To do this, the sound is sampled thousands of times a second. At each sampling, the amplitude of the wave is noted and converted to a binary representation. . . .

The data on a compact disk is recorded as a series of closely spaced pits in the surface of the disk. The pits are arranged in a spiral track whose total length is more than 3.5 miles. To play back the CD, a laser retraces the spiral track, starting at the center. When it hits a pit the light is scattered; when it hits a smooth spot it's reflected.
—Steven Lubar

effects of digitized sound. We'll take a look at several recent copyright amendments that were designed to address the copyright problems.

Whatever Happened to the Audio Rental Stores?

In the 1980s, video rental stores proliferated across the country.* Why had there never been *audio* rental stores? Probably because of the poor quality of used records. Once a record was handled a few times, it got

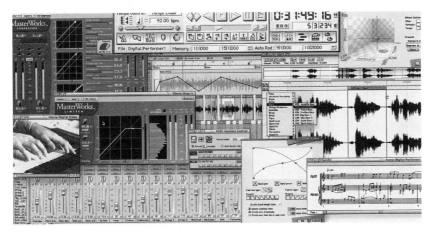

Playing with digitized music. The digitizing of sound allows for its manipulation in ways not previously possible. Using the music sequencer software controls, a musician/engineer can rearrange or alter the notes (bottom right) or the sound wave itself (center right).

*Video rental stores, see p. 69.

scratches and pops and hiss, and who would want to rent a worn-out used record?

Well, the CD changed all that. CDs were not "indestructible," as originally billed; you can easily prove that with a steel soap pad and just a little ingenuity. But if you take reasonable care of your CDs and put them back in their cases, then they can last virtually forever. Their quality doesn't deteriorate in normal use, since the laser beam that reads the CD makes no physical contact with the CD itself.

So, in the early 1980s, alongside the emerging video rental stores, there began popping up audio rental stores, where you could rent a CD for a dollar or two a night. Most consumers only owned one video recorder, and so were not set up to make copies of rented *movies* in their homes. But most home music systems had a tape deck right alongside the CD player, so that making tapes of rented CDs was as simple as pressing a button. To facilitate copying (and make a little extra money), the audio rental stores also sold blank audiotapes.

As you might expect, the record companies felt that the unauthorized audio rental stores could have a disastrous effect upon the sale of CDs. But a simple copyright doctrine stood in the way. Under U.S. copyright, once a manufacturer sells a particular copy of a copyrighted work, then anyone else may resell or give away or rent that particular copy without paying any further copyright royalty. This is known as the "first sale" doctrine,* which provides that the copyright owner effectively "exhausts" its rights upon the "first sale" of a particular copy of a work. It is this principle that allows the video rental stores to exist, without storeowners having to pay copyright royalties for the privilege of renting out videos.

The upshot of all of this was that the record companies were able to convince Congress that audio rental stores were a bad thing. What Congress did was to pass an amendment in 1984 to make an exception to the first sale doctrine so that it wouldn't apply to sound recordings. In other words, the amendment made clear that record companies *retained* the exclusive right to rent their works, and could prevent purchasers of their records (even stores) from commercially renting out their sound recordings—records, tapes, or CDs. This 1984 amendment is the reason why audio rental stores virtually don't exist in this country.

*First sale doctrine, see p. 167.

Why Can't I Make Copies from Copies of My CDs?

The second major response to the digitizing of music was the Audio Home Recording Act of 1992. Here's the problem. Inexpensive and easy-to-use cassette tape recorders had been around for decades, and everybody understood that lots of people made tape copies of music in their homes. Never mind that these recordings were technically copyright infringements, there was nothing anybody could do to stop the copying that took place in private homes.

But the situation was tolerable for one basic reason. No matter how much the technicians tweaked the technology, tapes were still not as good as the originals. Or if they did come close, it was still true that if you made a copy of a copy, the sound quality started deteriorating. And whether or not that's true, record companies seemed to be selling more CDs and prerecorded tapes than at any time in history, and it was hard to believe the hysterical outcries of such an apparently successful industry.

Now introduce the digital audio tape recorder. What it records is not the soundwave, but a bunch of ones and zeroes, ons and offs, that can be used to digitally reproduce the original recording exactly. And I mean exactly. Whether or not the tape perfectly captures reality, it *does* perfectly capture the original recording, because it records, digit for digit, the same sequence of electronic bits. And unto the second and third generations, and forever. The tenth copy of a copy will sound just as good as the original.

So, when the first such recording devices were introduced in the late 1980s, the record companies threatened to bar their sale by bringing suit under copyright. For a variety of reasons, the manufacturers held off selling the digital audio tape recorders in this country. In addition to the fear of litigation, there was the recession, which didn't bode well for the introduction of a major new technology; there was the problem of incompatible systems (and no one wanted to get into a technology war on the level of the Beta-VHS competition); and there was the fact that some of the companies that would sell the new devices were still doing quite nicely selling CD players, and it didn't seem wise to introduce one technology before realizing the full potential of the previous one.

Whatever the reason for the delay, it did give the parties time to negotiate a deal. What they came up with was an industry-sponsored compromise that was presented to Congress as acceptable to both the

Congress misses the market.

In passing the new home recording amendment, Congress obviously anticipated that the new digital audio tape systems would be the next major technology in the music industry. But it didn't work out that way. For one reason or another, hardly anybody bought the new digital tape machines. Instead, the technology that caught on like wildfire in the later 1990s was the MP3 format for storing and sending digital music over the Internet.

Diamond Multimedia Systems was the first company to market a portable device for storing and playing MP3 files captured from the Internet. The files could be stored on the Rio's "hard drive," or on memory cards that could be played on the Rio at a later time or on someone else's Rio. The Recording Industry Association of America (RIAA) brought suit against Diamond, claiming that the device failed to comply with the audio home recording amendment, because it didn't have a serial copy management system (and Diamond didn't pay the royalty that it would have had to pay if the device were covered by the statute).

The federal courts refused to grant an injunction, on the ground that the Rio was not a recording device; while it could store one copy of MP3 files, it had no capability for making additional copies. Why would you need a serial copy management chip if you couldn't make serial copies (copies of copies) anyway? But, argued RIAA, if the Rio were not covered by the amendment, then the consumers were getting their right to make a "free" home copy without having to pay the price—the compulsory licensing fee—that the statute had contemplated. The technology had simply developed in ways not anticipated by Congress.

manufacturers of the new digital audio tape machines, and the music and record publishers. Congress ultimately adopted the deal in the form of the 1992 home recording amendment.

There are three major components to the new statute. First, all digital recording devices must incorporate something called the "Serial Copy Management System." This is a special chip that allows for the making of a first-generation copy of a digitally recorded work, but places a special signal on any copies that tells the chip not to make any further copies. In other words, you can copy the original, but you can't copy the copy. Second, the statute provides for a new royalty fee of up to $8 per digital recording machine and 3 percent of the price of all digital audiotapes or disks used in such machines. These royalties are to be collected not from consumers, but from the manufacturers or importers of the machines and tapes, and distributed to copyright owners whose musical works and sound recordings are presumably being copied. Third, since royalties are being paid by the manufacturers or importers of the new recording devices and media, the copyright owners agreed to forever waive the right to sue consumers for copyright infringement using audio recording devices in their homes.

Although this package may appear to give the record companies a real windfall, in fact there are several substantial limitations. For one thing, there's the Serial Copy Management System: it does prevent second-, third-, and later-generation copies, but it still allows users to make as many *first*-generation copies as they want. So, for example, I can still buy one copy of a CD, record it digitally, give the original to a friend, who records it digitally, who gives the original to a friend, who . . . well, you get the idea. The Serial Copy Management System doesn't prevent users from making multiple copies, it only prevents them from making copies of copies.

And this business about not suing anyone for home recording of music—that represents a wonderful gift for home users. Prior to the 1992 amendment, there was no "home use" exception for home taping, much as some people seemed to think there was. Well, now there is a specific home use exception. Effectively, the record companies just gave away any claim of copyright infringement for home taping of any kind. All the music publishers and record companies get is a share of the $8 royalty per digital machine, and the 3 percent royalty per digital tape or disk. Why did they give up their right to sue? Because it wasn't worth much; there was no effective way to enforce the right anyway.

The new amendment adds a dozen pages of complicated and technical regulations that only a lawyer can understand and appreciate. But the important point is that copyright has adapted, and with a statute that the affected industries agreed to in advance.

Having lost the preliminary round, RIAA ultimately settled with Diamond, on Diamond's promise to work with RIAA on the Secure Digital Music Initiative—a successor to the MP3 format that can protect against unauthorized copying. As this book went to press, RIAA was bringing lawsuits against various parties for distributing or facilitating the unauthorized distribution of MP3 files over the Internet. One suit is against the creators of "Napster," a program that doesn't directly make or store MP3 files, but allows for systematic tracking and exchanging of MP3 files among various users. I'm not about to predict how these cases will come out. But I am fairly certain that the music industry will be fighting the unauthorized "free" MP3 music sites that are ubiquitous on the Internet, and shifting most of its inventory to the newer, secure formats.

Digital Audio Transmissions

Congress has recently responded to the digitization of music in a third major context. Here's the concern: now that music is digitized, it can be sent over telephone or cable lines and through computer networks. Yes, I know you could always "send" music over telephone lines, but the quality of the music received would be about like listening to Beethoven through a paper cup. What I'm talking about is sending a stream of computer signals from which the music can be reconstructed at the other end. When you play the music on your computer or other receiver, voilà, it sounds just as good as the original.

The future is now. People connected to the Internet are already exchanging digital files containing pictures, music, video clips, you name it. Some companies have launched new subscription services that distribute music and video virtually on demand. There's a big potential market here, and—you guessed it—the record companies are afraid that people will simply download their music, instead of buying CDs. That could put the CD manufacturers out of business. And if they're out of

Music and video Internet services.

Real Player and other music playing programs can be used to play "streaming" audio of words or music. The radio stations listed here have authorized the use of their sounds, but hundreds of unauthorized streaming audio and video MP3 formatted sites are also widely available.

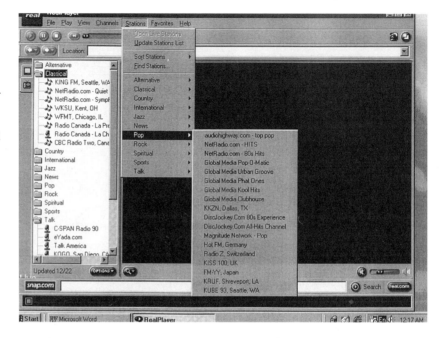

business, who's going to pay the musicians and sound engineers who keep the music flowing?

The legislation passed by Congress to deal with all of this is the Digital Performance Rights in Sound Recordings Act of 1995. It's got several features, and it gets even more complicated than the earlier music amendments to copyright. To simplify a bit (and to update for further amendments made in 1998, discussed below), it divides the performance of digital music into three categories.

The first category is nonsubscription broadcast transmissions, for which no royalties have to be paid to the sound recording copyright owners. As explained by the sponsors of the amendment, it "does not apply to" and would not create copyright liability for "traditional radio and TV broadcasts, or to background music services, such as Muzak or 3M, nor does it apply to public radio, restaurants, department stores, hotels, or amusement parks." (These services have traditionally had to, and will continue to, pay ASCAP and BMI

Performance rights in sound recordings.

Prior to the 1995 amendments, there were no performance rights in sound recordings. A radio station or dance hall or store could play music from sound recordings, and would have to pay a performance right to the owner of the copyright in the underlying music, but would not have to pay anything to the owner of the copyright in the sound recording.

With the 1995 amendments, there now *are* performance rights in sound recordings, but limited to the right to certain digital performances, as described in the text and the accompanying chart.

for performance rights in the underlying music, but not anything to the owners of copyright in the sound recordings.)

The second category is certain other digital transmissions, including services in which a subscriber pays a fee but doesn't control what music is played. In this context, Congress has provided that the copyright owners have to allow such uses for prenegotiated fees—another "compulsory license."* Such fees currently amount to about 6 to 7 percent of gross revenues from residential music services.

The third category is interactive digital subscription services, or services that allow a subscriber, for a fee, to listen to music either on demand, or on a schedule that allows for easy digital taping of the music. The owners of copyright are granted full control over such services, so that they can decide to license such services for a fee, or prevent such services in order to protect their CD sales.

What we're left with is a complicated and technical amendment that, again, only a lawyer could really love. But everyone criticizes copyright and other laws for being too slow to respond to technology and new crises, so this is perhaps a refreshing attempt by Congress to face the problem and nip it in the bud before vested interests make regulation difficult.

As a matter of fact, shortly after passage of the 1995 amendment, a dispute arose about whether music "webcasting" or "streaming" audio on

Categories of Accountability
Under the Digital Performance Right
In Sound Recordings Act of 1995*

Category	Accountability	Notes
Non-subscription broadcast transmissions	No copyright liability	No fees to record companies for "traditional" types of performances, even if digital.
Certain other digital transmissions	Compulsory license fee applies	Record companies can't prevent the use of their recordings if the user pays the fees.
Interactive digital subscription services	Full copyright liability	Presumably the record companies won't authorize this unless they are compensated enough to cover the displaced sales of CD's or other sound recordings.

* As amended, 1998. This chart applies only to the copyright in the record or CD itself. Users of copyrighted music must make separate arrangements to pay the owners of the underlying musical copyright.

*Compulsory licenses, see p. 184.

the Internet was within the compulsory license, or was completely exempt. It became obvious that there were ambiguities in the amendment; and only three years later, the section was completely rewritten (as described here) in the Digital Millennium Copyright Act to make clear that such real time "streaming" audio is not exempt, but subject to the compulsory license. The technology is changing so rapidly that frequent updates to the law will probably become the norm.

The Digital Millennium Copyright Act of 1998* contained many other provisions that greatly expanded the protection of digitized information, including music. A fuller treatment of that complicated statute, however, must await our discussion of the Internet in chapter 5.

Used CDs: Sorry, No Protection

It's not the case that copyright has expanded or should expand to cover every possible effect of digitized music. For example, because CDs retain their sound quality for so long, there has developed a market in used CDs that goes beyond the market that ever existed for used vinyl records.

**Sources of Revenue
For Sound Recordings***

Use of copyrighted work	How payments made
Sale of records, tapes, CD's, etc.	Direct payment to sound recording manufacturer.
Motion pictures, television, home video	Synchronization or other fees separately negotiated.
Sales of audio digital recording devices and media	Statutory fee to be paid to sound recording copyright owners.
Performances	Only for certain digital performances (see the chart on categories of accountability).

* This chart applies only to the owners of copyright in the record or CD itself, usually the record company. The *performers* who make sound recordings get paid whatever is provided in their contract with the record companies - usually a set fee or a percentage of the revenue received. The new statutes providing compulsory licensing fees for audio digital recording devices and media, and for non-interactive subscription transmissions, specifically provide for payments to be made directly to performers as well as the record companies.

*Digital Millennium Copyright Act, see p. 112.

Some authors have suggested that the used CD market undermines the new CD market, and that Congress should adopt a new amendment to the first sale doctrine that would prevent the resale as well as the rental of CDs. This suggestion apparently goes too far. Congress has not attempted to prevent the resale of old CDs. A record company just has to live with the fact that when it sells, say, a million copies of a particular CD, some tens or hundreds of thousands of those very CDs may be sold on the used CD market, thus theoretically reducing further initial sales. The record company just has to charge enough upon the first sale to recover the value for the full useful life of the CD. So there's still a balance between the interests of copyright owners and copyright users— copyright users may not commercially rent out their records, tapes and CDs, but they *may*, if they want, resell them for whatever someone else is willing to pay.

CONCLUSION

So that's a whirlwind tour of copyright in one of the fields most heavily affected by the new technologies. Perhaps not surprisingly, many of the legal issues raised by the introduction of new technologies have been addressed by specific legislation. Congress first created the exclusive right to make mechanical reproductions of music in 1909, and created exclusive rights in sound recordings themselves in 1971. Congress clarified and cautiously extended copyrights in separate amendments in 1984, 1992, 1995, and 1998. But expanding protection is not the only option. In some cases, Congress has withheld its power to expand copyright, and in other cases the owners of copyright have been able to achieve the results they wanted through private negotiations or the application of general copyright principles. Whether by amendment or otherwise, copyright has hardly stood still, and indeed may have changed more in the past few decades than it had in the previous two centuries.

The kinetograph.
Thomas Edison (right) demonstrating the kinetograph (motion picture camera), with the assistance of George Eastman, who helped develop the film used in the early motion picture machines. The inventors look a bit older than they did when they made their inventions; they posed at a 1928 Eastman garden party for this endorsement of a camera not of Edison's making.

The kinetoscope.
An early kinetoscope parlor in San Francisco, about 1899.

The "peephole" machine, showing the continuous, circulating loop of film.

CHAPTER THREE

Movies and Television

MOTION PICTURES

In 1893, Thomas Edison patented the first efficient motion picture viewer, the kinetoscope. A customer could drop a penny into the kinetoscope, turn the crank, look through the viewfinder, and enjoy a short movie loop. In the 1890s and 1900s, kinetoscope parlors spread like crazy across the country. Although Edison didn't immediately pursue his invention beyond this early version, in 1896 the American Mutoscope and Biograph Company produced the first projection of moving images onto a screen. Hollywood, here we come!

Ben-Hur

In 1880, Harper Brothers published a book written by General Lewis Wallace, a colorful figure who had been a major general during the Civil War, and later governor of the New Mexico Territory. The book was *Ben-Hur; A Tale of the Christ,* and it was tremendously successful.

In 1907, the Kalem Company produced the first of several movie versions of *Ben-Hur.* It advertised the motion picture under the name "Ben-Hur"—"Positively the most superb moving-picture spectacle ever produced in America in sixteen magnificent scenes."

Edison misjudges the market.

As he had with the phonograph, Edison misjudged how the market was to develop. He thought the money was in the kinetograph and the kinetoscope; he didn't think people would want to sit in audiences to see an image on a screen.

The Edison profits came from the sale of machines and prints, not from exhibition to the general public. . . . From the Edison viewpoint, one machine for every viewer was more to be desired than a hundred or more viewers for every machine.

–*Wonderful Inventions*

The patent wars.

For the first ten years, the use of the new movie cameras and projectors was tied up in a protracted patent war between Edison and other inventors. In 1907, Edison formed the Edison Licensee Group. In 1908, this group joined with the Biograph Company to form the Motion Picture Patents Company, which was able to dictate royalties for the creation and showing of motion pictures.

General Lew Wallace.
Wallace commanded the Middle Division VIII Army Corps during the Civil War. The photograph is by Mathew Brady. A statue of Wallace stands in the Hall of Statuary of the U.S. Capitol in Washington, D.C., Indiana's contribution honoring one of its outstanding citizens.

***Ben-Hur*, the photo-play.**

Back in 1899, General Wallace and Harper Brothers had realized the dramatic potential in *Ben-Hur,* and had arranged with Marc Klaw and Abraham Erlanger, part of Broadway's notorious "theatrical syndicate" at the turn of the century, to have the book adapted into a theatrical production. The play ran for over a dozen years on Broadway. It featured an ocean scene in which the waves were recreated by stagehands waving large pieces of cloth, and a chariot race using live horses on stage, running on an elaborate treadmill in front of a moving panorama.

The contract provided that Harper Brothers would own the copyright in the play, but that Klaw and Erlanger would have the exclusive right of "producing" the work "upon the stage," or "performing" the "dramatic version" so written. After the successful theatrical run, and after the successful suit against Kalem, Harper Brothers sued Klaw and Erlanger to prevent them from making a motion picture version of the play, since Harper Brothers wanted to make their own version free of their theatrical contract. In 1916, the district court that heard the case observed that, at the time of the contract, "the moving picture art was . . . in its infancy," and hardly within the contemplation of the parties. So who owned the right to make movies of the play under the existing

There was one problem—Kalem had not bothered to get permission from Harper Brothers, the owners of the copyright in the book. Not surprisingly, Harper Brothers sued Kalem Company for copyright infringement. The case was ultimately appealed to the Supreme Court, which found that the movie version of *Ben-Hur* infringed upon the copyright in the book.

Kalem raised several interesting defenses. It argued (1) that the visual depiction of a story could not infringe the copyright in the book, which consisted only of words and not visual images; (2) that the pantomime action contained in the silent movie used only the unprotectable ideas, but not the protectable expression,* found in the book; and (3) that, even if the display of the motion picture might infringe on Harper's exclusive right to perform the work dramatically, the distribution of the motion picture was not itself such a public performance.

Justice Oliver Wendell Holmes, in the Supreme Court opinion, rejected all of these fine distinctions. As

*Ideas v. expression, see p. 188.

early as 1856, Congress had amended the copyright act to grant copyright owners the exclusive right to "act, perform, or represent"* a dramatic work "on any stage or public place." An earlier case, *Daly v. Palmer,* had held that a live pantomime within a play could be copyrighted, and would be infringed by the use of a similar scene in another play even if no words were used in either scene. As Holmes concluded, "drama may be achieved by action as well as by speech," and if a live pantomime infringed a copyright, then a motion picture pantomime would also infringe. (The Daly case

contract? The court held that technically Harper Brothers had not conveyed the motion picture rights, since such rights were not contemplated at the time of the contract. But in a decision applying the wisdom of Solomon to the new technology of the twentieth century, the court read into the contract an implied contract by Harper not to undertake any activities that might interfere with Klaw and Erlanger's theatrical rights. "Neither party . . . can produce a photo-play of Ben-Hur except by bargain with the other."

Bargain they did! The New York theater syndicate was able to get Goldwyn Pictures to pay a royalty of 50 percent of the gross receipts for the privilege of making its classic silent film. Although the movie was a smash success, grossing over $9 million, the hefty royalties actually left the movie company $850,000 short of recovering its costs. However, the legend established the reputation of the new Metro-Goldwyn-Mayer company for years to come.

***Ben-Hur,* the Broadway play.**
The production of *Ben-Hur* on stage was a triumph of theater technology as well as acting. Shown here are the elaborate ship scene, and a chariot from the race scene. The latter was staged in front of a moving panorama, with the chariot and horses running on a treadmill, rigged so that the chariot could lose a wheel during the race.

 *Public performance, see p. 168.

The Kalem Company.

The Kalem Company, founded in 1907 by George Kleine, Samuel Long, and Frank J. Marion (K, L, and M), was headed by three men of broad experience in the movie business. Kleine was the successful importer of European productions and owner of Kleine Optical Company, Long was the inventor of much of the machinery used to process and duplicate exposed film, and Marion was a former director and studio chief for Biograph. In the first years of production, the Kalem Company turned out a standard list of undistinguished comedies and melodramas. . . . Most were predictable, and all were less than one reel in length. By late 1909, the company had discovered the appeal that audiences found in standard melodramas set in exotic locations. Early excursions were among the palms in Florida, and later California, where the climate facilitated winter production schedules that were impossible to carry out in the New England states.

—*Wonderful Inventions*

Record of a Sneeze.
This is not the first movie ever made, but it is the earliest existing copyrighted motion picture, and the earliest copyright registration for a movie, *Record of a Sneeze.* The series of pictures, running in sequence top to bottom, was made by W. K. L. Dickson in the Edison laboratory in West Orange, New Jersey, in 1893. It depicts Fred Ott, an employee of Edison's Kinetoscope Company. Many early movies, whose original movie stock has deteriorated or been lost, have been painstakingly reconstructed from the copyright registrations of such still photos.

was important to the analysis, since motion pictures at the time were of course silent.) Kalem ultimately settled the case by paying $25,000 and withdrawing the film from circulation.

Even before the Kalem case found copyright infringement in the making of movie adaptations of copyrighted works, early film producers had registered their copyrights in movies as a series of individual photographs, by depositing either copies of the filmstrips or paper prints made from the filmstrips. Early cases upheld these copyrights under the category of photographs.

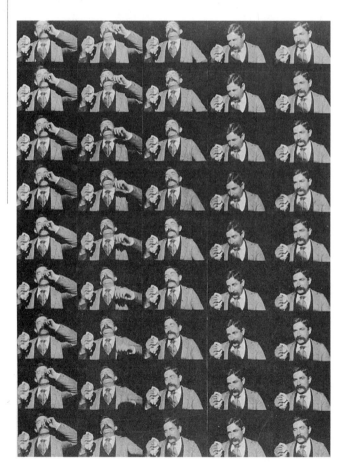

So, in contrast to the case of sound recordings, the existing copyright statute was broad enough to handle the legal issues raised by the invention of motion pictures. The major turning points, it seems, took place back in 1856, when copyright was expanded to cover dramatic rights, and in 1865, when copyright was expanded to cover photographs.* It took only a small further step—that is, a small step for an innovative judge—to find that copyright covered motion pictures, which embodied *dramatic* works in a *photographic* form. In 1912, without much discussion or controversy, Congress specifically added motion pictures to the growing list of works subject to federal copyright. The legislation was more a ratification than a change of the law.

TELEVISION

Broadcast Television

No one person is responsible for the invention of television; it was developed by incremental improvements from the 1880s to the 1930s, when a workable television set was first made available to the public. A traditional video camera scans a picture and converts it to a beam of electrons that varies in darkness and lightness with the intensity of the image. In the United States, the

Early copyright protection.

Copyright protection was crucial to the continued investment in movies, and, for a period of time when such protection looked dubious, Edison held back from movie production.

Because Sigmund Lubin had been selling duplicates of Edison films . . . the inventor sued the Philadelphia producer for copyright infringement. No sooner had *Life of an American Fireman* been completed than the courts declared Edison's method of film copyright invalid. (The judge wanted each frame of film submitted separately, a hopelessly time consuming and expensive task!) Without legal protection for his investment, Edison halted serious film production for five months and dismissed the stage director George Fleming. . . . Porter [working for Edison] did not resume filmmaking until that summer, after a higher court reversed the earlier decision and upheld Edison's procedure for copyrighting films.

—Charles Musser

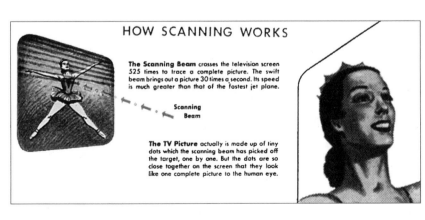

How scanning works.

 *Photographs, see p. 136.

Pioneers of radio and television.
Guglielmo Marconi, the father of wireless communication (right), with David Sarnoff (left), a
major promoter of radio and television. Sarnoff
began his career as a wireless operator. He gained
national attention when, for seventy-two hours, he
relayed the names of *Titanic* survivors rescued by
the *Carpathian*. As an employee of the American
Marconi Company, Sarnoff developed plans for a
"radio music box." At the time, most people dismissed his proposals. Later, Sarnoff became an
executive, and eventually president, of the Radio
Corporation of America, which acquired the assets
of American Marconi. Sarnoff oversaw the establishment of the National Broadcasting Company.

Television at the 1939 World's Fair.
Franklin Roosevelt (A) and a video camera (B) at
the New York World's Fair.

> In April 1935 the Radio Corporation of
> America announced a million-dollar appropri-
> ation for television demonstrations. . . . RCA
> picked a target date and site for the unveiling:
> the 1939 World's Fair in New York. . . . On
> April 30, the formal opening, Franklin D.
> Roosevelt became the first President in office to
> appear on television. RCA sets with five- and
> nine-inch picture tubes went on display at the
> fair, followed later by sets with twelve-inch
> tubes. Prices ranged from $199.50 to $600.
> Crowds stared at the flickering scenes: plays,
> snatches of opera, kitchen demonstrations;
> comedians, singers, jugglers, puppets. But by
> now the world was on the brink of holocaust,
> and as the United States geared for World War
> II, television gradually faded from the public
> eye. Most of the 23 stations in operation during
> May 1940 went off the air. Sets disappeared
> from the market. A few went into police stations
> to be used as training aids for air-raid wardens.
> —National Geographic Society

By post-Depression standards, $600 was a lot of
money; a new Ford four-door sedan could be
bought for about the same price.

standard television image has historically consisted of 525 lines scanned 30 times per second. The television set then receives the electronic signal, and converts it back into an image by projecting the beam, 525 lines, 30 times per second, across the picture tube. For color television, the beam is broken down into three component parts, which make up the primary colors from which all the other colors may be reproduced.

The miracle part of this process was not just in capturing or reproducing images, but in delivering images to locations far removed from the source. This was the technology of radio—wireless communication—first developed by Guglielmo Marconi in 1895. Because of the intervening depression and World War II, however, it was not until the 1950s that commercial television really caught on. This new technology allowed millions of viewers to see programs from just about anywhere in the country, using their own receivers in the comfort of their own living rooms. People didn't have to go to the movies; the movies came to them.

As revolutionary as the technology was, it too posed no major problems for copyright. Although the medium was of course different, television programs were, for copyright purposes, just like movies. The basic principles of copyright* worked just fine. But a later television technology *did* require a legislative response—cable television.

> **Movies for television.**
>
> Theatrically released movies were not generally shown on commercial television until the 1960s. Prior to that time, the owners of motion pictures were reluctant to make their movies available "for free," for fear of undermining their theatrical audience. As with the record manufacturers a generation earlier, their fears were probably warranted. As Samuel Goldwyn is said to have quipped, "Why should anyone pay to see a bad picture in a theater when he can see one for nothing at home?" In 1946, only ten thousand television sets had been sold; by 1951, there were twelve million sets in American homes. During that same period, total movie company profits plummeted from what was then an all-time high of $119.9 million (based upon box office receipts of $1.69 billion) in 1946, to only $31.4 million in 1951.
>
> By the 1960s, however, the increasing profits to be made from commercial television release of their movies were too great to be ignored, and the movie studios essentially decided that if they couldn't beat television, they would join it. Not only did they begin releasing their movies for television, at ever increasing prices, but most of the major studios began making movies specifically for television.

Cable Television

Curiously, the aspect of television programming that threw a monkey wrench into existing copyright was not broadcast television but cable television. Originally, cable did not deliver the "premium" channels available today, but simply received and boosted existing television programming using a "community antenna." The problem was that the cable operators didn't pay anything for the programs that they retransmitted to their customers. In 1966, United Artists Television, the owner of copy-

 *Basic principles of copyright, see Part Two.

Early cable television.

I grew up in Paragould, Arkansas, a town about ninety miles from Memphis, Tennessee, at the time the closest city with television stations. My early experience of television in the 1950s was that reception was generally poor, and that for some stations, the reception would fade in and out. There was no guarantee that just because a program came in when it started it would still be viewable twenty minutes later.

The revolution came in 1965, when Paragould Cablevision, Inc., built a community antenna, and charged customers a $10 hookup fee and $5 per month for the privilege of connecting to the antenna through cable. For the first time, pictures came in consistently. For the first time, we had meaningful access to all three national television networks, as well as the Memphis educational station. And for the first time, we could even view programming from such faraway places as Little Rock, Arkansas; Paducah, Kentucky; and Cape Girardeau, Missouri.

rights in several television programs, sued Fortnightly Corporation, a cable operator in the Pittsburgh viewing area. United Artists argued that Fortnightly infringed its copyrights when Fortnightly retransmitted these programs to its cable customers without obtaining a license. If an independent local television station had wanted to broadcast, for example, *Goldfinger,* a United Artists movie, they would have had to negotiate a licensing fee. Wasn't it unfair that Fortnightly should be able to make a profit by charging its customers to see the movie, when it didn't pay such a licensing fee?

The cable operators argued that to hold them liable for copyright infringement would effectively halt the development of cable television. They also argued that they didn't technically violate any of the exclusive rights of copyright.* They didn't actually create a "copy" of any programs, since the programs were transmitted in real time; they didn't "distribute" any copies, since there were no "copies" to distribute; and they didn't "perform"† the copyrighted work within the meaning of the copyright law.

The Supreme Court, in an incredible opinion, agreed with the cable operators that they did not infringe the United Artists copyrights. The Court divided the television world into broadcasters—who "performed" works, in the copyright sense—and viewers—who did not "perform." The Court then concluded that cable operators were more like viewers than like broadcasters, since, at that time, cable systems didn't control the content of programs, but passively received them and passed them on. In dissent, Justice Abe Fortas argued that, while the language of the act might not be entirely clear, it would be better policy to find in favor of the copyright owners until Congress could come up with a more balanced solution.

In the following years, it became obvious that cable television was not limited to the early "community antenna" model that had presented itself in the *Fortnightly* case. Instead, cable operators expanded into new territory, using satellite and microwave links to import signals from distant communities, particularly popular stations from major cities like New

*Exclusive rights of copyright, see p. 166.
†Exclusive right to perform, see p. 168.

York, Los Angeles, Chicago, and Boston. The cable operators relied on the *Fortnightly* case for the proposition that they were exempt from copyright liability. The movie studios, television networks, and stations whose programming was being taken argued that the *Fortnightly* case should not apply when a signal was imported from a distant community. This was not "enhancing" viewership within the normal service area, but making a profit by importing the television signal into a completely new television market.

The new argument was presented to the Supreme Court in 1974, in the case of *Teleprompter Corporation v. CBS.* The Supreme Court, however, stood by its analysis in *Fortnightly,* and found the cable industry still exempt from copyright liability. It also offered a more sophisticated defense of its position. Since most television programming in this country is financed not by direct payments from viewers, but by indirect profits from selling advertising, there is less economic harm to the copyright owner than might at first appear. After all, if a cable system delivers copyrighted programming to a wider audience, the original television station will be able to charge more for advertising. That's true, at least, for national advertising, since national advertisers like Procter & Gamble, or General Foods, will pay more to a television station or network when their advertising is delivered to a larger audience. But it isn't true for local advertising. The owner of a car dealership or a local restaurant in Boston is not likely to pay extra to have the advertisements seen by viewers in New York or Los Angeles.

Meanwhile, Congress was already in the midst of a major revision of copyright, to deal with among other things the cable issue. When Congress finally responded, it was in the form of a compromise. The 1976 Act overturned *Fortnightly* and *Teleprompter* by specifically providing that cable systems would be

The dexterity of Houdini.

This case calls not for the judgment of Solomon but for the dexterity of Houdini. We are here asked to consider whether and how a technical, complex, and specific Act of Congress, the Copyright Act, which was enacted in 1909, applies to one of the recent products of scientific and promotional genius, CATV. . . . Applying the normal jurisprudential tools—the words of the Act, legislative history, and precedent—to the facts of the case is like trying to repair a television set with a mallet. . . . Our major object, I suggest, should be to do as little damage as possible to traditional copyright principles and to business relationships, until the Congress legislates and relieves the embarrassment which we and the interested parties face. . . .

The opinion of the majority, in my judgment, does not heed this admonition.

– *Fortnightly Corp. v. United Artists Television, Inc.* (J. Fortas dissenting)

Importing distant signals.

By importing signals that could not normally be received with current technology in the community it serves, a CATV system does not, for copyright purposes, alter the function it performs for its subscribers. . . . The reception and rechanneling of these signals for simultaneous viewing is essentially a viewer function, irrespective of the distance between the broadcasting station and the ultimate viewer.

– Supreme Court, *Teleprompter Corp. v. Columbia Broadcasting System, Inc.*

A golden age of free premium television?

Here's a little story of audacity not within the realm of copyright, but from related technological regulation. Back in the 1980s, cable systems, as well as broadcast networks and premium cable networks, distributed their programming around the country by satellite transmissions. Under the existing law, it was perfectly legal for anyone with a compatible antenna to intercept these signals for free. With their backyard antennas, viewers could see not only hundreds of television channels, but even the channels, like Home Box Office, for which cable systems otherwise charged a premium, and even the network feeds to local stations prior to their formal broadcast, and prior to the addition of local commercials. Needless to say, many viewers had a field day. The number of people owning satellite dishes, primarily in rural areas, jumped from a few thousand in 1980 to over 3 million in the early 1990s.

Companies like Home Box Office and the television networks responded by scrambling their signals as they were transmitted by satellite. And here's where the audacity comes in. Many of the satellite dish owners, having invested hundreds or thousands of dollars in their dishes, began pressuring Congress to pass a law that would make it illegal for the companies to scramble their signals. Never mind that the companies' entire multimillion-dollar operations would be put in jeopardy; since the companies were using the "public airwaves," they weren't supposed to be able to protect their investment.

Congress was not persuaded, and allowed the companies to develop the technology that would protect their programming. The unauthorized descrambling of signals is now a violation of federal communications law as well as most state laws. But for the viewers

subject to copyright. But the Act also provided a compulsory licensing system to assure that cable operators would be able to get licenses at a modest fee. The cable compromise was very much like the phonorecord compromise of 1909,* providing for copyright liability, but subject to a compulsory licensing fee.

The funds raised by the compulsory license are distributed among all of the owners of copyright whose works have been picked up by cable. The allocation has become fairly standard from year to year. About 55–60 percent of all the money collected goes to "program suppliers," primarily motion picture companies (through the Motion Picture Association of America); about 20–25 percent to professional sports leagues; and the remainder to various other claimants. The total revenues available for distribution have increased substantially over the years, rising from $14 million in 1978 to about $200 million in 2000.

Whether one likes the compulsory license or not, it has served a useful function in allowing the sort of compromise that only a legislative body can provide. Indeed, the scheme has not only been retained but has been extended to cover satellite distribution, or "wireless," systems that provide cable-like services. The total royalties from such satellite distribution services were about $55 million in 1998.

THE VIDEOCASSETTE MARKET

The Test Case—Sony against the Movie Studios

Video recorders have been around since the 1950s. It was not until the 1970s, however, that the industry was able to shrink the equipment to an acceptable size, at an affordable price, and with the reliability and ease of use that made it suitable for the home market. The first

*Phonorecord compulsory license, see p. 38.

home video recorder, the Betamax, was introduced in 1975 by Sony Corporation. The Betamax lawsuit was introduced in 1976 by Universal Studios and Walt Disney Productions.

Universal and Disney argued that the use of the home recorder to tape their copyrighted television programs was copyright infringement. They realized that it would be pointless to sue individual Betamax users; instead, they aimed their arguments at Sony for supplying the equipment. The ultimate goal was to force Sony to agree to a licensing fee, much like the compulsory license compromises for music recording or cable television.

The first decision, however, in the district court of California in 1979, found that the home taping of television programs was a "fair use" of copyrighted works.* Even if not a fair use, the court decided that Sony should not be held liable for what its customers did with their Betamax machines. The public was free to buy and use video recorders, and Sony didn't have to pay anything to the owners of the copyrights in the programs that were being taped.

Next, the Ninth Circuit Court of Appeals in 1981 reversed the decision of the court below. The appellate court found that the home use of

who experienced it, the 1980s were a golden age of free premium television the likes of which may never be seen again. (Stay tuned, though. As of the year 2000, it looks like there's another golden age of free entertainment, this time music on the Internet. Take a look at page 120.)

The workings of a VCR.

A VCR must record much more information than an audiotape recorder. The way to do this is to move the tape by the recording head much more quickly. In a VCR, the record/playback head is mounted at an angle to the tape and spins [more] rapidly [than the tape] at the same time the tape moves. This records the signal in diagonal tracks across the tape, one track for each frame of the picture. The sound information and the synchronization signal that controls the pictures are recorded in two separate, linear tracks at the top and bottom of the tape.

—Steven Lubar

VIDEO RECORDER

LOADING POLES
RECORD/PLAYBACK HEAD
LOADING POLES
GUIDE ROLLER
GUIDE ROLLER
ERASE HEAD
AUDIO AND CONTROL HEAD
PINCH ROLLER
FEED SPOOL
DOTTED LINES REPRESENT TAPE IN RETRACTED POSITION
LOADING POLES GRAB TAPE AND BRING IT IN CONTACT WITH HEAD AND ROLLERS
TAKE-UP SPOOL
AUDIO SIGNALS
PICTURE SIGNALS
CONTROL SIGNALS
VIDEO CASSETTE

*Fair use, see p. 190.

ON WHICH ITEM HAVE THE COURTS RULED THAT MANUFACTURERS AND RETAILERS BE HELD RESPONSIBLE FOR HAVING SUPPLIED THE EQUIPMENT?

The Conrad cartoon, syndicated in many newspapers, including the *Philadelphia Inquirer.*

The video police.

Here's the public response to the Ninth Circuit opinion holding against Sony:

"It's so stupid it hardly bears comment," declared an editorial in the *Kinston* (North Carolina) *Free Press.* "Big Brotherism," said the *Salt Lake City Deseret News.* "Something misfired in the judicial process," concluded the *Wall Street Journal.* Enforcement would make "Prohibition look easy," opined a colum-

video recorders was not a fair use, and that Sony could be held liable for supplying a product whose primary and intended purpose was to tape commercial television programs, virtually all of which were copyrighted. As a result of this case, it looked as if the sale of video recorders might be legally barred, or at least delayed until some sort of licensing fee could be worked out.

The public response to the Ninth Circuit's decision was immediate and generally hysterical. Could it be that individual purchasers and users of video recorders were now copyright infringers? Several senators announced the next day that they would give the American people a Christmas present—a simple amendment providing that home taping would be exempt from copyright infringement. The cartoons and commentary overwhelmingly conveyed a sense of fear and outrage. The most prevalent image was that of a police officer or FBI agent whisking away home videotapers in handcuffs.

As a young copyright professor, I thought the opinion was absolutely correct. Of course, I explained hurriedly, this doesn't mean the end of the home video recorder. It just means, I explained, that the companies that make money from such recording will have to sit down and work out some arrangement to compensate the owners of copyright whose works are being copied. If there were something to bargain about, then I fully trusted that the parties would work out a deal to share the revenues from what would inevitably be a lucrative market for home television programs and movies. If they didn't work out a deal, then I fully trusted that Congress would work out a compromise, and come up with another of its compulsory licenses. But if the opinion had gone the other way, holding that home taping was not an infringement—if there were no leverage from a judicial victory—then I felt certain that there would be no incentive for Congress to pass a compulsory license, and some sort of disaster would befall the copyright owners whose works would be duplicated without compensation.

Shortly thereafter, the Supreme Court agreed to hear the case, and Congress decided not to act until the Supreme Court had its say. In January 1984, the Supreme Court issued its ruling: by a bare 5-to-4 majority, the Court reversed the Ninth Circuit and held for Sony. The American public got their Christmas present, a little late.

We'll consider the ramifications of this case shortly. But first, let's look at the other setting in which the movie producers got clobbered.

The Video Rental Market

Under the first sale doctrine,* once someone buys a particular copy of a copyrighted work, they may dispose of that copy however they want, including by sale or by rental. It's because of this doctrine that video rental stores can buy a copy of a movie, and then make money by renting it out over and over again, without paying any royalty above the price of the one copy. In 1984, the very year of the Betamax decision in the Supreme Court, the music recording industry managed to get Congress to pass an exception to the doctrine so that audio works may not be rented out without the authority of the copyright owner.† The movie industry originally had expected to be included in the amendment. But by now millions of people owned VCRs, and were used to the idea of renting movies cheaply. Congress was unwilling to pass a bill that threatened to end or "tax" a practice that people had gotten used to. In the end, the video amendment was severed from the audio amendment: the audio amendment passed, but the video amendment did not. In 1990, the computer software industry was also successful in getting an exemption to the first sale doctrine, barring rentals of computer programs;‡ but still video rentals were not included.

Why the disparate treatment? There are at least two possible answers. One, a sort of "conspiracy theory," is that the video dealers

nist for the *Los Angeles Times.* The *Martinez* (California) *News-Gazette* contended that the decision, "carried to its logical extreme . . . would forbid singing a copyrighted song to one's self in the shower." A cartoon in the *Philadelphia Inquirer* showed a VCR and a revolver side by side and asked the question, "On which item have the courts ruled that manufacturers and retailers be held responsible for having supplied the equipment?" Countless cartoonists and columnists—and Johnny Carson, in a sketch for "The Tonight Show"—imagined frantic households being visited by "Video Police" or detectives from the "Betamax Squad." Tom Shales, the TV critic for the *Washington Post,* imagined himself as an underground videotaper in the dread year 1984. "It is the third year of our persecution, oh my brothers, oh Betanauts and Betalogues and fellow members of the Betanese Liberation Front," he wrote. "Still, they come, the gray men in the greatcoats, the storm troopers in their clodhoppers. . . ." In the long history of its offenses that much-maligned branch of government the judiciary had probably never issued a decision that attracted more abuse and less sympathy.

—James Lardner

*First sale doctrine, see p. 167.
†Audio exception to first sale doctrine, see p. 48.
‡Computer exception to first sale doctrine, see p. 88.

The economics of the video market.

The video market was definitely affected by the lack of a video rental royalty. Producers of video works had to decide whether a work was intended primarily for the "sales" market or the "rental" market. If for the former, then the producers would have to charge a low enough price—in the $10 to $20 range—to encourage hundreds of thousands or millions of sales. If they believed that the video would do better in the rental market, then the producers would charge a higher fee, as much as $50 or $60 per video, knowing that the primary buyers were video rental stores and that they had to charge enough on the "first sale" to compensate for all the rentals of the particular copies sold. If the producers could "differentiate" these markets—charge a high fee for videos in the "rental" market, and a low fee for those in the "sales" market—the result would be that more video works would be available for sale to consumers at a cheaper price.

simply outflanked the movie industry in lobbying efforts. And as with most conspiracy theories, there's also a possible rational explanation. Everyone understands that many people who rent audio works are going to make copies of them, so that they can listen to them over and over. It is assumed, however, that most people don't make copies of videotapes, because they don't generally watch video works repeatedly, or because it takes two video recorders to make a copy of a videotape, and most people either don't have two video recorders or wouldn't normally go to the trouble of hooking them up to record from one to the other. It's debatable whether these assumptions are still true today. Children, for example, are very likely to watch favorite programs repeatedly, and many households now have more than one video recorder. (It's still a good bet, though, that most consumers haven't figured out how, or don't care to go to the trouble, to hook up the two VCRs. But that's probably only because it's so cheap to rent the tapes anyway.)

In any event, the copyright owners of movies and television programs got neither the license for home video recording nor the rental amendment that they said was necessary for their continued survival. Those of us who were sympathetic braced for the disaster that we predicted would occur.

Guess what? The disaster never came. Instead, the VCR turned out to be one of the most lucrative inventions—for movie producers as well as hardware manufacturers—since movie projectors. Video rental stores had to buy lots of copies of hit movies, and so the movie companies still made a bundle. As the economy was strong in the 1980s and 1990s, more people bought movies than appeared likely to do so in 1984. Indeed, movie companies soon made more from video release of their movies than they did from theatrical release. Of course, they didn't make as much as they would if they could charge for every single copy, or for every single rental. But the market was big enough that everybody in the chain could make money.

Victory at Last!

Don't yet write the obituary for the movie industry. In December 1996, the United States and most other countries signed a new international treaty sponsored by the World Intellectual Property Organization (WIPO). Among other things, it provided that all countries were supposed to protect exclusive rental rights in audio, computer software, *and* video works. There was an exception, if it could be demonstrated that the market for rentals was sufficient to protect the interests of the copyright owners. The signing of the treaty did not obligate the United States to amend its copyright law (instead, the United States hoped that it would get other countries to upgrade *their* laws), but it did focus the inquiry upon the market effect on copyright owners of movies. If it were determined that the first sale doctrine undermined the ability of the movie producers to make a fair return on their investment, there might yet be legislative changes in the statute.

Some legislative changes have already occurred. The Digital Millennium Copyright Act of 1998* has a new provision governing the analog video recorder market: after the middle of 2000, manufacturers are required to include in all analog video recorders a chip that recognizes the "macrovision" copy protection system used by many movie companies in their videos. It's now illegal to circumvent such protection systems or to sell equipment that can circumvent such systems, and the penalties for violating the statute are severe. The act thus allows movie producers to physically protect movies released on VHS video (the successor to the Beta format), to prevent copying. Movie producers can be expected to increase their use of such copy protection schemes. Although broadcast television stations and basic-tier cable television services are prohibited from encoding their programming, pay-per-view and subscription services will be allowed to add the electronic protection to their programming. No one yet knows

---

"Completely snookered."

James Lardner wrote an account of the VCR wars for the *New Yorker* that was later expanded into a thorough and fascinating book, *Fast Forward: Hollywood, the Japanese, and the VCR Wars* (1987). Lardner colorfully documents the motion picture industry's loss of the battle in the courts, in Congress, and in the hearts of the American citizenry. Some of the chapter headings suggest the dynamics: "Outgunned," "Pigs Versus Pigs," and "Completely Snookered."

Looking back on the collapse of the movie industry's lobbying efforts, [Jack] Valenti agreed with Dale Snape's assessment. "You've got to be proconsumer, and we were never able to show that we were proconsumer," he said. He singled out the press as another big headache. The *New York Times*, the *Wall Street Journal*, and the *Washington Post*, had come out against the rental bill, as they had against the royalty. "We got completely snookered—just absolutely destroyed—in the press!" Valenti exclaimed. . . . "But I suppose we lost this battle when those cartoons appeared about video police coming into your homes. The cartoonists killed us. We became objects of ridicule. Molière once wrote that most men don't object to being called wicked, but all men mightily object to being made ridiculous, and the Molière line is quite relevant today."

—James Lardner

---

*Digital Millennium Copyright Act, see p. 112.

The economics of the new video market.

In recent years, the video market has actually been moving in the direction of allowing movie companies to get a percentage of the revenues directly from video rentals. The problem with running a successful video store is to have enough of the "hit" movies immediately, when they are in demand. Blockbuster Video has arranged for this by negotiating with the movie companies to allow for the making and stocking of lots of new release videos at a relatively cheap cost per video, in exchange for granting the movie companies a percentage of the rental revenues. The resulting market looks very similar to what would exist if the movie companies had an exclusive rental right that survived the "first sale"—except that the video stores probably get a better deal, because of the leverage of the first sale doctrine. The arrangement also has the effect of giving Blockbuster a tremendous advantage over video stores that are not in a position to make similar deals with the movie companies. Blockbuster can "guarantee" that major new releases will be available immediately, while stores without profit-sharing arrangements can't afford to buy too many new releases, because of the high cost of the inventory and the relatively short shelflife of most movies today.

whether such encoding will become the norm, or whether consumers will simply boycott subscription services that don't allow for videotaping of their programs. Stay tuned for future developments.

And, as explained in the sidebar, "The economics of the new video market," movie producers have already worked out ways of getting a bigger "piece" of the video rental action. With such arrangements, the movie producers are effective partners with the video stores. We've come a long way since the Betamax case.

High Definition Television

In the 1990s the television industry developed, and the Federal Communications Commission approved, a new HDTV (high definition television) standard that will completely replace the old NTSC (National Television System Committee) standard. It's based upon the digital encoding of programming information. The new HDTV standard scans the equivalent of 1125 lines per frame, exceeding the resolution of 35-millimeter movies, and far surpassing the quality of the NTSC standard.

This digital technology makes it easier to copy, reproduce, and alter television programs, and, as with other digital works, each copy retains the same quality as the original. The technology thus raises some of the same seemingly intractable copyright concerns as it did in the case of music.

As we'll study in more detail in chapter 5 (after analyzing computer programs and the Internet), the fix for this problem is already in place. In 1998, Congress passed the Digital Millennium Copyright Act, which makes it illegal, except in certain circumstances, to gain access to digital copyrighted works that are protected by electronic protection systems. So, as movies follow music and computer programs into the digital age, and as the movie industry develops hardware and software systems to block access to and block copying of their works, the law supports their efforts.

CONCLUSION

While movies and television may have appeared to be technologies that would test the limits of copyright, it turns out that, for the most part, the fit between copyright and the video technologies has been fairly smooth. In the case of movies and television, the basic principles of copyright seem to have accommodated the technologies. In the case of cable, when the fit didn't seem to work, Congress responded with a special compromise to balance the interests of copyright owners and the cable industry. And even in the case of the new video market, both analog and digital, it looks as though Congress has been able to fix the problem. Miracle of miracles, the market has managed to adapt quite nicely, or well enough. The technology in this field has turned out not to be copyright's enemy, but its friend.

High definition television, (right) compared to the previous standard television (left). The high definition version uses twice the number of scan lines, making it comparable in resolution to film.

CHAPTER FOUR

The Computer

Functions of the Computer

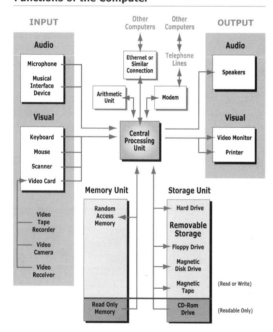

THE WORKINGS OF THE COMPUTER

Probably no technology has had a more profound effect upon copyright, upon the creative process, or for that matter upon our lives, than the computer. Before getting into the intricacies of copyright, however, it will be helpful to spend just a little time exploring what computers are and how they work.

The Hardware

The real guts of most computers is the *central processing unit,* or CPU. (The italicized key phrases are illustrated in the diagram on the this page.) Basically, this central processing unit is a very fast traffic cop. It receives information, in the form of electronic impulses, and reroutes it to other parts of the computer. These impulses are simply electronic on/off switches. Ultimately, all the information a computer receives, stores, manipulates, and sends is simply electronic impulses that are either "on"—there is an electrical charge stored in a particular place in the computer—or "off"—the relevant location in the computer does *not* have an electrical charge. The CPU does its magic by handling an amazingly large number of operations in a very short period of time—about a billion operations per second on the most recent generation of computers.

Another important function of the computer is the simple storage and retrieval of electronic impulses in what is called the *memory unit* of the computer. The memory unit stores the electronic impulses so that they can be retrieved by the central processing unit at a later time.

There are different types of memory in computers. *Random access memory,* or RAM, is basically short-term memory that's stored in such a way that it's immediately accessible to the central processing unit. In most computers, the electronic impulses in RAM must be constantly recharged. Think of RAM as live electricity flowing through the system. Turn off the computer, and the flow of electricity ceases—the information stored in RAM disappears. This form of memory is very good for information you want to access and process very quickly, but it isn't very good for storing a word processing document until you need it next Thursday.

For that longer-term memory, you need some form of *storage unit* that will reliably retain the information well after the computer itself is turned off. One storage device is a *hard drive,* which basically records a copy of the electronic impulses on platters that spin within the computer. Other storage devices are magnetic tapes or floppy drives, magnetic disks or optical disks, or CD-ROMs, all of which store the information on a separate medium that can be removed from the computer and reinserted at a later time, or can be transferred to other computers to share the information encoded on them.

Some information is so critical to the operation of the computer that you want it always to be accessible, and not normally altered. Such critical information is

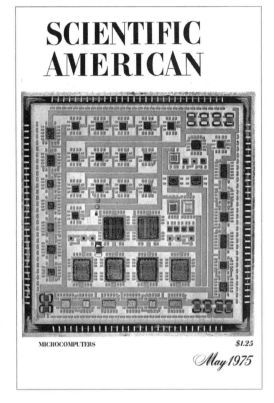

Only $1,295!
This is a picture of a complete general purpose computer, here about actual size, from the cover of *Scientific American* (May 1975). The computer was made by Teledyne Systems Company from chips manufactured by National Semiconductor Corporation. The two largest chips, in the center, were integrated circuits containing what at the time was the remarkable capacity of six thousand transistors each. These two chips controlled the four slightly smaller chips devoted to arithmetic and logic circuits, and the numerous other chips. The computer, mounted on a ceramic wafer and with six glass-insulated conducting layers, communicated with the outside world through 120 leads, 30 on each side. The cost of the computer at the time was $1,295.

usually contained in a permanent storage unit known as *read-only memory,* or ROM. Think of ROM as the hard-wired circuits that can't normally be changed by the user of the computer. (You might notice that the line between computer memory and storage is not at all a fine one. For reasons that may be more historical than functional, read-only memory and random access memory are usually considered memory units, while hard drives and removable media are usually considered storage.)

Other parts of the computer are the *arithmetic unit,* which can add, subtract, multiply, divide, and perform other advanced calculations; *input* devices, such as a keyboard, a mouse, a microphone, a midi (musical interface device), or various devices that allow the computer to recognize video images from a television receiver or video camera or video recorder; *output* devices, such as a computer monitor, a printer, or speakers; and connections to allow the computer to communicate with other computers through direct connections or over telephone lines. Once computers can access telephone or other long-distance lines, they can be linked via global networks like the Internet, so that practically any computer can access any other computer, wherever located.

Computer Programs

At the end of this chapter, we'll take a look at the profound effect computers have had on a broad range of creative works. For most of the chapter, however, we're going to focus upon the protection of a new form of creative work: the computer program that controls all of the information inside a computer and makes it work its magic.

What, exactly, is a computer program? In the words of the Copyright Act (as amended in 1980), a computer program is "a set of statements or instructions to be used directly or indirectly in a computer in order to bring about a certain result." There are several different ways of categorizing computer programs. One traditional distinction is between *object code* and *source code.* Object code is simply the program as it's stored in the computer, the ones and zeroes, the ons and offs that tell the computer precisely what it's supposed to do. This is the language that only a computer would love. Even a sophisticated computer programmer can't really decipher all these ones and zeroes, and doesn't usually write programs directly in object code. Instead, the programmer usually writes in source code, a more abstract, or "higher," programming language, such as Basic or C or PASCAL, and uses a computer program, a *compiler,* to convert the humanly intelligible source code into the computer-intelligible object code.

A simple programming example will illustrate the distinction. Let's say I want to write a simple computer program that will ask the user for two numbers, and then respond by calculating their sum. Here's how the program might look in an old version of Basic, a relatively straightforward programming language that unfortunately is hardly ever used anymore:

```
10 Input A
20 Input B
30 Let C = A+B
40 Print "The sum of your two numbers is "; C
```

Here's what this program would accomplish on a computer that was set up to run Basic. At lines 10 and 20, the program would stop and wait for the user to input two numbers (that's what the instruction "Input" is defined to do in Basic). It would then select a portion of its memory, give the memory locations the titles "A" and "B," and store the two numbers in those locations. In line 30, the computer would go to the locations labeled "A" and "B," take the numbers previously stored there, send them to the arithmetic unit for addition, and store the result in a portion of memory labeled "C." In line 40, it would print out literally the words in quotation marks, followed by the number that is now stored in the portion of memory previously labeled "C." On a computer screen, the running of the program would look something like this, with the underlined portions entered by the user:

? <u>12</u>

? <u>23</u>

The sum of your two numbers is 35

This Basic program is relatively easy for people to understand and work with, because it's written in source code. In fact, human beings could work with this program, analyze it, and discuss it without ever entering it into a computer. As entered into any particular computer, however, it's reduced to computer instructions—or object code—that implement the above Basic program on a particular type of computer.

Of course, computer programs get much more sophisticated than our example. Programs have been written that will allow word processing, graphic image processing, sound processing, and video processing on a sophisticated level. The cutting edge of the technology is usually reflected in the games. It was only in the early 1970s that the first commercial computer video game was made available to the

Pre-Pong.
In 1972, Magnavox released Odyssey, a "totally new dimension in television entertainment for the entire family." One of the dozen games it could play was a Ping-Pong game that preceded the video arcade hit, Pong.

Pac-Man.

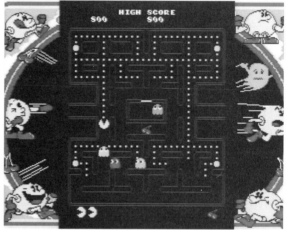

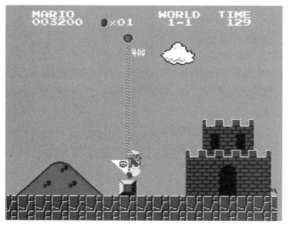

Super Mario Brothers.

Super Mario 64.

public. That game, Pong, was basically little more than a light blip that was moved around the screen to simulate a Ping-Pong game. What I think of as the second generation of computer games were games like Pac-Man, a program that could move simple imaginary characters around a relatively stationary two-dimensional grid. We might think of the third generation of games as the Mario Brothers type game, a still basically two-dimensional game, but with characters that moved around with much greater fluidity and sophistication: Mario walked across two-dimensional side-scrolling backgrounds, and interacted with those backgrounds. The fourth generation of games is represented by StarFox or Star Wars or Super Mario 64, in which the background scenery constantly changes so as to simulate a three-dimensional view of a virtual space. It's hard to even imagine the amount of information—the hundreds of millions of operations per second—the computer has to process in each frame, at the rate of many frames per second, in order to create a realistic image that "puts" the viewer into the scene displayed on the computer monitor. The position of practically every pixel on the screen has to be recalculated, based upon the complicated three-dimensional contours of the "characters" and background of each scene.

HOW DO WE PROTECT THE INVESTMENT?

As the games and word processing and business programs have become more and more complicated, the investment in developing them has increased dramatically. Today, the development of a new computer program can cost millions of dollars and hundreds of thousands of programmer-hours. If you're a developer who spends all that time and energy to bring your program to market, you certainly don't want to have teenage kids send free copies of your latest version of MegaDoom to all their friends over the Internet, or have business executives distribute dozens or hundreds of copies of your latest version of MegaWord to all the employees over the company's network, for free. You expect to get compensated, and you probably wouldn't develop the software if you didn't think you would be compensated.

During the 1960s and 1970s, programmers began asking how they could protect their creations in the marketplace. One method that's met

Can computer programs be patented?

Gary Benson and Arthur Tabbot sought a patent on a computer program that converted binary-coded decimal (BCD) numerals into pure binary numerals, and back again. Since computers use binary numbers, but people are better able to understand decimal numbers, or even binary-coded decimal numbers, such a program was absolutely essential to the running of most modern computers. If the patent were granted, it would be the computer program equivalent of a patent on transistors or on semiconductor chips.

When their patent application was rejected by the patent office, Benson and Tabbot sued Robert Gottschalk, the acting commissioner of patents. The case went to the Supreme Court, which in 1972 held that the computer program was not patentable. As stated by Justice Douglas:

> A procedure for solving a given type of mathematical problem is known as an "algorithm." The procedures set forth in the present claims are of that kind; that is to say, they are a generalized formulation for programs to solve mathematical problems of converting one form of numerical representation to another. . . .
>
> It is conceded that one may not patent an idea. But in practical effect that would be the result if the formula for converting BCD numerals to pure binary numerals were patented in this case. The mathematical formula involved here has no substantial practical application except in connection with a digital computer, which means that if the judgment below is affirmed, the patent would wholly pre-empt the mathematical formula and in practical effect would be a patent on the algorithm itself.

with some success is the development of physical copy protection systems. That is, you write the program so that it won't work unless the user types in the proper password or serial number, or inserts a disk containing a legitimate copy of the program. The problem with using such physical protection is that many legitimate users are unhappy with the system. What happens if you forget the password, or if you don't happen to have the original program disk when you want to run the program from your hard drive? Can you make backup copies to protect against the possibility that something might go wrong with your initial disk? What most software companies learned during the seventies and eighties is that legitimate users complained strenuously about overly burdensome copy protection systems; and so, most companies abandoned all but the most straightforward of such systems.

Some companies tried patent protection* of their programs, but there were several problems. The level of creativity required to get a patent is too high, and most computer programs don't qualify. In any event, it usually takes about a year or two to get a patent, and in the software business, one year and you're obsolete. And the Supreme Court, in a fascinating early case, held that a computer program—or at least the program in that case—was simply a mathematical algorithm, and not an "invention" subject to patent.

Some companies tried trade secret law.† If you only disclose your program to people who agree not to further disclose it, you can legally enforce their promises not to disclose. This worked for some computer setups, where the software supplier retained some control over the use of the software program. But it didn't work very well for the new desktop computers, where copies of the software were sold to the users, and could be studied and sometimes deciphered by them.

As we saw in some detail in chapter 1, copyright is an effective method of protecting creative works,

*Patent protection, see pp. 128 and 219.
†Trade secret protection, see p. 224.

designed to encourage the making of such works by granting certain exclusive rights in them. Why not bring computer programs within the scope of copyright protection? After all, copyright has been around for a long time, and it seems to work. It's easy to get a copyright, because you don't have to go through any particular qualifying applications. The threshold of copyrightability is pretty low. All you have to do is create something original—that is, that you figured out yourself, and didn't simply copy from someone else.

In recent years, the patent office has begun granting patents for computer programs, particularly ones that are part of methods of doing business. Some of these patents are controversial, and it remains to be seen how extensive such patent protection will be in the future.

There are some conceptual problems in using copyright as the form of legal protection to cover computer programs. Under the "works of utility" doctrine,* functional works are not the proper subject of copyright protection. Under that doctrine, how can copyright protect a computer program, the purpose of which is to run a machine? Computer programs are simply different from most creative works: while copyrightable works are generally designed for human communication, isn't communication with a machine something of a different order?

Some commentators suggested that computer programs didn't fit neatly into any of the existing forms of legal protection of creative works—patent, copyright, trade secret, or anything else. What we needed, these commentators suggested, was some new form of protection designed specifically to protect computer programs.

To cut a long story short, all of this, by now, is actually ancient history. For the most part, we've opted to treat computer programs as creative works protectable under the copyright laws. This might not be obvious from the Copyright Act itself, since the Act does not list computer programs as one of the eight categories of works covered by copyright. But one of the categories of works is "literary works," and literary works are defined to include works "expressed in words, numbers, or other verbal or numerical symbols or indicia." During the congressional discussions leading up to the 1976 Copyright Act, Congress concluded that computer programs were within the definition of "literary works," even though computer programs clearly had features that were unlike those of any literary works that had previously existed. So, whether or not it seems intuitive, and whether or not the statute seems clear,

 *Works of utility, see p. 185.

The argument for copyright protection: the Commission majority (1978).

The cost of developing computer programs is far greater than the cost of their duplication. Consequently, computer programs . . . are likely to be disseminated only if:

(1) The creator can recover all of its costs plus a fair profit on the first sale of the work, thus leaving it unconcerned about the later publication of the work; or

(2) The creator can spread its costs over multiple copies of the work with some form of protection against unauthorized duplication of the work; or

(3) The creator's costs are borne by another, as, for example, when the government or a foundation offers prizes or awards; or

(4) The creator is indifferent to cost and donates the work to the public.

The consequence of the first possibility would be that the price of virtually any program would be so high that there would necessarily be a drastic reduction in the number of programs marketed. In this country, possibilities three and four occur but rarely outside of academic and government-sponsored research. Computer programs are the product of great intellectual effort and their utility is unquestionable. The Commission is, therefore, satisfied that some form of protection is necessary to encourage the creation and broad distribution of computer programs in a competitive market.

The conclusion of the Commission is that the continued availability of copyright protection for computer programs is desirable. This availability is in keeping with nearly two centuries' development of

computer programs are "literary works," and, as such, they are protected by copyright.

Even as Congress passed the 1976 Copyright Act, it established the National Commission on New Technological Uses of Copyrighted Works (CONTU) to analyze, among other things, the appropriateness of the copyright approach. That commission concluded that computer programs were and should be copyrightable, and recommended a minor amendment to the Copyright Act that Congress adopted in 1980.* The amendment created a "limitation" on the copyrightability of computer programs by specifically allowing users to make archival, or backup, copies of programs, and to make minor adaptations necessary to get programs to run on their particular machines. These exceptions would hardly have been necessary unless computer programs were otherwise already covered by the Act. So, while the statute still does not say in so many words that computer programs are copyrightable, the 1980 amendment, by carving out a limited exception, implicitly confirms that they are. To be sure, there was a well-reasoned dissent to the CONTU report, as well as periodic negative comments by various commentators over the years. But by now it's a done deal: computer programs are copyrightable.

The only remaining question is not *whether* computer programs should be protected by copyright, but *to what extent* they should be protected. This is not an easy question, since computer programs are not obviously or easily amenable to analysis under traditional copyright principles.

Let's turn to two of the leading cases in which the courts have proven themselves able to resolve the tough issues. We'll look later at the ways in which Congress has felt it necessary to change the existing laws in order to accommodate the particular problems raised by protecting computer programs.

*1980 computer amendment, see p. 88.

THE COMPUTER COPYRIGHT CASES

Apple Computer, Inc. v. Franklin Computer Corp.

American copyright doctrine during which the universe of works protectible by statutory copyright has expanded along with the imagination, communications media, and technical capabilities of society.

One of the great success stories of the computer industry is that of Apple Computer, Inc., which developed the Apple II, one of the first more or less user-friendly desktop computers. The computer was assembled in 1976 by a couple of enterprising kids in their parents' garage using standard parts that were readily available, designed around the new, cheap 6502 chip manufactured by Mostek. Within months, dozens of companies were developing software to run on Apple's new machine. The big breakthrough for Apple came with the development of the first truly successful spreadsheet program, VisiCalc, in 1979. In its first year, VisiCalc was available only on the Apple; and it was so successful that it resulted in the sale of many Apple computers to businesses and individuals who wanted or needed to have VisiCalc.

Shortly after Apple introduced its computer, Franklin Computer Corporation tried to duplicate Apple's achievement. It designed its computer, the Franklin Ace 100, around the same 6502 chip that Apple had used. Franklin realized early on that it would be very difficult to compete with Apple and other existing computer manufacturers. When first introduced, a new computer would have virtually no software that it could run, while the existing computer manufacturers had the advantage of hundreds of programs already up and running. Franklin's solution was to make its computer "Apple-compatible." That way, Franklin could plug into the existing software and peripherals that were already designed to run with Apple computers. To achieve compatibility, Franklin thought it was not enough to simply use the same computer chip that Apple used; it also had to duplicate some of the Apple operating

The Apple prototype—using a Mostek 6502 microprocessor, four kilobytes of memory, and a cassette recorder for storage of programs and data—can now be viewed in the Smithsonian Institution.

The first commercial Apple computer, with its own keyboard, monitor, disk drives, and power supply.

The argument against copyright protection: John Hersey's dissent (1978).

In the early stages of its development, the basic ideas and methods to be contained in a computer program are set down in written forms, and these will presumably be copyrightable with no change in the 1976 Act. But the program itself, in its mature and usable form, is a machine control element, a mechanical device, which on Constitutional grounds and for reasons of social policy ought not to be copyrighted.

The view here is that the investment of creative effort in the devising of computer programs does warrant certain modes of protection for the resulting devices, but that these modes already exist, or are about to be brought into being, under other laws besides copyright: that the need for copyright protection of the machine phase of computer programs, quite apart from whether it is fitting, has not been demonstrated to this Commission; and that the social and economic effects of permitting copyright to stand alongside these other forms of protection would be, on balance, negative.

The heart of the argument lies in what flows from the distinction raised above, between the written and mechanical forms of computer programs: Admitting these devices to copyright would mark the first time copyright had ever covered a means of communication, not with the human mind and senses, but with machines.

system. That is, in developing the software to run its machine, Franklin copied various portions of the computer programs Apple used to run its machine.

Without yet getting to the legal arguments, Franklin's practical assessment may have been correct. It might be possible to write an operating system that would make Franklin's computer look very much like an Apple. But unless it were precisely the same, it would be hard to guarantee that a program that ran on an Apple would run on a Franklin. For example, a program like VisiCalc, written to run on the Apple operating system, might be written on the assumption that certain specific operating instructions, like telling the printer to print a copy, or telling the monitor to move a pointer, were controlled by instructions at particular locations in the Apple operating system. These are known as "entry points," the precise locations within an operating system where specific instructions can be found. If Franklin wrote its own operating system, then some of the critical entry points would be at different locations. So if you tried to run VisiCalc on a Franklin, and VisiCalc tried to make a call to the location where it expected printer instructions, and those instructions weren't there, then your computer would crash.

In order to achieve Apple compatibility, Franklin simply copied parts of Apple's operating system. And, no surprise, Apple sued Franklin for copyright infringement of its computer programs. Apple's argument was straightforward: Computer programs are copyrightable; copying and distributing are exclusive rights of copyright; so Franklin's copying and distributing* of Apple's computer programs are a copyright infringement.

Franklin made several counterarguments. It could hardly argue that computer programs weren't copyrightable, since that, at least, was clear from the 1976 Act and its legislative history. Instead, Franklin argued, more specifically, that *these* computer programs weren't copyrightable for three somewhat overlapping reasons: (1) they existed in

*Copying and distribution, see p. 167.

the Apple computer in object code, and object code, as part of a machine, was a "work of utility,"* and therefore not copyrightable; (2) some of the programs were embedded in the ROM of the Apple computer, and ROM, as part of a machine, was not copyrightable; and (3) the programs were part of the operating system, and, as such, a functional part of the computer; as part of the "process, system, or method of operation,"† under section 102 of the Act, it was not copyrightable. Although the district court was sympathetic to Franklin's arguments, the Third Circuit Court of Appeals ruled in favor of Apple on the copyrightability issues. The programs were copyrightable even though they were in object code, even though they were embedded in ROM, and even though they were part of an operating system. The court held that there was no basis for making the distinctions Franklin had urged: computer programs were copyrightable no matter what form they might take. Franklin ultimately settled the case for a large cash payment, undertook to develop a separate operating system, and then proceeded to fail in the marketplace.

So what is a company like Franklin to do? It's theoretically entitled to make a new computer using the same chip Apple used. But if the computer can't be made Apple-compatible, then there will be no software to run on the new machine, and it will have a difficult time getting out of the starting gate. Apple thus gets an indirect benefit from a lot of programs that are not written by Apple at all, but by third parties to run on Apple machines. Well, the court was unsympathetic to this argument, stating that "Franklin may wish to achieve total compatibility with independently developed application programs written for the Apple II, but that is a commercial and competitive objective," which did not enter into the consideration of whether Apple was entitled to copyright in its operating system.

Another argument against copyright protection: Office of Technology Assessment (1986).

Although the copyright law adopts a uniform approach to protected works, not all types of information-based products are the same, nor can they be treated as if they were. A list of stock and bond prices, for example, differs from the musical score or a motion picture, and both of these are distinct from a computer program. In the case of stock prices, the value is in the information itself—the number of shares traded and the daily fluctuation in prices. The value of a musical score, in contrast, lies in the way it sounds to an audience— the appeal of its melody, rhythm, and harmony. And computer programs are valued for what they do—their effectiveness at performing a given task in a computer.

This analysis has identified three types of copyright works: *works of art, works of fact,* and *works of function.* . . . It is these differences that pose problems for the uniform application of copyright principles to all three categories. . . . In theory . . . copyright law cannot be successfully applied to computer programs. On the basis of the recommendations of the CONTU Commission, and without legislative debate, Congress determined that computer programs could be copyrighted as "literary works" under Section 102 of the 1976 Copyright Act. Although the issue of whether computer programs could or should be either copyrighted or patented was the subject of considerable legal controversy, it is now dormant. . . . [T]he courts have resolved these questions in favor of copyright protection for computer programs.

*Works of utility, see p. 185.
†Process, system, or method, see p. 188.

Two kids in a garage.

The two "kids" did have jobs. Steve Wozniak (affectionately known to his friends as "Woz") was an engineer at Hewlett-Packard, and Steve Jobs worked part-time at Atari.

Woz had designed a single-board computer around the Motorola 6800 microprocessor. While the 6800 was fairly powerful, it was also fairly expensive at $175. In 1976, a small company called MOS Technology announced a pin-for-pin replacement for the 6800 called the 6502. Although it performed many of the same functions as the 6800, it cost only $25.

Woz purchased a 6502 chip and immediately began work on a programming language—BASIC—for the new chip. Once the programming was complete, Woz redesigned his original 6800-based computer to accommodate the new 6502 chip. He and Jobs named the machine the Apple computer. Working from Jobs's garage, Woz designed circuitry to connect a video monitor and keyboard to the computer. . . . By the end of 1976, Wozniak had designed and built a much-improved computer, the Apple II. The Apple II was a single-board computer like the Apple I, but the Apple II went several steps farther. The Apple II had the BASIC programming language built in, and it also had the ability to display text and graphics in color.

—Les Freed

Apple Computer, Inc. v. Microsoft Corp.

Apple's next breakthrough was the development of the Macintosh computer in 1984. The Mac, as it came to be known, represented the first major successful use of a graphical user interface to run a desktop computer. Instead of typing in archaic lines of code that were gibberish to the uninitiated, the idea of the Macintosh was that major computer functions were represented by images, or icons. The user could run the computer by simply clicking on pictures. For example, to open a particular application, you didn't have to type in the name of the program you wanted to run, but, using a pointing device known as a mouse, you just moved a cursor to a picture of the program and clicked twice. To open a file, or a work in progress, you just double-clicked on a visual representation of the file. The images were laid out on the screen in ways that allowed for their easy manipulation. You could store files in folders, and folders in folders, to organize your programs and data. You could click on "windows" that contained different groups of programs and data, and move the images from one window to another. You could open windows to work on them, and close them to clear them away from the screen while you worked on something else.

One of the people who admired this new graphical way of running computers was Bill Gates, the person who at age seventeen had developed the DOS operating system that ran the IBM computer, as well as most other desktop computers. In 1983, Gates's company, Microsoft, developed the Microsoft Interface Manager as a graphical overlay to the existing DOS operating system. The problem was that the program didn't work very well, particularly when compared with the Macintosh operating system that was introduced the following year. In 1985, Microsoft signed a licensing agreement with Apple, under which Microsoft was allowed to incorporate certain features of the Macintosh interface into its new program. Although it took several more years to get it right, Windows 3.0, released in 1990, finally seemed to answer most of the problems with earlier versions of the program.

Windows 3.0 was an immediate success, and eventually became the most successful computer program ever written. It made the awkward DOS operating system almost manageable. It also made Microsoft look like a monopoly, leading to one of the largest antitrust lawsuits since the breakup of AT&T—but that's the subject of a book on antitrust.*

Apple, by this time regretting its licensing agreement, claimed that the new version of Windows was not included within the earlier arrangement, and sued Microsoft for copyright infringement. This suit, however, was completely different from its earlier suit against Franklin. While Franklin had clearly copied portions of Apple's actual computer program—its operating system—Microsoft did not copy any of the actual code from the Apple operating system. Microsoft basically wrote a completely different computer program that nonetheless copied the *effect,* or the "feel," of a Macintosh.

Microsoft raised several defenses, based upon some of the basic copyright principles we'll discuss in Part Two. It argued that what it had taken was merely the "idea" of Apple's graphical user interface, not any of the actual expression,† or code. It had taken some of the functional elements, but the functional elements, under the works of utility doctrine,‡ were not protected by copyright. Microsoft also argued that certain of the features in the Macintosh operating system were not original• to Apple, but in fact owed their origin to earlier prototypes, particularly the Xerox Corporation's Star computer. And many of the features, Microsoft argued, were covered by its earlier licensing agreement with Apple.

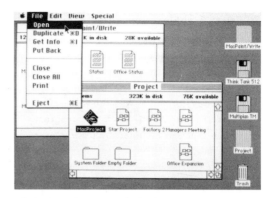

The original Macintosh desktop, showing icons representing folders, applications, and documents, and windows showing and controlling open applications.

Microsoft Windows 3.0.

  *Antitrust, see p. 222.
†Idea-expression, see p. 188.
‡Works of utility, see p. 185.
•Originality, see p. 127.

The first graphical user interface.

Many of the principles of the graphical user interface had already been worked out by the Xerox Corporation on its Star computer. For various reasons, the Star computer was not itself successful, but it was the inspiration for both the Macintosh and Windows programs that have come to dominate the personal computer market.

Narrowing the scope of protection.

A leading case has held that, in determining whether one computer program infringes another, the test is not the usual one of "substantial similarity," described in chapter 7, but a special three-part test. First, in the "abstraction" step, a court is supposed to "dissect the allegedly copied program's structure and isolate each level of abstraction contained within it." Second, in the "filtration" step, a court is supposed to "examine the structural components at each level of abstraction" to determine whether they are uncopyrightable as idea, "required by factors external to the program itself," or "taken from the public domain." (This filtration is supposed to reduce the program to the "golden nugget" of protectable expression.) And third, at the "comparison" step, the court is supposed to compare the infringed program to the "golden nugget" that survives the above analysis, to determine if there is any substantial similarity.

This test, announced in the case of *Computer Associates v. Altai,* is about as abstract and metaphysical as the law gets. Even the court admitted that "[t]o be frank, the exact contours of copyright protection for non-literal program structure are not completely clear." Yet the court clearly contem-

In a series of decisions in the federal district court in California, Apple basically got trounced. The court concluded that most of the elements of Apple's graphical user interface were not protected by copyright, either because they were not original with Apple, because they were functional, or because they were covered by the original licensing agreement.

There are other computer copyright cases, but they are basically consistent with the Apple cases. Copying of computer code generally constitutes a copyright infringement, but copying of the "idea" of a computer program does not. Of course, the problem in many cases is in deciding what constitutes "idea" and what constitutes "expression"—and on this point, courts sometimes disagree. Yet, despite the early doubts and the not-so-perfect match, courts have found that the basic principles of copyright—originality, works of utility, the idea-expression distinction, substantial similarity, and fair use*—also work just fine in determining the copyrightability of computer programs.

THE COMPUTER COPYRIGHT AMENDMENTS

Even while the courts were tackling some of the tough issues raised by the decision to include computer programs within the scope of copyright, Congress was also fixing some of the problems that it thought should not have to await judicial resolution.

The Exception for Archival and Adaptive Copies

In 1980, Congress passed an amendment to the Copyright Act that created a limited exception to the rights of copyright in computer programs.† The amendment specifically allows purchasers of computer programs to make backup copies for archival purposes, and

---

*Originality, see p. 127; works of utility, p. 185;
   idea-expression, p. 188; substantial similarity, p. 151; fair use, p. 190.
†1980 amendment, see p. 82.

to make adaptations necessary to get the program to run on a particular machine. Of course, if the computer program comes with some sort of physical copy protection system, it might not be possible for the user to make such copies; but the making of such copies, for the purposes specified in the amendment, would not otherwise violate the copyright law.

The Special Protection for Computer Chips

Back in 1984, before it was clear that copyright would or could be made to effectively protect computer programs, the computer industry convinced Congress to pass a statute creating exclusive rights in computer semiconductor chips. A semiconductor chip is defined in the statute as a product "having two or more layers of metallic, insulating, or semiconductor material, deposited or otherwise placed on, or etched away or otherwise removed from, a piece of semiconductor material in accordance with a predetermined pattern." These chips are usually made of silicon crystal, and the patterns are etched into the chips in layers so that they interact like miniature electronic circuits, connecting miniature transistors (that is, circuits that control other circuits). The chips are made up of as many as a dozen or more layers: each layer is designed by making a large-scale "mask work," which functions something like a photographic negative in that it allows the making of copies. The images produced from the mask works are miniaturized and embedded one on top of the other to make the three-dimensional semiconductor chip. It's these chips that form the guts of virtually all computers manufactured today. Their main feature is that they are tiny: a sophisticated chip like the Intel Pentium CPU chip measures only 1.5 square inches, yet contains 3.1 million transistors.

The problem, as far as the computer industry is concerned, is that it's relatively easy—or at least in 1984 it was relatively easy—for someone

plates that application of its test will result in a narrow range of protection for computer programs. As explained by the court, "If the test we have outlined results in narrowing the scope of protection [for computer programs], as we expect it will, that result flows from applying, in accordance with Congressional intent, long-standing principles of copyright law to computer programs." The net result is that computer programs are protected under copyright, but not as liberally as other types of copyrighted works.

A limited exception for computer programs.

Notwithstanding the provisions of section 106, it is not an infringement for the owner of a copy of a computer program to make or authorize the making of another copy or adaptation of that computer program provided:

(1) that such a new copy or adaptation is created as an essential step in the utilization of the computer program in conjunction with a machine and that it is used in no other manner, or

(2) that such new copy or adaptation is for archival purposes only and that all archival copies are destroyed in the event that continued possession of the computer program should cease to be rightful.

–Copyright Act

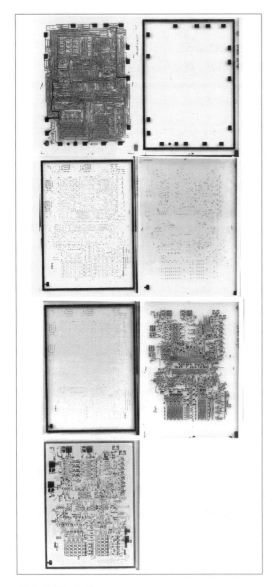

The first microprocessor chip, the Intel 4004, containing 2250 transistors on a single chip.

An engineer working on a mask work.

"Mask Works."
These mask works are more than just the blueprints for a semiconductor chip: they are the "negatives" that are used to actually make the chip. Engineers shine light through the mask works as they build up the layers that make up the chip. Shown here are the mask works from the Intel 4004 chip.

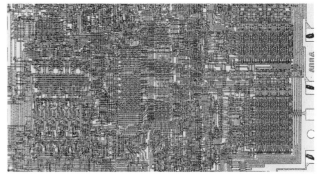

The final product: the 4004 chip (detail).

to take a semiconductor chip, effectively strip away the layers, and use the chip as the model for making a limitless number of copies. So, what takes months or years and maybe millions of dollars to develop, can be copied and mass-produced in a matter of weeks or days. Congress understood immediately that such practices, if widespread, would destroy the computer industry. Its response was the Semiconductor Chip Protection Act of 1984, which granted exclusive rights to the developers of semiconductor chip products.

The new law was based loosely upon copyright principles. For example, only original works were protected, borrowing the lesser standard of originality* from copyright, rather than the higher standard of novelty from patent. Some features were different from copyright. For example, the period of protection was only ten years, much less than in the case of copyrighted works generally.† Although the act was codified in chapter 9 of title 17 of the U.S. Code, right after the Copyright Act that comprised chapters 1 through 8, it was decided that semiconductor chip products should be treated separately from copyright. There were at least two reasons for doing this: first, it was thought that separate treatment would avoid possible distortions of basic copyright principles to make them fit the new type of work. And second, if such protection were included under American copyright law, it might trigger U.S. treaty obligations‡ to give equal protection to foreign creators of such works even though their own countries didn't grant similar protection to U.S. citizens. By keeping the law separate, the United States could withhold protection for foreigners, or could negotiate to get other countries to specifically pass reciprocal laws.

Curiously, the Semiconductor Chip Protection Act has turned out not to be all that important. Registrations for mask works were below expectations, and in the first ten years after its passage, there was only one reported case brought under the act. Why should this be? To some extent, the evolving technology of semiconductor chips may have made it more difficult for others to make copies anyway. Or maybe it's just that copyright protection of computer programs has developed so effectively and

Reasons for the exception (subsection 1).

Because of a lack of complete standardization among programming languages and hardware in the computer industry, one who rightfully acquires a copy of a program frequently cannot use it without adapting it to that limited extent which will allow its use in the possessor's computer. The copyright law, which grants to copyright proprietors the exclusive right to prepare translations, transformations and adaptations of their work, should no more prevent such use than it should prevent rightful possessors from loading programs into their computers. Thus a right to make those changes necessary to enable the use for which it was both sold and purchased should be provided.

– Final Report of the National Commission on New Technological Uses of Copyrighted Works

*Originality, see p. 127.
†Duration of copyright, see p. 205.
‡International treaties, see p. 242.

Separate protection for mask works and semiconductor chips.

The Committee decided that the formidable philosophical, constitutional, legal and technical problems associated with any attempt to place protection for mask works or semiconductor chip designs under the copyright law could be avoided entirely by creating a sui generis form of protection, apart from and independent of the copyright laws. The new form of legal protection would avoid the possible distortion of the copyright law and would establish a more appropriate and efficacious form of protection for mask works. Rather than risk confusion and uncertainty in, and distortion of, existing copyright law as a result of attempting to modify fundamental copyright principles to suit the unusual nature of chip design, the Committee concludes that a new body of statutory and decisional law should be developed. It should be specifically applicable to mask works alone, and could be based on many copyright principles, and other intellectual property concepts; it could draw by analogy on this statutory and case law framework to the extent clearly applicable to mask works and semiconductor chip protection, but should not be restricted by the limitations of existing copyright law.

—House Committee Report

so rapidly that semiconductor chip protection just isn't that attractive anymore. If you manufactured such a product, would you be more interested in the ten-year protection of your chip, or the ninety-five-year protection of the contents of the chip? (Actually, there's no need to choose; both types of protection are granted.)

In any event, while the Semiconductor Chip Protection Act was initially praised as a model for "sui generis" statutes—separate statutes for particular types of creative works—such special protection has turned out not to be nearly as effective as the protection afforded under the more general principles of copyright.

The Computer Software Rental Amendment, 1990

The "first sale" doctrine* provides that, once a purchaser has bought a copy of a copyrighted work, the purchaser normally may resell, rent, or otherwise dispose of that particular copy of the work, so long as the purchaser doesn't make further copies. This caused problems in the music industry because, it was thought, the rental of records or CDs inevitably led to the home copying of those works. Congress responded to the problem in 1984 by making an exception to the "first sale" doctrine for CDs and sound recordings:† while purchasers of such works could resell them, purchasers were prohibited from renting them.

In 1990, the computer software industry was successful in convincing Congress that it should be afforded similar treatment to sound recordings. If companies were allowed to purchase computer programs and rent them to the public, then the public would very likely use such rentals to make copies of the computer programs that would displace sales. For example, if you could rent a copy of Adobe Photoshop for, let's say, $20, and it costs about $500 to buy a copy, then you might be awfully tempted to simply make a copy from the one that you'd rented. To prevent this, Congress

*First sale doctrine, see p. 167.
†1984 audio rental amendment, see p. 48.

amended section 109 of the Act to extend the exception to cover computer programs as well as sound recordings: "[N]either the owner of a particular phonorecord nor any person in possession of a particular copy of a computer program . . . may, for the purposes of direct or indirect commercial advantage, dispose of, or authorize the disposal of, the possession of that phonorecord or computer program . . . by rental, lease, or lending. . . ."

But, you say, your kids rent copies of the latest version of Super Mario or Final Fantasy, or other Nintendo or Playstation video games, from the local video rental store. That's because of an exception to the exception. The exclusive rental right for computer programs created by section 109 does not apply to "a computer program embodied in or used in conjunction with a limited purpose computer that is designed for playing video games. . . ." What does that mean? It means that a video store *can* rent video games that run on dedicated systems, like the Nintendo system, from which they cannot normally be copied. If your kids rent such games, they can't easily make copies of them, and so the rental does not lead to a copy that displaces a sale.

LOOK WHAT I CAN DO NOW!

So far in this chapter, we've been looking at how copyright has come to embrace and protect computer programs, the new type of creative work that makes computers do what they do. But computers have raised a much broader issue for copyright.

As we've seen in the previous chapters, copyright protects books and magazines, music and records, plays and movies, and now, computer programs. We'll explore many other types of protected works in chapter 6. With the advent of the computer, however, all of these works are being digitized to make them accessible to the computer. We create our literary works on computers, using word processors to manipulate the words and letters as part of the creative process, and to store vast amounts of information on new media such as disks and CD-ROMS. Using image scanners and digital cameras, or plugging our video recorders and camcorders into our computers, we capture pictorial and photographic images, even moving images, in pixels that can be displayed and manipulated on a computer screen and stored in ever smaller amounts of space. Using

My favorite early CD-ROMs. Below are some of my favorite early CD-ROMs, illustrated at less than half actual size. They each contain up to 650 megabytes of information. The first contains the complete works of Shakespeare, with so much room left over that it includes the entire works *twice*—once in Elizabethan English and once in contemporary English.

The second contains a map of virtually every street in the United States, viewable at varying scales. I was able to find the very street where I grew up in Paragould, Arkansas! Street maps are now available basically for free on the Internet.

The third CD-ROM contains the complete Microsoft Encarta multimedia encyclopedia from a few years ago, one of many encyclopedias now on CD-ROM that contain the equivalent of dozens of volumes of their book counterparts. (The more recent versions are on two or more disks, because of extensive use of interactive media that take up more space than does text.)

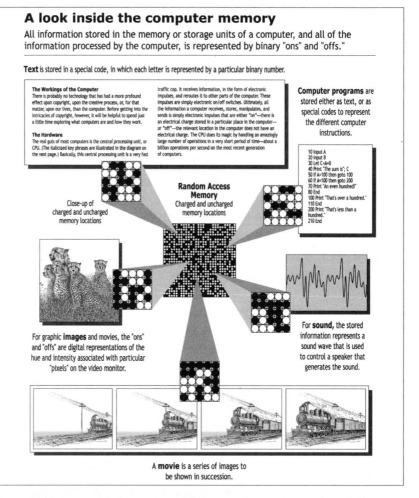

A look inside the computer memory

All information stored in the memory or storage units of a computer, and all of the information processed by the computer, is represented by binary "ons" and "offs."

Text is stored in a special code, in which each letter is represented by a particular binary number.

The Workings of the Computer
There is probably no technology that has had a more profound effect upon copyright, upon the creative process, or, for that matter, upon our lives, than the computer. Before getting into the intricacies of copyright, however, it will be helpful to spend just a little time exploring what computers are and how they work.

The Hardware
The real guts of most computers is the *central processing unit*, or CPU. (The italicized key phrases are illustrated in the diagram on the next page.) Basically, this central processing unit is a very fast traffic cop. It receives information, in the form of electronic impulses, and reroutes it to other parts of the computer. These impulses are simply electronic on/off switches. Ultimately, all the information a computer receives, stores, manipulates, and sends is simply electronic impulses that are either "on"—there is an electrical charge stored in a particular place in the computer—or "off"—the relevant location in the computer does not have an electrical charge. The CPU does its magic by handling an amazingly large number of operations in a very short period of time—about a billion operations per second on the most recent generation of computers.

Computer programs are stored either as text, or as special codes to represent the different computer instructions.

```
10 Input A
20 Input B
30 Let C=A+B
40 Print "The sum is"; C
50 If A>100 then goto 100
60 If A<100 then goto 200
70 Print "An even hundred!"
80 End
100 Print "That's over a hundred."
110 End
200 Print "That's less than a
    hundred."
210 End
```

Random Access Memory
Charged and uncharged memory locations

Close-up of charged and uncharged memory locations

For graphic **images** and movies, the "ons" and "offs" are digital representations of the hue and intensity associated with particular "pixels" on the video monitor.

For **sound**, the stored information represents a sound wave that is used to control a speaker that generates the sound.

A **movie** is a series of images to be shown in succession.

musical interface devices (midis), we "sample" music electronically, reducing sound itself to pure information that can be captured, stored, manipulated, and copied with remarkable consistency and fidelity.

It's the digital revolution. If you could look inside the memory of a computer, you'd see all the electrical impulses, stored in a binary code of on/off switches. If you saw these electrical or magnetic impulses, you couldn't immediately tell whether what you saw stored in any part of the computer was words, images, sounds, or computer programs. But the computer itself keeps track of what type of information is stored where, and can easily transform the information back into the words, images, and sounds that make sense to us as humans.

With the computer, we can create works, copy them, distribute them, perform them, and transform them. As we'll see in chapter 7, these are precisely the exclusive rights that are supposed to be protected by copyright. Clearly something has got to change in how we think about these creative works.

We'll get back to some of these basic questions. But first, we'll look at the Internet, the popular new way of distributing the vast amounts of information we've accumulated and digitized.

CONCLUSION

It's interesting to contrast the legislative response to new technologies in the context of music, television, and computer programs. As we saw earlier, Congress adopted highly technical regulatory schemes to handle some of the big copyright issues raised by digital technology in the music industry. Relatively few new laws were required for motion pictures and television. In this chapter we've seen that although Congress has adopted some amendments to handle specific prob-

A favorite graphics program.
Using Adobe Photoshop, I scan old family pictures into my computer, touch them up or alter them, and then print them out in improved form. In this picture of my grandmother (third from left) and three of her sisters, I have enlarged and enhanced the image. You may also notice that the car has disappeared with a few waves of the magic Adobe wand. (It's debatable whether cutting out my grandfather, and the car—from which my father can date the picture precisely—is an improvement, but the point is that you can do what you want.) If you don't have the equipment for doing this yourself, your local photography store will be glad to correct pictures, even erasing old friends, putting together new ones, or, as advertised in one local store, enlarging the size of the fish you catch.

Another favorite program.

Another favorite program is Kai's Power Goo, with which a user can manipulate pictures in all sorts of fascinating ways—again, all because the information is stored in digital form that can be readily altered. With apologies to the artist, here is a relatively mild distortion of the *Mona Lisa.* Many wilder variations are available using the tools pictured here—grow/shrink, move, smear, smudge, nudge, mirror toggle, smooth, and ungoo, which undoes any of these effects. Using another set of tools, the user can bulge, twirl, rotate, stretch, spike, or "static" the image, or unwind any of these effects. Don't ask what these tools do; finding out is half the fun. Using the sliding switch at the left, the user can ease the effects in and out of the image. Or the user can record a succession of different images at the bottom, and the program creates a smooth "goovie" moving from one distortion to another. All of this is of course good clean fun, since Leonardo da Vinci is dead and the *Mona Lisa* is in the public domain. But what if the artist is alive and the original work is still copyrighted? Stay tuned for further developments.

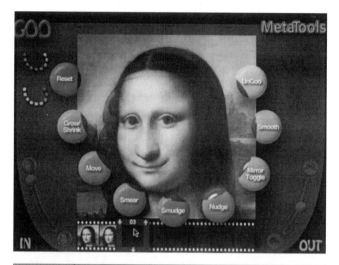

3-D rendering program.

Using Ray Dream Studio, my daughter, Claire, constructs three-dimensional models in which the instructions for reproducing characters, objects, and background are stored as basic information. By relatively easy manipulation, the characters can be moved around, seen from different perspectives, or strung together over time to make animated movies. Shown here is "Trish," a cartoon cat.

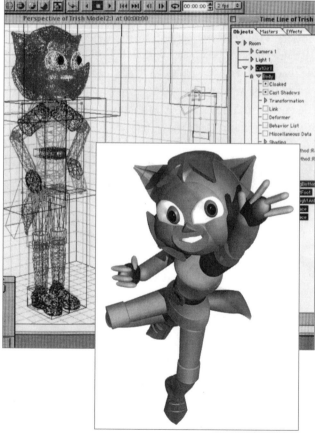

lems in administering copyright in computer programs, for the most part it's the courts that are deciding the major computer copyright issues, and they're
doing so on traditional copyright principles, not the
legislation directed specifically at protecting computer
programs. This may seem surprising, given the number
of commentators who had originally argued that computer programs were just too new, too different from
traditional notions of copyright, to expect a workable

International context.

Article 10 of the international Agreement on
Trade-Related Aspects of Intellectual Property
(1994) provides that "Computer programs,
whether in source or object code, shall be
protected as literary works under the Berne
Convention." For more on the 1994 agreement, see p. 244.

solution to be developed. Yet a reasonable balance has been struck, and
it seems to be working fairly well. Indeed, the United States has been so
successful in developing standards for protecting computer programs
that it's even begun exporting the concept. While many European and
other countries had originally balked at the notion of treating computer
programs as within the subject matter of copyright, the United States has
recently prevailed upon most of the rest of the world to protect computer programs under copyright.

It's my own opinion that the treatment of computer programs,
leaving the tough issues to be developed by the courts based upon general
copyright principles, has led to a more satisfying and nuanced resolution.
As we face the copyright issues raised by other new technologies, such as
the Internet, I would argue that the preferable approach is not to run to
Congress for quick fixes to every tough question, but, if possible, to allow
a little time for the courts to work out the issues.

CHAPTER FIVE

The Internet

THE TELEGRAPH AND THE TELEPHONE

"Hurrah for the Yankee experiment."
Physicist Alfred Mayer, a Henry protégé, recounted the following story of Henry:

> I shall never forget Henry's account of his visit to King's College, London, where Faraday, Wheatstone, Daniell and he had met to try to evolve the electric spark from the thermopile. Each in turn attempted it and failed. Then came Henry's turn. He succeeded: calling in the aid of his discovery of the effect of a long interpolar wire wrapped around a piece of soft iron. Faraday became as wild as a boy, and jumping up, shouted: "Hurrah for the Yankee experiment."

It's a wonderful story, but it's apocryphal, or at least exaggerated. Henry *had* impressed his European colleagues. But, as explained by Alfred Moyer, Henry's recent biographer, "Besides portraying Henry as outshining his inept London colleagues and winning their praise, this version of the King's College episode misassigns Faraday's particular coil to Henry and Henry's celabratory leap to Faraday."

Parallel to the technological developments described in the previous four chapters was the development of long-distance point-to-point communication. The first telegraph was actually developed by Joseph Henry, a remarkable American scientist who didn't receive adequate credit for this as well as several other key inventions and insights. He developed the first electromagnetic telegraph in 1831; but he didn't patent his invention because he thought that scientific knowledge should be free to everyone. The person who ultimately got the patent, and who is commonly credited as the inventor of the telegraph in 1837, was Samuel F. B. Morse. In fact, Morse's early models were not very effective, and it was only through the patient assistance of men like Henry that Morse was able to get his signals to travel over a distance, without degradation, using a system of electrical relays.

In 1843, Morse obtained a $30,000 government grant to demonstrate his telegraph. He strung an experimental line between Baltimore and Washington, and scooped all other services on the news of the day. Within a few years, telegraph wires were hung around the country, and people got the news of the Mexican

Men of Progress.
This is a detail from an 1862 painting by Christian Schussele of the leading scientists and inventors of the day. The setting is fictional, since the inventors were never assembled at one time; but Schussele did travel around the country to have each of them sit for him. Reclining to the right of the table is Samuel F. B. Morse, demonstrating his telegraph. To the left of the pole, leaning against it, almost apart from the rest, is Joseph Henry. Seated at the left is Charles Goodyear, inventor of vulcanized rubber.

War, and later the Civil War, by what one newspaperman called "the lightning wire." By 1861, a wire linked San Francisco to New York, and everything from news to prices on the stock exchanges was instantly communicated from coast to coast.

Laying a cable that would join America to Europe was an even more daunting task than the transcontinental cable. It required solving the problems of insulation against the hostile sea, and laying a continuous cable for thousands of miles that could not rely on relays to boost the signal or access to allow periodic repairs. After an expenditure of millions of dollars and years of frustrating failures, including a particularly bitter experience with an 1858 cable that first seemed to work, and then went dead, Cyrus Field finally was successful in laying the first transatlantic cable on July 27, 1866.

The next major breakthrough in communication at a distance was Alexander Graham Bell's telephone, invented in 1876.* Bell demonstrated his invention that

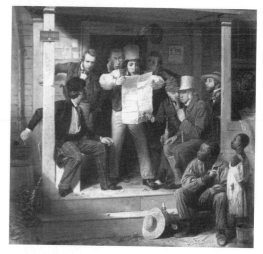

News by lightning wire.
Newspapers featured the latest reports of the Mexican War by what one correspondent called "News by Lightning Wire." Until the invention of the telegraph, information about a distant war arrived only days or weeks or months after the event—hardly "news" at all.

*The invention of the telephone, see p. 129.

A meanness of soul.

Morse went on to reveal a meanness of soul, for he never acknowledged Henry's help and, indeed, during prolonged litigation with Jackson over priority, tried to maintain that Henry had never helped him. Henry, testifying at the trial, was easily able to prove the contrary. . . . [W]hen the Hall of Fame for Great Americans was first opened in 1900 on the campus of New York University, Morse was made a charter member. The authentically great American, Henry, was not elected until 1915.

—Isaac Asimov

year at the Centennial Exhibition in Philadelphia. The following year, Joseph Henry had Bell demonstrate the invention at a meeting of the Philosophical Society in Washington, D.C. By 1879, stock in the newly formed Bell Company hit $995 a share. All of a sudden, Bell and all who had early invested in his company were rich.

Almost a century after all of these developments, in 1962, the United States launched the Telstar 1 satellite, the first communications satellite capable of both receiving and transmitting electronic signals, and for the first time allowing telephone, television, and other signals to be communicated directly between Europe and the United States.

Some of Bell's early telephone designs.
The voice vibrated a diaphragm that converted sound into electrical signals that traveled over wires; the electrical signals then controlled a receiver at the other end, to convert the electrical signals back into acoustical vibrations.

Telstar.
Telstar 1, launched in 1962, was the first communications satellite capable of both sending and receiving radio, television, and telephone signals.

What were the copyright implications of these new technologies? We have seen the effects of radio and television broadcasting and the adjustments such technologies brought about in copyright. But for point-to-point communication, the copyright implications were very few. For the most part, the telegraph was used to transmit breaking news, not creative works. And, unlike the other media reviewed earlier, telephone communications generally took place between two individuals at a time, and usually involved spontaneous conversation rather than copying the creative works of others.

While point-to-point telephone and even satellite communications don't by themselves raise any particular copyright problems, try adding the telephone and satellite communications to the digital media.* Do we have a problem yet? Imagine that what's being communicated over the telephone lines and satellite links is not individual conversations, but files of text, music, video, and computer programs, and the copyright implications become obvious.

INTERNET–THE TECHNOLOGY
The Birth of the Internet

The Internet is a global communications network linking computers around the world. It was created in 1969 as ARPANet (Advanced Research Projects Agency) for the U.S. Department of Defense. The network was designed to break information into separate packets and send the packets over various routes from computer to computer, rerouting the information as necessary to circumvent the breakdown or failure of parts of the system. In the first year, there were four host computers connecting Stanford, UCLA, UC–Santa Barbara, and the University of Utah. In 1981, several academic institutions formed BITNET, a wide-area network to serve

The ignorant and inexperienced.

Mark Twain, in his autobiography, tells of how he barely escaped becoming a millionaire. He had lost large sums of money investing in various patents, and so had resisted the temptation when an agent for Bell offered to sell him as much stock as he wanted in the new company for $500.

About the end of the year (or possibly in the beginning of 1878) I put up a telephone wire from my house down to the *Courant* office, the only telephone wire in town, and the *first* one that was ever used in a private house in the world.

That young man couldn't sell *me* any stock but he sold a few hatfuls of it to an old dry-goods clerk in Hartford for five thousand dollars. That was that clerk's whole fortune. He had been half a lifetime saving it. It is strange how foolish people can be and what ruinous risks they can take when they want to get rich in a hurry. I was sorry for that man when I heard about it. I thought I might have saved him if I had had an opportunity to tell him about my experience.

We sailed for Europe on the 10th of April, 1878. We were gone fourteen months and when we got back one of the first things we saw was that clerk driving around in a sumptuous barouche with liveried servants all over it—and his telephone stock was emptying greenbacks into his premises at such a rate that he had to handle them with a shovel. It is strange the way the ignorant and inexperienced so often and so undeservedly succeed when the informed and the experienced fail.

*Digital media, see p. 93.

the academic community. In 1990, after ARPANet and various other networks had connected over 300,000 host computers, ARPANet was decommissioned as a project of the Department of Defense and allowed to develop as a civilian enterprise.

In that same year, The World was the first commercial service provider for the Internet, allowing individual subscribers to connect their computers to the system by telephone dial-up. By 1992, the number of host computers connected to the Internet had surpassed 1 million; by 1998, there were nearly 50 million Internet users in the United States; and by 2000, Internet users were estimated at over 133 million in North America, and 228 million in the rest of the world.

Chat Rooms, Instant Messages, Phone Calls, and Videoconferencing

There are some Internet uses that, like the telephone, don't raise serious copyright concerns because they don't usually involve the transfer of information copyrighted by others. For example, one of the popular Internet pastimes is participation in chat rooms, in which many people "chat" with each other in real time. They don't actually talk at all, but instead type messages on their computers that pop up simultaneously on the computers of all other participants in the "chat room." The dynamics of chat rooms can be fascinating, particularly to first-timers. Given the lag time it takes to type coherent responses, most chat rooms don't consist of a single conversation, but are more like several conversations taking place around a common topic.

Chat rooms can represent anything from a real-time simulation of a *Star Trek* battle to communications about developing natural or political disasters. Some chat rooms are set up on particular on-line services, such as American Online, and are available only to subscribers of that particular service; Internet Relay Chat (IRC) rooms are available to anyone who has access to the Internet. Since chat rooms are conducted in real time, they usually don't involve the attachment of files that might contain digitized copyrighted works. Instead, to the extent that everyone responds spontaneously, they presumably own the copyright in their own contributions. Of course, there is the possibility that others in the chat room will "steal" this expression and pass it on, but at least the participants who voluntarily contribute to a chat-room conversation know that their contributions are available, with little control, to anyone on the Internet.

Instant messaging is the process of typing messages that appear instantaneously not on lots of computers but only on one, or a few selected computers. It's like having a private chat room with only one other person at a time. Instant messages are not saved on the recipient's computer: if the recipient is not on-line when the message is sent, it won't be received. To let subscribers know when their friends are on-line, many service providers maintain a "buddy" system that allows subscribers to list the people they want to chat with. The system notifies the subscriber whenever any of the subscriber's "buddies" is on-line, so that instant messages may be sent.

Some service providers maintain hybrid systems that allow messaging at different levels simultaneously. For example, America Online provides "town meetings" in which famous speakers can talk to thousands of subscribers simultaneously. All subscribers see what the featured guests type (or what someone types for them), but only a few of the audience responses are forwarded to the guest, in order to avoid totally flooding the guest with communications. Subscribers can be assigned "rows" of "seats" when they sign on, and their responses will be visible only to members of their own rows. The system is designed to balance the value of interactivity against the burden of communications overload.

A more recent development is that of real telephony, in which users may actually talk to each other instead of just typing messages. The telephony software picks up sounds from a microphone, converts the sounds into electrical signals, and sends the signals in packets over the Internet. The recipient must have compatible software that converts the packets back into sounds and plays them on the recipient's computer. Acceptable voice quality requires a relatively high-speed Internet connection. With sufficiently fast connections, it is also possible to connect a video camera, so that users with the proper equipment and software may see each other while they talk. This technology, called *videoconferencing*, can connect two subscribers, or several at once.

Entrepreneurial taking.

As the World Wide Web, with its graphical user interface, became the dominant component of the Internet, some entrepreneurs figured out that there was money to be made by taking the contents of the chat rooms and making them available on Web sites. The money was made by adding a layer of advertisements. It's an interesting question whether such entrepreneurs are violating the copyright of Internet users whose posted messages they have appropriated.

Given the tremendous amount of "bandwidth" required to send real-time video images over the Internet, it's pretty much pushing the existing technology to send a video image to a single recipient at a time. Currently under development is a new technology known as the Multicast Backbone, or MBone, that would provide sufficient bandwidth to deliver "multicasts" to thousands of recipients at a time. The multicast would begin as a single file, and be duplicated only as it got out onto the Internet to be delivered to the many subscribers.

In any event, the most common current uses of chat rooms, instant messages, telephony, and videoconferencing are to transmit spontaneous typing, talking, and gesturing. While it's certainly possible to recite poetry or send unauthorized copies of CDs, movies, or television programs, the quality of the messages, processed in real time, ranges from unacceptable to barely acceptable to acceptable, and probably doesn't yet threaten existing methods of distributing most copyrighted works.

E-mail

The most popular use of the Internet is to send electronic mail, or e-mail. It is estimated that e-mail volume surpassed 1 trillion messages in 1995, and is approaching 7 trillion messages in the year 2000. The sender addresses text and other messages to recipients by typing in their unique e-mail addresses. The message is broken down into packets and sent over the Internet following the TCP/IP (transmission control protocol/Internet protocol) standard, usually in a matter of seconds or minutes. If the recipient is on-line when the message is received, the recipient may be notified of the incoming e-mail. If the recipient is not on-line, then the message is stored in the recipient's assigned "inbox" until the next time the recipient logs on to the recipient's own network or service provider. At that time, the recipient may "read" the e-mail, save it for later, respond to it, delete it, or forward it to yet another recipient.

In some ways, e-mail might be thought of as simply a very fast mail delivery service, raising no more copyright concerns than the regular mail that has existed for centuries. The difference is that with e-mail, you can send messages to dozens, hundreds, or thousands of people at a time. You can keep subscription lists of people you contact regularly. You can have people subscribe to a mailing list by sending a message indicating they

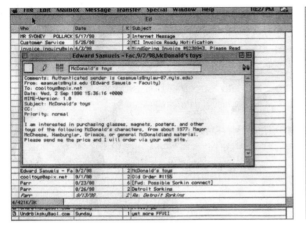 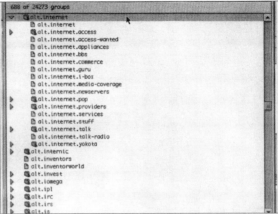

want to receive e-mails from a particular source or on a particular topic. And e-mail isn't just text anymore. Most e-mail programs and services allow the sender to attach a digitized file, which can be just about anything—a picture, sound, video clip, or computer program. Given the ease with which such information can be scanned, uploaded, or otherwise input to the computer, it's easy to see why the Internet is fast becoming the primary means of distributing information—including copyrighted works—around the world.

Newsgroups

You can think of newsgroups as bulletin boards where anyone connected to the Internet can post messages or read messages posted by anyone else. Newsgroups are divided into categories, covering any topic that a participant is able to imagine. There are tens of thousands of newsgroups, running the gamut, including sex-related newsgroups, arts and recreation, astrology and genealogy, science and fantasy, computers and movie star "fan" groups. For many newsgroups, there are so many postings that messages are only maintained for a week or two (although they may be "archived" on selected sites if anyone is interested in donating the space to accommodate the older messages). Depending upon the software, users who access the newsgroups may see the messages grouped together with those to which they respond, creating "threads" of messages that cumulatively respond to earlier messages. Users may browse

E-mail.
Shown here, in the front window, is an e-mail message ready to be sent at the press of a button. In the background window you can see a list of some of the e-mail messages I have recently sent and received.

Newsgroups.
Just a few of the thousands of newsgroups available on the Internet. Unopened folders, with arrows pointing to the right, contain subfolders of other newsgroups.

any newsgroups they want, or may "subscribe" to selected newsgroups so that they automatically receive all updates whenever they start the newsgroup program. Some newsgroups even offer to e-mail all of the postings to subscribers.

Just as in the case of e-mail, newsgroups thus allow the dissemination of messages to limitless numbers of people at one time. And just as with e-mail, the newsgroup messages may contain digital attachments that represent pictures, sound, video, and computer programs, all organized by topic to make it easy for those interested in the topic to receive the information.

Transferring Files

One of the major uses of the Internet is to transfer files from one computer to another. One way of doing this is through the Internet's FTP, or File Transfer Protocol. An FTP site maintains a list of available files, and a computer program that allows subscribers to download the files. Because of their frequently large size, files are normally compressed in order to minimize the amount of time it takes to transfer them: they are decompressed by the user upon receipt. The files can contain anything that can be digitized—articles, forms, photographs and other images, sound, video clips, and computer programs.

Keeping track of all the information available on a given topic can be a mind-boggling task. In 1991, programmers at the University of Minnesota developed a program called "Gopher," named after the school mascot and also suggesting what the tool does. It keeps track of collections of information and databases, allowing users to find and retrieve files on topics they want (digging through the mounds of information like a gopher). The advantage of Gopher is that it is menu-driven, so that you don't have to know how to program in order to use it; and it is able to retrieve data stored in many different formats.

Another use of the Internet is telnet, which allows a user to remotely access other computers. A student or employee can use telnet to gain access to specific computers at school or work, and run programs that reside on those computers. Or a library, for example, can set up a telnet site to allow users to run programs from within the library's computer that will access information on that computer. Users don't have to have or download the card-catalogue software to their own computers; instead, they use the library's software running on the library's computer.

The vast amount of information available on the Internet can also be tracked through agents (also called spiders, robots, or just 'bots). These agents are automated programs that gather information for a user without their intervention, and then make the information available when the user wants it. For example, an agent might regularly check for updated news items, particular stock information, or all recent articles on a particular topic.

The World Wide Web

The proliferation of different protocols and programs for storing and sending information over the Internet made accessing information somewhat intimidating to the average user. Back in 1989, Tim Berners-Lee, a scientist at CERN, the European Particle Physics Laboratory, had suggested a way to let all users, but particularly scientists, browse each other's papers on the Internet. He developed a code known as Hypertext Markup Language (HTML) and a protocol known as Hypertext Transfer Protocol (HTTP) that could be implemented on any computer. He also developed a Universal Resource Locator (URL) system for naming, locating, and retrieving documents, pictures, and other media over the Internet. Using the URL system, a user could retrieve data from newsgroups, FTP sites, and Gopher pages, as well as other types of sites. And the beauty of HTML was that it also contained the instructions for formatting the information on a page, no matter what computer the user happened to be running.

In 1991, Berners-Lee, using the system he had developed, launched the World Wide Web. It opened up the Internet to true multimedia capability. Using the relatively straightforward HTML language, just about anybody with a computer and a place to store the information could create a Web page, or series of interrelated pages, that could be accessed by anybody else on the Internet. In 1994, Marc Andreessen and James Clark founded Netscape Communications, which distributed an easy-to-use netscape browser for accessing Web pages. The browser became the Internet connection of choice for millions of users, and by 1995, Netscape went public with an initial public stock offering valued at over $2 billion.

Tim Berners-Lee, the father of the World Wide Web.

The Internet and the World Wide Web.
The Internet is the infrastructure that connects various local area networks of computers (at universities, companies, and government agencies) to each other to form a global network of networks. It's not connected by any particular type of transmission lines, but consists of all ways in which computers are connected to other computers—including telephone lines, cable, fiber optics, microwave dishes, and satellite links.

The World Wide Web is a subset of the Internet, but it doesn't exist in any particular location on the Internet. Rather, the World Wide Web is simply a protocol for exchanging information, and a system for identifying the location of particular items of information on any of the computers linked by the Internet. To view the http code for any Web site, simply click on *view page source*, or *view source* in your browser.

The following year, Sun Microsystems introduced Java, a programming language that could be run on any type of computer. Using "applets" (small applications programs), Java allowed Web pages to incorporate true multimedia, such as animations or interactive programs. Within a few short years, major computer programs, such as word processors, began incorporating the ability to script Web pages using Java applets. Microsoft got interested in the Internet market, developed its own browser, Internet Explorer, and incorporated the browser into its new operating system so that accessing the Web was supposed to be just like accessing files on one's own computer. (Microsoft's actions became part of the focus of the Justice Department's antitrust lawsuit against the company in 1998.)

One of the main methods of navigation around Web pages is through what are known as hypertext or hyperlinks. Using hypertext or hyperlinks, users can click on a word, phrase, button, or icon on a Web page, and automatically be forwarded to the hyperlinked page. In this way, a Web author can organize a system for navigating from one of the author's pages to another, or to other pages located on different Internet servers. Now getting text, pictures, sound, animation, video clips, computer programs, or any other type of file is just a click of a mouse away.

HOW DO WE PROTECT THE INVESTMENT?

The Internet has encouraged among some users the belief that many or most people should share their creative works for free, or in a free-for-all environment. These people claim that the Internet, which was purportedly designed to withstand nuclear attack, treats censorship or regulation as a malfunction, or damage to the system, and simply routes around it. Not only will intellectual property laws cease to operate, we're told, but government as we know it will become obsolete. These users look on with amusement or disdain as Wall Street developers search frantically for the "killer app," or *any* application, that can make money from the Internet. The major concern of the free-Net users is how to protect their revolutionary and truly egalitarian technology from being co-opted by business.

At the same time, the Wall Street developers look on with envy at the few entrepreneurs who actually *do* manage to start up a company, and in a few years take it public for millions or billions of dollars in a marketplace pumped up with Internet hysteria. The heroes are Andreessen of Netscape, Bezos of Amazon.com, Case of America Online, and Filo and Yang of Yahoo!, who made fortunes as their companies emerged literally from nowhere. For business, it's like the early days of radio or television, as the industry tries to figure out how to use the new technology to make money, and whether the money will be made by a relatively free service supported by advertisers, by a pay-for-use service, or by new business paradigms tailored to the new technology.

It's a great boon to society that organizations that are in the business of distributing information for free, such as NASA, the New York Public Library, museums or government agencies, or companies that want to disseminate information or advertising about their products, now have a newly efficient means for doing so. And it's a boon to society that people who have similar interests in just about any topic can find each other and share their information and opinions. But at least some of the artists and writers, composers and programmers who create the pictures and words, sounds and sites that make up the Internet are trying to figure out how to protect their investment in creativity.

Although the courts have begun to handle some of the resulting legal issues, they have been joined by the administration and Congress, by international copyright organizations, and by the industries themselves, all of whom have rushed in to fine-tune the law rather than wait for the courts to work it out themselves. In 1998, Congress passed and President Bill Clinton signed the Digital Millennium Copyright Act, which has reshaped

Go to bed, Mikey!
The gauntlet was laid down by business in a series of television commercials for Lotus Domino in 1996–97. My favorite was one in which Denis Leary, as an unlikely spokesperson for Lotus, business, and capitalism in general, smart-mouthed Mikey (played by Jeremy Blake Collins).

Mikey: I wrote this letter. Dear Lotus. I think the Web should be used for surfing and having fun. Not for business. Business is boring. Mikey Powers.
Denis Leary: You know what, Mikey? Guess what? You're a kid. You can't vote, you can't drive, you can't handle the fact that big companies are using the web to save a billion dollars and get their products to market faster. All you care about is fooling around on your computer, right? Well, who pays for that fancy computer, eh? Your parents. How do they make money. . . ? Business. So you know what, Mikey? Go to bed!

Yahoo!

> As a PhD candidate for Electrical Engineering at Stanford University, [David] Filo and his colleague Jerry Yang began developing a way to store and list their favorite sites on the Internet. Using Yang's computer for the Web site list and Filo's computer as the search engine, they formed a comprehensive collection of sites, and developed codes and software to fuel their new invention. In April 1994, they formally launched Yahoo!, which has become the leading brand name on the Internet . . . . and the most popular destination on the World Wide Web.
>
> *–Computing Dictionary: The Illustrated Book of Terms and Technologies*

the contours of copyright to fit the Internet. We'll get to some of the substance of that law in the next section. But first, let's review the brief history that has led to the recent statutory amendments.

The first volley came from the Clinton administration, in the form of a White Paper by the Working Group on Intellectual Property Rights of the Information Infrastructure Task Force. The Working Group argued that some form of legal protection for creative works on the National Information Infrastructure (NII) was necessary if the NII was to develop its full potential. (Although the Working Group talks about the NII and GII, the National and Global Information Infrastructures, which may develop in a variety of ways, I will use the term *Internet* to refer to the structure in both its existing and developing forms.) However, the Working Group concluded that relatively few amendments to copyright were necessary, since basic copyright principles covered most of the major problems. Indeed, over half of the massive report was basically a copyright primer, demonstrating how the existing copyright structure was up to the task.

The Working Group did recommend several specific amendments to bolster copyright, most of which we'll discuss in the next section. But the major proposed solution was a technological one: set up a legal system that will allow copyright owners to protect themselves.

There are developing technologies that can encrypt copyrighted works, or otherwise control access to them, or that can be used to keep track of uses of such works. The proposal of the Working Group was to make it illegal to circumvent such copyright protection systems, or tamper with any copyright management information. In this way, those owners of copyrighted works who want their works to be available without limitation, or who are willing to trust to their ability to enforce copyright on the Internet, are free to supply their works in a way that allows open access. But for authors, composers, artists, and record and movie companies that want to release their works only in protected formats, the law will support their efforts.

The White Paper proposals, at least as characterized by the Working Group, were for relatively modest adjustments to a law that was for the most part already in place. Other parties, however, did not see it that way. For example, the Internet service providers were alarmed at some of the early cases that suggested they might be liable for infringing activities of their subscribers, and at the stance taken by the Working Group that they could be held liable under existing principles of contributory copyright infringement.* The service providers appealed to Congress for an exemption that would treat them more like telephone companies, which are not generally liable for illegal conversations that take place over their systems.

Other scholars and some users of the Internet also opposed what they saw as unprecedented intrusion into what was to them the emerging communications system of choice. They urged Congress not to define copyright too strictly, but instead to accommodate a broad range of exceptions and a broad sense that much of the communication on the Internet was protected by fair use. In any event, the proposal that was supposed to be modest ended up getting bogged down in a Congress that was getting conflicting signals from important constituencies.

The debate quickly shifted into an international forum. The administration was instrumental in getting the issue addressed by the World Intellectual Property Organization (WIPO). Cynics would claim that the administration simply chose to take the tough Internet issues to the international forum in order to do an end run around Congress, which was not buying the administration proposals. Cynicism aside, it made a lot of sense to address the issues internationally because the problem was an international one, and America's major trading partners were as eager for a resolution of the problems as was the United States.

The net result was that WIPO acted more quickly than Congress. In December 1996, it adopted two treaties clarifying copyright on the Internet. The United States, which signed the new treaties, took the position that its own laws were in compliance with most of its obligations under the proposed treaties, and that only relatively minor amendments would be required to U.S. law in order to bring it into compliance with the new international standards. So the administration went back to Congress, this time asking for ratification of the international treaties,

A typical declaration.

Some of the revolutionary observations are generally attributed to Mitch Kapor, creator of Lotus 1-2-3, and more recently a cofounder of the Electronic Frontier Foundation. Another typical declaration:

> Notions of property, value, ownership, and the nature of wealth itself are changing more fundamentally than at any time since the Sumerians first poked cuneiform into wet clay and called it stored grain. Only a very few people are aware of the enormity of this shift, and fewer of them are lawyers or public officials.

> −*Wired* magazine

*Contributory liability, see p. 177.

Where's the content?

The Working Group was chaired by Bruce Lehman, the commissioner of patents and trademarks, as part of the Information Infrastructure Task Force, chaired by Ronald Brown, secretary of commerce. The White Paper they wrote reflected input from "the private sector, public interest groups, Congress, and State and local governments." Formally entitled *Intellectual Property and the National Information Infrastructure,* it was released in draft form as the "Green Paper" in July 1994, and in final form as the "White Paper" in September 1995.

> [T]he full potential of the NII will not be realized if the education, information and entertainment products protected by intellectual property laws are not protected effectively when disseminated via the NII. Creators and other owners of intellectual property rights will not be willing to put their interests at risk if appropriate systems—both in the U.S. and internationally—are not in place to permit them to set and enforce the terms and conditions under which their works are made available in the NII environment. Likewise, the public will not use the services available on the NII and generate the market necessary for its success unless a wide variety of works are available under equitable and reasonable terms and conditions, and the integrity of those works is assured. All the computers, telephones, fax machines, scanners, cameras, keyboards, televisions, monitors, printers, switches, routers, wires, cables, networks and satellites in the world will not create a successful NII, if there is no *content*. What will drive the NII is the content moving through it.
>
> —White Paper

and for what was described as modest implementing legislation.

By the end of 1998, Congress passed the new law as the Digital Millennium Copyright Act. One minor problem along the way, however, was that the modest proposals had grown to approximately sixty tightly packed, single-spaced pages of definitions, clarifications, exceptions, and highly regulatory language that were nearly incomprehensible to most readers. While I've described some of the previous technical amendments as ones that only a lawyer could love, I know of no lawyers who love the new act. Reading it is about like reading a technical journal in a foreign language.

THE DIGITAL MILLENNIUM COPYRIGHT ACT

Copyright Protection Systems and Copyright Management Information

The Working Group had identified several technologies that were capable of protecting works on the Internet. For example, certain commercial on-line services, dial-up bulletin boards, and businesses are available only to users who identify themselves as authorized to use the services by typing in a valid user ID and password. Furthermore, encryption techniques can provide for the "scrambling" of information so that it may be decoded only by authorized users. These encryption techniques guarantee that certain transactions, such as banking or credit card transactions, are secure against anyone who might otherwise obtain access to the information as it is forwarded from computer to computer over the Internet.

In addition to systems that control access, there are other systems that allow anyone to access files, but embed special information in the files. For example,

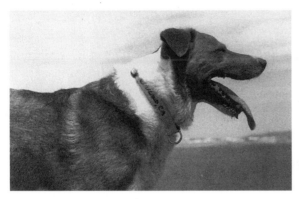 

digital "signatures" can be used to authenticate that a particular file was sent by the proper sender, and has not been altered. A related system is digital "watermarking," which incorporates into a file identifying information that cannot easily be dissociated from the file—so-called copyright management information about authorship, copyright ownership, date of creation, and terms and conditions of authorized uses. Using robots or spiders to prowl the Web, a copyright owner or organization can search for infringing uses of works incorporating the particular watermark.

All such systems for protecting or allowing the detection of copyrighted works in digital form, primarily on the Internet, would be pointless if users simply unlocked the locked files or stripped the relevant codes. The purpose of the new WIPO treaties, and the provisions of the Digital Millennium Copyright Act, is to make it illegal to circumvent such copyright protection or copyright management information systems.

The relevant provisions are set forth in a new chapter of the copyright law, chapter 12, which is technically separate from the rest of the statute. That is, the chapter has its own civil and criminal remedies, apart from the preexisting provisions governing copyright generally. And the potential criminal penalties are high: anyone who violates the rights in copyright protection

Digimarc watermarking system.
Above is an illustration of the Digimarc watermarking system. The picture of the dog has embedded within it the photographer's Digimarc watermark. As described by Ben Long in *Macworld* magazine, the watermark "adds a simple code to your image, distributed throughout the image and disguised as image noise," which you can see on the right. "Because it's in all parts of the picture, it cannot be cropped away." It theoretically survives printing out and rescanning. The Digimarc, readable by Photoshop and most other major professional image-editing programs, provides basic information about the artist and the work of art, including an assigned ID number registered with the Digimarc company. Photoshop can access the ID number on the Internet, thus revealing further information about the copyright owner and licensing arrangements. The Digimarc encoded image can then be tracked on the Internet by using MarcSpider, a Digimarc program that constantly scans the Web for copies of marked works.

One is reminded of Edward R. Murrow's poignant words on his telecast of New Year's Day, 1952: "This instrument can teach. It can illuminate; yes, it can even inspire, but it can do so only to the extent that humans are determined to use it to those ends. Otherwise, it is merely lights and wires in a box."

No need for a new coat.

> With no more than minor clarification and limited amendment, the Copyright Act will provide the necessary balance of protection of rights—and limitations on those rights—to promote the progress of science and the useful arts. Existing copyright law needs only the fine tuning that technological advances necessitate, in order to maintain the balance of the law in the face of onrushing technology. . . .
>
> The coat is getting a little tight. There is no need for a new one, but the old one needs a few alterations.
>
> —White Paper

or copyright management information systems "willfully and for purposes of commercial advantage or private financial gain" can be fined up to $500,000 and imprisoned for up to five years for a first offense. For subsequent offenses, the penalties double. My advice: whatever your attitude toward the appropriateness of the law, just don't do this!

However, lots of exceptions and qualifications got added in the circuitous route to passage. For example, there are elaborate definitions, clarifications, exceptions, and exceptions to exceptions, to cover law enforcement, intelligence, and other government activities; authorized encryption research and security testing; and certain "reverse engineering" to allow minor modifications in order to make computer programs run on particular systems or to assure "interoperability" with other programs, or to allow the alteration of "personally identifying information" about the user. Under the new law, libraries would be able to circumvent systems in order to determine whether they wanted to make the copies to which they are entitled under section 108 of the Act.*

Once Congress got started on the list of exceptions, its members apparently began to worry that there were some exceptions that should be in the statute that they had not yet thought about. So they set up a mechanism under which the Librarian of Congress would periodically hold hearings to determine if there were other "classes of works" that might be "adversely affected" by virtue of the protections provided in the statute. The Librarian would then have the authority to carve out new exceptions. Congress even provided a two-year grace period before enforcement of many portions of the statute, postponing actions against violators until the year 2000, to give the Librarian sufficient time to review the first set of proposed exceptions.

It should be noted that the copyright protection systems are not solely an Internet phenomenon. The Digital Millennium Copyright Act is just as applicable to CD-ROMs or other storage media as it is to the Internet, and is designed to protect music, images, movies, and other data whether on the Internet or elsewhere. Indeed, one of the specific provisions of the amendment deals with VCRs.† The Digital Millennium

*Library photocopying, see p. 20.
†VCRs, see p. 71.

Copyright Act requires that manufacturers of VCRs make their machines so that they recognize and abide by copyright protection systems on certain video broadcasts and prerecorded videotapes and disks.

Limitation of Liability for On-line Service Providers

One of the hottest issues for the Internet is the potential liability of on-line service providers for the infringing activities of their customers. The on-line service providers argue that they simply supply the equipment allowing users to connect to the Internet, and do not actively control, nor should they be encouraged to interfere with, the content of materials posted on their systems.* They claim that they are like telephone companies, not liable for any illegal content in the communications of their customers; or like Sony in the Betamax case,† not liable for any potentially infringing activity undertaken by customers using their equipment.

Others argue that the service providers are in a very different position from telephone companies or VCR manufacturers, more like publishers and radio and television broadcasters, liable for the content of the material they publish even if they do not knowingly infringe copyright. Unlike Sony in the Betamax case, the service providers frequently have the ability to control or delete the content of infringing postings or Web sites, or to block access of their customers to such sites. Since the individual infringers are frequently anonymous, or use on-line pseudonyms that make it nearly impossible to track them down, copyright infringement would be unenforceable on the Internet if the service providers were not held accountable.

A handful of early cases, though very much flavored by their specific facts, found that bulletin board operators and Internet service providers could be found liable for copyright infringement for the uploading and downloading of infringing works on their systems. In some cases, it was clear that the operators and service providers were encouraging and even economically benefiting from such activity; but in other cases, operators and service providers were held liable even though they had no knowledge of the specific infringing activities. Needless to say, bulletin board

U.S. compliance with WIPO.

It was the position of the United States that we were already in compliance with several of the WIPO provisions that were designed to get other countries to raise their level of protection. For example, the articles requiring that countries protect computer programs and databases, to the extent that they represent original compilations, were essentially the American standards of protection.

*Contributory liability, see p. 177.
†Betamax case, see p. 67.

A funny thing happened on the way to the forum.

The major relevant provisions of the WIPO treaty requiring the United States to amend its law were stated concisely in Articles 11 and 12:

Article 11

Obligations concerning Technological Measures

Contracting Parties shall provide adequate legal protection and effective legal remedies against the circumvention of effective technological measures that are used by authors in connection with the exercise of their rights under this Treaty or the Berne Convention and that restrict acts, in respect of their works, which are not authorized by the authors concerned or permitted by law.

Article 12

Obligations concerning Rights Management Information

(1) Contracting Parties shall provide adequate and effective legal remedies against any person knowingly performing any of the following acts knowing or, with respect to civil remedies having reasonable grounds to know, that it will induce, enable, facilitate or conceal an infringement of any right covered by this Treaty or the Berne Convention:

    (i) to remove or alter any electronic rights management information without authority;

    (ii) to distribute, import for distribution, broadcast or communicate to the public, without authority, works or copies of works knowing that electronic rights

operators and Internet service providers became concerned about their potential liability for infringements on the Internet.

The Working Group recommended against any specific exceptions for on-line service providers. With hindsight, that position, as much as anything else, was responsible for the unfavorable reception of the White Paper proposals as submitted.

In any event, the Digital Millennium Copyright Act now specifically protects the Internet service providers in several carefully described circumstances. For example, service providers are not liable for "transitory digital network communications" that they simply forward "through an automatic technical process without selection of the material by the service provider" from a customer to its intended destination. (Service providers thus aren't generally liable for forwarding infringing e-mail.)

If a customer posts information so that it "resides on a system or network" run by the service provider, without the service provider's knowledge that the information is infringing, then the service provider is generally not liable. The provisions are incredibly intricate; but they do exact the cooperation of the service providers to assist copyright owners in limiting copyright infringements. If the service provider is notified of a claimed infringement, the provider must generally respond "expeditiously to remove, or disable access to, the material that is claimed to be infringing." Furthermore, a copyright owner may obtain a subpoena from an appropriate court requiring a service provider to reveal the identity of any of its subscribers accused of violating the copyright. Such procedures ought to allow the copyright owner to proceed against the proper party.

Another exception protects the process known as *system caching*. Let's take a look at this problem. Most computers have their own built-in "caches"; that is, the computer programs, such as Web browsers, automatically store copies in RAM of recently accessed images and materials, so that if the user wants to go back to a site that's already been accessed, the images and information can be reloaded virtually instantaneously. System providers use similar caching systems. When a customer clicks on a Web page, effectively requesting the service provider to connect the customer to a specific address, the service provider usually connects directly to that location. However, for sites that are frequently accessed by lots of customers, it is faster for the service provider to set up a "cache"—a copy of the requested site—so that the cached information can be accessed more quickly.

The service providers argue that such system caches speed their services, and actually reduce congestion on the Internet by allowing many requests for information to be satisfied using the provider's cache instead of going back repeatedly to the Internet. Some copyright owners have objected that such caching systems constitute copyright infringement, since they result in the making of copies that the copyright owner does not control. Congress, however, agreed with the service providers that system caching should be allowed, by creating an exception to specifically exempt such systems.

However, there are circumstances in which system caching might in fact cause harm. For example, if a Web site constantly updates material, requests for information that are satisfied by routing the request to a previously stored system cache might fail to update the information as frequently as is necessary, and result in the users' receiving outdated information. Or if a Web site makes money by charging advertisers for the number of "hits" to the site, the use of system caching might result in an undercount in the number of hits—hits to the cache would not be recorded. Therefore, there are elaborate provisions in the new act requiring that the system providers comply with "rules concerning the refreshing, reloading, or other updating of the material when specified by the person making the material available online in accordance with a generally accepted industry standard data communications protocol for the system or network."

management information has been removed or altered without authority.
(2) As used in the Article, "rights management information" means information which identifies the work, the author of the work, the owner of any right in the work, or information about the terms and conditions of use of the work, and any numbers or codes that represent such information, when any of these items of information is attached to a copy of a work or appears in connection with the communication of a work to the public.

How did these relatively straightforward provisions get turned into page upon page of technical jargon? See the accompanying text.

Name and password.

The most common elements of such systems involve authentication of the user desiring access to the server. Typically, the server will require entry of a user name and a password. More elaborate mechanisms, however, have been developed. For example, some servers do not grant access once a user is verified, but rather, they terminate the connection and reestablish it from the server to the registered user's site. . . . Other systems are being implemented that use more elaborate authentication systems. For example, a number of companies are developing hardware key systems that require the user, after establishing a preliminary connection, to verify that connection by inserting a hardware device similar to a credit card into the user's computer system. That device then sends an indecipherable code to verify the identity of the user.

           —White Paper

Does the New Statute Work?

The Digital Millennium Copyright Act is not traditional copyright at all: rather, it's a new paradigm, reinforcing the copyright protection and copyright management information systems that are adopted by the copyright owners themselves. The new act protects the package, rather than the content. It has some precursors. When Congress extended copyright protection to sound recordings,[*] it covered the "package" in which copyrighted music or other recorded sound might be embedded. And when Congress passed the Semiconductor Chip Protection Act,[†] it focused more on the package than on the content of the semiconductor chips.

Will the new paradigm work? It's too early to say. Some early computer software manufacturers relied upon electronic protection systems to prevent copying of their works. But legitimate users of most software, particularly business software, objected to cumbersome

"Wow, thanks. I'm a big fan. I've downloaded all your stuff."

---

*Sound recordings, see p. 44.
†Semiconductor Chip Protection Act, see p. 89.

copy protection systems, and tended to buy programs that didn't have such elaborate protections. The marketplace favored open access, and buyers voted with their dollars. So it's possible that, despite the copyright protection systems supported by the Digital Millennium Copyright Act, buyers will simply boycott or avoid buying products that have overly cumbersome protection systems.

The international community, in adopting the WIPO treaties, and the United States Congress, in adopting the Digital Millennium Copyright Act, were obviously concerned about the possible negative effects of digitized information. Once text, images, sound, and movies are digitized, it's simply too easy to make copies and disseminate them around the world at the touch of a button.

Some scholars, however, warn that something is going to be lost by protecting the packages in which creative works are contained. Under traditional copyright principles, not all copying of works constitutes copyright infringement. Some works aren't subject to copyright protection;* certain aspects of works, such as ideas and facts,† are not protected; certain uses of works, such as those denominated a fair use,‡ are simply not infringements; and even protected works, after a certain period of time, go into the public domain.˙ If a work is electronically protected against duplication and access, however, it will prevent some uses of works that would have been allowed under traditional copyright. Copyright has always been directed at copying and other specific infringing activities, and mere "access" to a copyrighted work has never been barred under copyright. But the new act prevents not only the copying of works, but even access to works. And once access is controlled by electronic protection systems, it's impossible to get at even the parts that are supposed to be available for use by the public.

For example, what does it mean for a work to go into the public domain after the expiration of copyright if it's still under electronic lock and key? Of course, just because a work is in the public domain doesn't guarantee that the public has access to copies; copyright in unpublished letters eventually expires, but that doesn't mean that the public will neces-

A dangerous precedent?

The Working Group believes it is—at best—premature to reduce the liability of any type of service provider in the NII environment. . . . If an entity provided only the wires and conduits—such as the telephone company, it would have a good argument for an exemption if it was truly in the same position as a common carrier and could not control who or what was on its system. The same could be true for an on-line service provider who unknowingly transmitted encrypted infringing material.

It would be unfair—and set a dangerous precedent—to allow one class of distributors to self-determine their liability by refusing to take responsibility. . . .

—White Paper

---

*Subject matter of copyright, see chapter 6.
†Ideas, see p. 188; facts, p. 187.
‡Fair use, see p. 190.
˙Duration of copyright, see p. 205.

A golden age of free music?

As of 2000, it might look like the Internet has outpaced the law. MP3 music is widely available on the Internet, and the record industry seems powerless to stop it. The Recording Industry Association of America (RIAA) has been busy bringing suits to stop the dissemination of recording/storage devices like the Rio (for downloading and listening to musical MP3 files) and Internet sites like Napster (that make it possible for subscribers to easily exchange MP3 files). At the moment, it's not clear how successful the RIAA will be in these suits.

But guess what? The fix is already in. It's the Digital Millennium Copyright Act. The legal framework is already in place that will make it illegal to copy or access protected works. The secure format is not yet in place, but it probably will be by the time you read this book. Enjoy all the music that's been put out there in unprotected form, because the free ride will be over. In five years or so, when the new music is in a secure format, we'll look back nostalgically at all the free music we got from the "pre-protection" days.

Sound familiar? It's like the 1980s when people bought backyard dish antennas and picked up satellite video transmissions before they were scrambled (see page 66). Except that all the music that's out there in unsecure form will still be around for a long time to be duplicated over and over in unauthorized MP3 files. I suspect, however, that our kids will discover some new musical style that absolutely requires that they go out and buy the new music, whatever it is. The old "free" music just won't be the same.

sarily get access to the works. Or if a museum has physical control over access to an artwork that's in the public domain, it can still prevent the making of copies of the work. But now we're going to be generating lots of works that are under a lock and key that may long outlive the life or the scope of the copyright.

The whole protection system is premised upon the assumption that, if works are not subject to the safeguards provided in the new act, companies will simply not disseminate their works in digital formats; and that it is ultimately a boon to the public that works should in fact be made available in such new and useful formats. Some of the specific exceptions that were added to the Digital Millennium Copyright Act paralleled or were inspired by some of the traditional limitations on copyright, but the fit is not precise. Presumably, that's why a procedure has been set up for periodically reviewing the system and making additional exceptions. Whether the price we're going to have to pay to encourage the creation and dissemination of digital works is worth it, in terms of cost, complication, and possible overreaching of protection, has yet to be determined.

LET'S NOT FORGET THE BASIC PRINCIPLES OF COPYRIGHT

Lest you think that the Digital Millennium Copyright Act covers all situations on the Internet, let's take a look at a recent case that illustrates something about the fundamental nature of the Internet that makes it different from all other forms of communication.

In 1996, TotalNEWS, a start-up company on the Internet, introduced one of the most useful Web sites of the year. Their Web site, reproduced on the next page (shown accessing a Fox News site), allowed "one-stop"

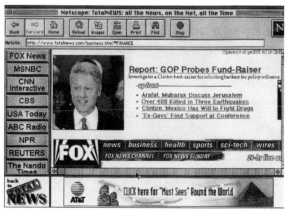

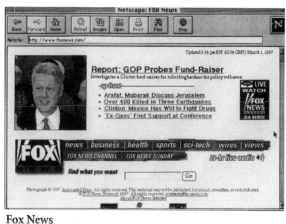

TotalNEWS   **Fox News**

news access. From the TotalNEWS site, customers could access news, either by typing in topics and getting cross-links to hundreds of separate Web news sites on those topics, or by clicking on one of the news buttons at the left of the page to access the news reporting service of any of the news services listed. TotalNEWS maintained no news of its own, but was strictly a conduit for accessing news from the linked sites.

TotalNEWS used what was known as "framing" technology to access the other sites from within a separate frame of the TotalNEWS site. For example, the illustration above right shows the way a customer would view the Fox News site on a particular day if he or she went directly to that site. As you can see, the same Fox site was reproduced on the TotalNEWS site in a "frame" that represented a portion of the TotalNEWS site; the other frames for accessing other news sites remained along the left side, and the TotalNEWS ads remained in their own frame along the bottom of the page. Customers could "move around" the Fox site within the TotalNEWS site by clicking on the arrows or margins at the right of the TotalNEWS frame. There was also an option to bring the inner frame to the "front" window, in a full-sized frame, but there were no instructions on how to do this, and many people may never have figured out how to do it or even realized that it could be done.

Several of the other news services sued TotalNEWS for copyright infringement. They complained that the framing technology cut off portions of their pages, so that their pages were not presented to the customers as they were designed to be presented. For example, by displaying the Fox site in a smaller frame within the TotalNEWS site, the initial view cut off the Fox News ad on the right, the Fox search engine ("find what you want"), and the Fox links at the bottom of the page. The other news companies particularly objected that their sites were displayed inside a frame that contained TotalNEWS' advertisements, sometimes covering up their own ads. Furthermore, if customers liked a particular page, and pressed the "Bookmark" button so they could come back to that page later, they were actually bookmarking the TotalNEWS site rather than the other site. For example, if a customer liked the Fox News site, pressed "Bookmark," and later came back to the bookmarked site, he or she would be at the TotalNEWS Home page (www.totalnews.com) rather than the Fox News site (www.foxnews.com)—and with the general TotalNEWS inner frame rather than the inner Fox News frame.

For its part, TotalNEWS argued that it didn't actually make a copy of the other news sites: instead, their Web site simply contained a URL (universal resource locator) address (such as www.foxnews.com) that instructed the user's Web browser to link to the other site directly. As explained in the TotalNEWS "disclaimer,"

> TotalNEWS provides a link to other sites maintained by third parties. As such, for your convenience, TotalNEWS facilitates access to news and news related sites on the Internet.
>
> Due to the use of the frames technology on browsers that support it, even though the TotalNEWS URL might be displayed as the current URL, users are actually directly accessing the third-party web sites. TotalNEWS does not modify, copy, reproduce, republish, transmit, upload, post, broadcast, rewrite or redistribute information found on the third-party web sites. All data is sent from the corresponding web site directly to the user's browser without any intervention from TotalNEWS.

Rather than contest the case, TotalNEWS agreed to stop using the framing technology; now, whenever a user clicks on a news service button, he or she "leaves" the TotalNEWS site, and is linked to the new site in a full-sized frame. In exchange, the other news companies agreed to give TotalNEWS a "linking license." Since the case was settled, it is unclear whether such a linking license would have been required but for the settlement.

The case illustrates one of the features of the Internet that is bound to raise questions in the future, and which is not dealt with by the Digital Millennium Copyright Act. Once any person or company assigns a universal resource locator to a picture, or text, or any other digital file, authors of any other Web sites can use that same URL name to make the image, text, or other file appear to "exist" on their page. That is, it's now possible to make what appear to be copies of other people's works on one's own Web site without having to "modify, copy, reproduce, republish, transmit, upload, post, broadcast, rewrite or redistribute" them. And if you don't make or distribute a copy, or publicly perform or display it* (beyond the display caused by the creator's own URL), then you haven't infringed any copyright, have you? Well, there is still the exclusive right to make a derivative work;† and the "placement" of a work onto a different site, so that it appears different to the user, is arguably the creation of a derivative work, even if no copy is ever made.

In another variation on the theme, some Web authors are quite careful to set up their sites in a particular sequence, so that the user sees, for example, the Home page first (explaining the company philosophy), and then particular explanations and disclaimers in a particular order before getting into the "inner" Web pages. What if someone else upsets that scheme by making links not to the company's Home page, but to one of the inner pages? On the one hand, how can anyone complain about having "traffic" sent to their site? On the other hand, isn't it a violation of the expectations of Web authors to have others link to their sites in such a way as to defeat their carefully structured sequence of pages?

The Internet is a fascinating place, and I suspect it will be generating novel questions of law faster than Congress can possibly deal with the specifics. That's why it's important that the Digital Millennium Copyright Act is not the only law on the subject. Many of the issues will be decided by the parties, lawyers, and courts applying basic copyright principles of law, just as they have for years.

CONCLUSION

There are other provisions of the Digital Millennium Copyright Act,‡ but you've probably gotten the point by now: yes, copyright is capable of dealing with the new technology. But no, there isn't necessarily a pretty or

*Exclusive rights of copyright, see p. 166.
†Derivative works, see p. 168.
‡Other DMCA provisions, see pp. 25 and 71.

neat solution to the problems. Even Congress seemed aware that this was only the first pass, and provided that the Register of Copyrights and other members of the Department of Commerce should report back to Congress the effects of the amendments, and any recommendations for further change. I personally lament how technical the recent copyright solutions have become. But the point is, solutions are available. The Internet is not the death knell for copyright, but simply an opportunity for modification.

Indeed, the digital distribution of copyrighted works offers not only a threat to copyright interests, but also the seeds of a technological solution. The Digital Millennium Copyright Act protects copyright protection systems and copyright management information. The administration, Congress, the international community, and the industries themselves envision an era when the computer software and the copyright management information can provide for more efficient tracking of the use of copyrighted works, and more efficient licensing mechanisms. Technology, on balance, is neutral to copyright interests; in some ways it's a threat, but in some ways it's a boon, just another market to be exploited. In any event, copyright is alive and well on the Internet.

PART TWO

Copyright Basics

CHAPTER SIX

What Does Copyright Protect?

ORIGINALITY

Some sense of the range of copyright can be gleaned by looking at the many types of works covered by the current copyright statute. These include books, drama, dance, music, sound recordings, pictures, photographs, sculpture, architecture, movies, and computer programs. Later in this chapter, we'll take a closer look at each of these types of work, and see how they each came to be added to the list of works eligible for copyright.

However, the key language of the statute is not in the categories, but in the section defining the subject matter of copyright. According to the statute, "Copyright protection subsists, in accordance with this title, in original works of authorship fixed in any tangible medium of expression, now known or later developed, from which they can be perceived, reproduced, or otherwise communicated, either directly or with the aid of a machine or device."

Under this statute, there are thus two core concepts: "originality" and "fixation." The latter, "fixation," is relatively easy to understand. It requires that a work, to be protected under the federal statute, must be recorded in some way, so that it exists in at least one copy.

Fixation.

Under the [Act] it makes no difference what the form, manner, or medium of fixation may be—whether it is in words, numbers, notes, sounds, pictures, or any other graphic or symbolic indicia, whether embodied in a physical object in written, printed, photographic, sculptural, punched, magnetic, or any other stable form, and whether it is capable of perception directly or by means of any machine or device "now known or later developed."

– Conference Report on the Copyright Act of 1976

The Act requires an *authorized* fixation. The one exception is that, since 1994, a live musical performance is protected, under federal law, against *unauthorized* fixation, as described at p. 170. Live spoken performances, or live conversations, are not covered by the Act, though they may be protected under some state theories of protection, as described generally at p. 222.

Originality.

As colorfully explained by Judge Learned Hand in *Sheldon v. Metro-Goldwyn Pictures*, a 1936 appellate court decision, "Borrowed the work must not be . . . ; but if by some magic a man who had never known it were to compose anew Keats's Ode on a Grecian Urn, he would be an 'author,' and, if he copyrighted it, others might not copy that poem, though they might of course copy Keats's [since Keats's work is now in the public domain]." The problem is that no one would believe the man: the burden of proving independent creation might simply be too high.

The more difficult concept is that of "originality." Congress intentionally left the term "original works of authorship" undefined, but indicated in the Conference Report that "it is intended to incorporate without change the standard of originality established by the courts under the [previous] copyright statute." Thus, in order to understand the concept, it is necessary to have some knowledge of earlier statutes and earlier cases.

That the threshold of copyrightability is quite low is made clear by a long line of cases, including a 1903 Supreme Court case in which Justice Oliver Wendell Holmes suggested that almost any creative effort, however modest, would suffice:

> The [work] is the personal reaction of an individual upon nature. Personality always contains something unique. It expresses its singularity even in handwriting, and a very modest grade of art has in it something irreducible, which is one man's alone. That something he may copyright. . . .

(Another famous quote from the case, *Bleistein v. Donaldson Lithographing Co.,* can be found on p. 142.)

The low level of creativity required by the "originality" standard can be best understood by contrasting it with the relatively high standard of creativity required for patents.* A patent is the exclusive right to "make, use or sell" a "new and useful process, machine, manufacture, or composition of matter." While copyright deals primarily with the aesthetic, patent deals with the functional. But patent rights are granted only sparingly. Before a *patent* is issued, the inventor must demonstrate that the invention is "novel"—that is, that "the world ain't never seen it before" (to paraphrase Busby Berkeley). The invention must be "non-obvious"—that is, not obvious "to a person having ordinary skill in the art" to which it pertains. By contrast, under the originality standard of *copyright,* an author gets a copyright in an independently created work even if the work is similar to a preexisting one, so long as the author did not in fact copy the preexisting work.

*Patent, see p. 219.

Dr. Nobel Price.
One of my favorite characters from the PBS program *Sesame Street* was "Dr. Nobel Price" (lower right), who would spend long years in isolation inventing some new contraption. As he was explaining it to Ernie or some other *Sesame Street* character—"it opens over your head and protects you from the rain"—any child would soon be shouting, long before Ernie pointed out the obvious, "It's an umbrella!" Poor Dr. Price, even if he hadn't ever seen an umbrella, and even if, in the copyright sense of the word, it was "original" to him, would not be able to patent it, because patent law requires a higher level of creativity. Independent creation does not assure patentability.

The higher patent standard.

The lesson was also learned, the hard way, by Elisha Gray, who lost out to Alexander Graham Bell for the patent on the first telephone. Bell filed his application in New York City at noon on January 14, 1876; Gray filed his application in the same place two hours later. The litigation upholding Bell's priority centered upon this two-hour difference, and upon whether Bell had sufficiently "reduced" his invention to "practice," as required by the statute, even though at the time of the application he did not have a working model of the telephone. In any event, Bell went on to develop the companies that became AT&T and the Bell Telephone system, and the stories of his first call to his assistant Thomas Watson and of his presentation of the telephone at the 1876 Centennial Exposition at Philadelphia have become a part of American folklore. Gray's consolation prize was not complete obscurity: together with his partner, E. M. Barton, he formed a manufacturing concern that developed into the Western Electric Co., which was ultimately taken over by the Bell Company to become the world's largest manufacturer of communications equipment.

Originality does require, however, at least *some* minimal level of creativity. For example, in a recent case, the Supreme Court held that a company that compiled a telephone directory, listing all of its customers alphabetically, could not get a copyright in the work. The directory was just a compilation of facts,* and facts themselves are not copyrightable because facts exist independently, and "do not owe their origin to an act of authorship." Although someone may copyright the original language in which facts are described, or an original "compilation" of facts, the compilation in the case of an alphabetical listing of customers and their telephone numbers did not involve sufficient creative choices to qualify the work as original.

*Facts, see p. 187.

Telephone books.

The Supreme Court stated, in *Feist v. Rural Telephone Service* (1991):

> We conclude that the names, towns, and telephone numbers copied by Feist were not original to Rural and therefore were not protected by the copyright in Rural's combined white and yellow pages directory. . . . [C]opyright protects only those constituent elements of a work that possess more than a *de minimus* quantum of creativity. Rural's white pages, limited to basic subscriber information and arranged alphabetically, fall short of the mark.

It is because of this doctrine and this case that the telephone companies have been helpless to prevent a plethora of new products and services using the information freely available from telephone books, such as complete United States–wide telephone directories on CD-ROM or the Internet.

The requirement of some minimal level of creativity reflects the policy of copyright that we generally want to reward those who have made some sort of contribution to "learning" or "art." As stated by Professor (later Judge) Benjamin Kaplan, "to make the copyright turnstile revolve, the author should have to deposit more than a penny in the box."

We'll now turn to the different types of work eligible for copyright. But we'll continue, in the context of each category, to explore the intricacies of the originality standard.

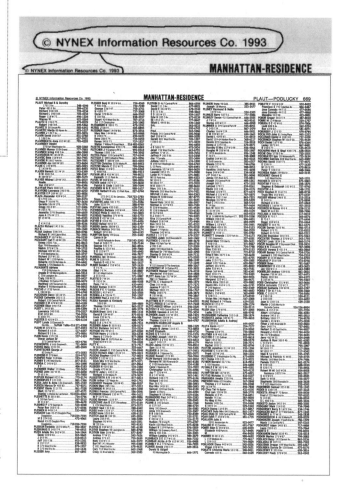

That persistent copyright notice.

Even after the Feist case made it clear that telephone directories were not copyrightable, many telephone companies continued to place copyright notices in their directories. In this directory, from 1993, NYNEX placed a copyright notice on every page, so that a photocopy of any single page would be sure to pick up the notice!

WHAT KINDS OF WORKS ARE PROTECTED?

Books, 1790

Books* have been protected under copyright since its inception. The 1976 Act makes clear that coverage extends not only to traditional books, but to all "literary works . . . expressed in words, numbers, or other verbal or numerical symbols or indicia, regardless of the nature of the material objects . . . in which they are embodied," including "books, periodicals, manuscripts, phonorecords, film, tapes, disks, or cards."

Maps and Charts, 1790

In addition to books, the only works specifically mentioned in the original 1790 copyright act were maps and charts. By "charts," Congress presumably did not mean tables of information, but rather navigational charts. But there's woefully little explanation of why Congress singled out these works for protection, other than the obvious value of rewarding the makers of maps and charts in a young country. Americans wanted to encourage the likes of Meriwether Lewis and William Clark to go out and chart uncharted lands (though Lewis and Clark's maps,† from the expedition paid for by the U.S. government,‡ were uncopyrightable, being government works).

What does it mean to make an "original" map? Some cases once suggested that originality required that the cartographer obtain the information for the map from direct surveying, by "the sweat of one's own brow." But the *Feist* case has clearly repudiated the premise that labor and effort can constitute or substitute for originality. Instead, originality consists of the "selection, arrangement, and presentation of the component parts" of a map, and has more to do with the design by which the information is presented than with the information itself.

Other writings.

As originally introduced in 1790, the copyright bill would have protected not only books, maps, and charts, but also "other writings"; at the last minute, the phrase "other writings" was dropped, leaving only books, maps, and charts. Of the twelve states that had passed copyright laws under the prior Articles of Confederation, only three had specifically included maps and charts, while four had also protected "other writings" or "other literary works."

Insurance against international litigation.

Some further insight into the inclusion of maps and charts can be gleaned by looking at what materials the Library of Congress first ordered when it was funded in 1800.

> The map question is intriguing. The book orders for the first quarter century are saturated with map purchases. At first glance they would seem to relate to the need to develop an unexplored country, but if you read the justifications it is apparent they were to be insurance against international litigation. It is clear that the early leaders all assumed the North American continent would be balkanized and ultimately end up as several different nations—either colonies or client states of their European parents. The legislators wanted all the proof they could get of where land claims had been made, borders set, settlements established—geographic precedents in ink and *dated*.
>
> –Charles Goodrum

*Books, see p. 15.
†Lewis and Clark map, see p. 215.
‡Government works, see p. 215.

The New York subway system.
Copyright 1964, New York
City Transit Authority.

The New York subway system.
Copyright 1972, New York
City Transit Authority.

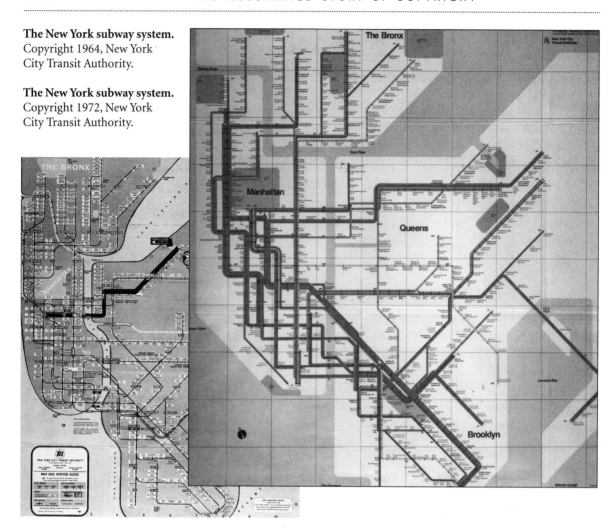

To see how this works in practice, let's take a look at two maps of the
New York subway system. The first was a special map highlighting the
1964 World's Fair, published by the New York City Transit Authority in
that year. Assume that you were hired to produce a new, clearer, more
graphically appealing subway map, and came up with the second map—
the one in fact published by the Transit Authority in 1972. Although very
differently presented, most of the information for the second map can
be derived from the earlier map, without any particular need for independent surveying or even verification. Is the new map sufficiently "original" to be eligible for copyright? Of course! The originality is in the

The Gallery of the Louvre, by Samuel F. B. Morse.
In the foreground you can see several artists doing what all artists do to learn their craft— copying the works of the masters (which, of course, Morse himself did here with a vengeance). Don't do this with modern painters whose works are still protected under copyright. You might add sufficient "original" elements to make your own creation otherwise copyrightable in its own right. But if the work is copied from a copyrighted work, it would also be a copyright infringement.

The Morse painting is described in a book published by The Metropolitan Museum of Art:

> Morse included such familiar masterpieces as Titian's *The Entombment,* Raphael's *La Belle Jardinière,* and Leonardo da Vinci's *Mona Lisa.* Morse regarded the painting, which he hoped would gain him a fair reward of money and fame, as an educational instrument, meant to benefit Americans who could not travel abroad to see the Louvre for themselves. The picture was unfinished when Morse left France late in 1832 on his historic passage to New York aboard the *Sully,* during which he conceived the idea for the electric telegraph.

On Morse's invention, see p. 98.

presentation, not in the information. So, obviously, what we are encouraging under copyright is not just the surveying of new lands and new systems, but also the development of new ways of representing those lands and systems.

Prints, 1802

In 1802, Congress provided that any person who "shall invent and design, engrave, etch or work . . . any historical or other print or prints" could obtain a copyright in the print. Interestingly, it was not until 1870 that paintings, drawings, and sculptures generally were added to the list; so why did Congress only grant protection for this much narrower category of etching or print? The statute obviously was designed to encourage the mass production of works, including not only original designs, but also copies of older paintings. Remember, this was all before photography. Classic art (mainly European masterworks) was known in this country almost exclusively through copies made and distributed by other artists, and it would make sense to encourage the "importation" of classic works by granting copyrights to those who "made" the imported versions. But what does it mean to make an "original" "etching" of a "historical" print?

The Blue Boy.
Gainsborough's *Blue Boy,* one of the Old Masters that was copied by Alfred Bell's mezzotint engravers. Alfred Bell's catalogue pictured several different mezzotint engravings of *The Blue Boy,* confirming that different engravers could indeed render different interpretations.

Some insight can be gleaned from more-recent cases. In the 1940s, Alfred Bell & Co., a British print producer and dealer, made and sold mezzotint engravings of several Old Masters, such as Gainsborough's *Blue Boy.* Cataloda Fine Arts, Inc., an American lithograph company, unable to gain access to the same paintings because of exclusive museum dealing arrangements, made lithographs of Alfred Bell's engravings. Alfred Bell sued for copyright infringement. But where was the "originality" in their engravings? Weren't they just copies of the works of Gainsborough and the other Old Masters, in which copyright, if it was claimed, would long ago have expired?

The district court in New York, and then the federal appellate court, had no difficulty in finding the requisite level of originality. The courts emphasized that the making of mezzotint engravings was a highly skilled craft that required creative choices, among other things in the pulling of a hand tool across the plate of the engraving, to properly imitate the texture of the original oil painting. No two mezzotint engravings are exactly the same, although of course the goal of each engraver is to reproduce as faithful a copy of the original work as the medium allows.

The appellate court discussed the meaning of the term "original" in this context:

> It may mean startling, novel or unusual, a marked departure from the past. . . . [But] "original" in reference to a copyrighted work means that the particular work "owes its origin" to the "author." No large measure of novelty is necessary.
>
> . . . A copyist's bad eyesight or defective musculature, or a shock caused by a clap of thunder, may yield sufficiently distinguishable variations. Having hit upon such a variation unintentionally, the "author" may adopt it as his and copyright it.

In a 1999 case, Bridgeman Art, Inc., held an exclusive license from dozens of art museums to distribute transparencies and license the printing of copies of many of the museums' Old Masters. Bridgeman sued Corel, Inc., claiming that Corel was selling prints that had been copied from Bridgeman's prints. The court held in favor of Corel on several grounds, including the ground that Bridgeman's transparencies were not entitled to copyright because they were photographic likenesses of public domain works. The copies they made, though perhaps

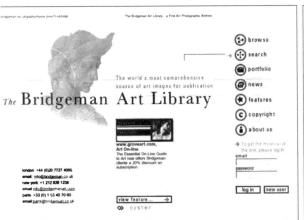

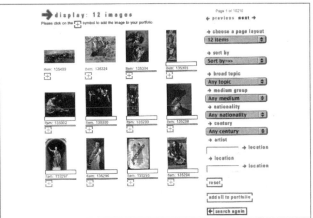

requiring some skill, had no distinguishable variations from the works that were in the public domain. The case raised some alarm among museum directors who have come to count on revenues they make by selling exclusive rights to make prints of works in their collection. The case makes clear that the only exclusive rights they have are in the distinguishable variations of the copies.

A tension is set up by this reasoning, however, that continues to plague copyright to this day. A historical print is protected under copyright because it is original; but it's not the originality of the print that we value. If we purchase a mezzotint engraving of Thomas Gainsborough's *The Blue Boy* (c. 1770), we don't want to find any "original" variations by the engraver; we *want* the work to be an exact replica of Gainsborough's. The same tension was evident to some extent in allowing maps and charts copyright protection: maps are protected only to the extent that they present information in an original way, yet we usually value the map not for the originality of the presentation but for the information conveyed.

Although expanded to include pictorial, graphic, and sculptural works generally, the 1909 act still sepa-

Bridgeman's transparencies for licensing.
Above is the Home page from the Bridgeman Web site, a modern source for transparencies of historical and contemporary images available for licensing. Bridgeman works with artists and museums to make their works available to a wide market. The digital market is now big-time: Microsoft has acquired the exclusive rights to hundreds of thousands of digital images, including (through Corbis, Inc.) the entire Bettmann Archives of historical photographs.

Mezzotint engraving.

Carol Wax documents how the process of mezzotint engraving, by capturing texture in unprecedented detail, was ideal for creating reproductions of oil paintings. The mezzotint became more popular, particularly in England, as a reproductive art than as a totally creative art. Wax describes the symbiotic relationship that developed between painters and the mezzotint engravers who, sometimes legally, sometimes illegally, mass-produced the painters' works. In England, the Hogarth Act of 1735 extended copyright protection to original engravings and etchings. In 1776, the English Act was amended specifically to protect reproductive as well as original engravings.

rately listed "reproductions of a work of art"; and the 1976 Act still separately mentions "art reproductions" as within the definition of "pictorial" works.

Music, 1831

Although music* was not specifically added until 1831, composers did register their sheet music before then under the category of "books." Since performance rights† were not granted in music until 1891, copyright during most of the nineteenth century effectively only protected the printing of sheet music.

Photographs, 1865

In 1865, Congress added "photographs and the negatives thereof" to the list of protected works. It's curious that photography was embraced within copyright so soon after its invention, five years before the inclusion of paintings and sculpture generally, and about a hundred years

Nobody cared anymore for war.
Mathew Brady was best known for his portraits of famous people and for his Civil War photographs. This picture is of a Napoleon gun from Cushing's Battery at Antietam in 1862. Despite his success, Brady died virtually penniless. He had cut back drastically on his successful portrait business for the much more costly and risky business of wartime photography. But with the completion of the war, it seems, nobody cared anymore for the pictures depicting it in such graphic detail. Although a collection of his Civil War photographs was eventually sold to the U.S. War Department for $25,000, most of that sum went to pay off Brady's creditors. Other Brady pictures appear on pp. 33, 58, 208, and 232.

*Music, see pp. 31 and 162.
†Performing rights, see p. 168.

before some major museums began to recognize photography as a serious art form. But it's obvious why Congress wanted to grant protection. During and after the Civil War, pioneering photographers like Mathew Brady were bringing back incredible photographs of the war and of American western expansion. Congress wanted to encourage such efforts, and copyright was the accepted vehicle for granting creative people rights in the works they created. It probably also helped that Brady had photographed portraits of many of the leading politicians of the day—Lincoln and his wife and his cabinet, Webster, Calhoun, Clay—and, in his lifetime, over a dozen past or current presidents. So the politicians would have been quite familiar with the photographic process and its incredible power.

Oscar Wilde, by Napoleon Sarony.

But are photographs the sort of "creative" works that copyright was intended to protect? After all, most photographers don't "create" their pictures so much as "capture" the images that already exist in nature.

Here's how the test case was brought to the Supreme Court. In the 1880s, Oscar Wilde gave a successful series of lectures throughout the United States. Napoleon Sarony, a New Yorker who specialized in photo-graphing visiting celebrities, took a series of portraits of Wilde in his "aesthetic lecturing costume." During the rest of Wilde's tour, the Burrow-Giles Lithographic Co. sold about eighty-five thousand unauthorized copies of the Sarony photographs. Sarony, of course, sued for copyright infringement. In 1884, the Supreme Court summarized the issue as one of constitutional dimensions: was a photograph a "writing" of an "author," within the Constitution?* If not, then Congress was without authority to include photographs within the copyright statute.

Burrow-Giles's argument was that "a photograph is the mere mechanical reproduction of the physical features or outlines of some object, animate or inanimate, and involves no originality of thought or any novelty in the intellectual operation connected with its visible reproduction in shape of a picture." In other words, it involved no "originality" of the photographer.

Photographs.

By writings in that clause [of the Constitution] is meant the literary productions of those authors, and congress very properly has declared these to include all forms of writing, printing, engravings, etchings, etc., by which the ideas in the mind of the author are given visible expression. The only reason why photographs were not included in the extended list in the act of 1802 is, probably, that they did not exist, as photography, as an art, was then unknown, and the scientific principle on which it rests, and the chemicals and machinery by which it is operated, have all been discovered long since that statute was enacted.

– Justice Samuel Miller,
from the Sarony case

This explanation is probably not the complete story, since the 1802 act did not include paintings and statuary either, even though they were clearly known to the people of the day.

*U.S. Constitution, see p. 13.

My first true visualization.

Ansel Adams, who specialized in taking pictures from nature, described in *An Autobiography* how he first began to "visualize" pictures when he photographed Half Dome at Yellowstone National Park:

> I began to think about how the print was to appear, and if it would transmit any of the feeling of the monumental shape before me in terms of its expressive-emotional quality. I began to see in my mind's eye the finished print I desired: the brooding cliff with a dark sky and the sharp rendition of distant, snowy Tenaya Peak. I realized that only a deep red filter would give me anything approaching the effect I felt emotionally.
>
> I had only *one* plate left. I attached my other filter, a Wratten #29(F), increased the exposure by the sixteen-times factor required, and released the shutter. I felt I had accomplished something, but did not realize its significance until I developed the plate that evening. I had achieved my first true visualization! I had been able to realize a desired image: not the way the subject appeared in reality but how it *felt* to me and how it must appear in the finished print. The sky had actually been a light, slightly hazy blue and the sunlit areas of Half Dome were moderately dark gray in value. The red filter dramatically darkened the sky and the shadows on the great cliff. Luckily I had with me the filter that made my visualized image possible.

"Luck" had little to do with it—Adams lugged forty pounds of equipment around Yosemite so he would have the right filter when he needed it. For an Adams photograph, see p. 160.

The Supreme Court conceded that "in regard to the ordinary production of a photograph," this may be true, but that, in Sarony's case, the photographer's contributions were considerable. The Court approved the district court's finding that the photograph in question was a

> useful, new, harmonious, characteristic, and graceful picture, and that plaintiff made the same . . . entirely from his own original mental conception, to which he gave visible form by posing the said Oscar Wilde in front of the camera, selecting and arranging the costume, draperies, and other various accessories in said photograph, arranging the subject so as to present graceful outlines, arranging and disposing the light and shade, suggesting and evoking the desired expression, and from such disposition, arrangement, or representation, made entirely by plaintiff, he produced the picture in suit.

Quite an early victory for the *auteur* theory! It almost sounded as if Wilde were only incidental to the creation of the Sarony photograph.

It is important to remember that, in the early years, photography was not as ubiquitous or as convenient as it is today. With "wet plate" photography, the photographer's plate—made of heavy glass—had to be processed before it dried, requiring photographers to literally carry their dark rooms with them if they ventured out of their studios. All of this changed only when George Eastman* developed the revolutionary "dry plate" method of photography in the 1870s, and the paper filmstrip in the 1880s. Then he introduced his famous Kodak box camera, along with a film developing service that allowed amateurs to take professional-looking pictures. The early photographers complained that now anyone could take "snapshots." They sounded about like the early radio or Internet fans

*George Eastman, see p. 56.

who in their days would bemoan everyone else nudging into their territory.

Although the Court distinguished Sarony's photograph from the "ordinary," later cases made clear that just about any photograph,* short of a photocopy, contains sufficient selection of elements to meet the threshold level of originality required by the Constitution and by the statute.

Drama, 1870

Congress first added "dramatic compositions" in 1870. We've already seen how the protection of dramatic works, including pantomimes,† was greatly expanded with the advent of motion pictures in the twentieth century.

Why did Congress add dramatic works only in 1870, even though drama had been known since at least the time of the ancients? To some extent, the snub may have reflected an eighteenth-century distrust, or even disdain, of the theater. (Alexander Cowie cites a "lack of affinity between Puritanism and art.") In colonial days, several states, and even the federal Congress under the Articles of Confederation, had passed laws prohibiting or severely limiting theater. It's also possible that there simply weren't many early American playwrights, so the need for protection did not appear strong (although it would be hard to prove whether the lack of playwrights produced the lack of protection or the other way around).

The breakthrough in attitude probably came about through the remarkable success of others in dramatizing Harriet Beecher Stowe's *Uncle Tom's Cabin* (written in 1851–52) without paying her any compensation. The injury was compounded by the fact that, at that time, translations were also not covered by copyright, so Ms. Stowe also received nothing for the hundreds of transla-

George Eastman as a young photographer.
This cartoon shows George Eastman as a young man, carrying all of the equipment that was required to take and produce photographs prior to his simplification of the process.

Unprotected by copyright.
John Anderson argued that "American drama begins with [Augustin] Daly" (the plaintiff in the pantomime case, p. 59). "Until Daly's time men of literary eminence could not be persuaded to take an interest in playwrighting because of the standards of production, because their work was unprotected by copyright and because the theatre had no interest in any quality beyond the effectiveness of a work on the platform."

*Photographs, see p. 159.
†Pantomimes, see p. 59.

Harriet Beecher Stowe.

Uncle Tom's Cabin.
(*Above right*) From the first
production in 1852,

> There were literally hun-
> dreds of theatrical compa-
> nies (some extraordinarily
> proficient, some atrocious
> and amateurish) which
> toured Uncle Tom's Cabin
> well into the early part of
> the twentieth century. It is
> said that Mrs. Stowe never
> made a penny from the
> dramatic adaptation.
> —Joesph and June
>   Bundy Csida.

This is the scene in which Eliza
crosses the frozen river, from a
1901 production.

tions of her works into other languages. Her injury was compounded
even further by the woeful state of international copyright protection.
These injustices were ultimately righted in the copyright amendments
of 1856 (covering translations*), 1870 (covering drama), and 1891
(improving international protection for foreign authors,[†] and thus trig-
gering better protection for American authors abroad). But all of these
came too late to help Stowe, whose rights were governed by the prior law.

Paintings, Drawings, and Sculpture, 1870

Also in 1870, Congress extended copyright to cover "a painting, drawing,
chromo, statue, statuary, and . . . models or designs intended to be perfected as works of the fine arts." It's not at all clear why it took Congress
so long to get around to the graphic arts, but it must have seemed somewhat illogical to protect photographs, on the ground that their creation
involved some level of creativity, but not paintings and sculpture, which
arguably required a higher degree of talent and creativity.

The reference to "fine arts" opened a Pandora's box that perhaps
helps to explain Congress's reluctance to get into the field in the first
place. Did the reference to "fine arts" limit only the immediately
preceding phrase, "models and designs," or did it imply that paintings,

*Translations, see p. 168.
†International protection, see p. 236.

drawings, and statuary were to be measured by a higher "fine arts" standard as well? In 1874, Congress attempted to clarify the coverage of the act by providing that "the words 'Engraving,' 'cut,' and 'print' shall be applied only to pictorial illustrations or works connected with the fine arts." Whatever this may reveal about Congress's intent to take the fine arts high road, it was somewhat undermined by specific provisions in 1882 for notice on "designs for molded decorative articles, tiles, plaques, or articles of pottery or metal." The question remained: was copyright available only for "fine" arts, and if so, how were judges supposed to draw the line between the fine and not-so-fine arts?

The definitive Supreme Court case came about as follows. The Courier Lithographing Co. created several circus posters advertising *The Great Wallace Shows.* Courier later sued the Donaldson Lithographing Co. for making unauthorized copies of three of Courier's works, apparently also for advertising use by Wallace. The lower courts, following the accepted wisdom of the day, held that mere "advertisements" were not eligible for copyright, and that there was nothing "useful" or "meritorious" about the work to make it deserving of such protection. Justice Holmes, however, scoffed at such an outcome. The circus posters clearly

The Great Wallace Shows. One of the circus posters produced by Courier Lithographing Company in 1898.

Uncle Sam.

Left, a metal replica of the original 1886 Uncle Sam mechanical bank (eleven inches tall), protected under a design patent that expired long ago. Right, a plastic replica (nine inches tall) that Jeffrey Snyder had made in anticipation of the bicentennial celebration, and in which he claimed copyright in 1975. The court held that Snyder's bank lacked sufficient originality, and was therefore not protected under copyright.

A dangerous undertaking.

It would be a dangerous undertaking for persons trained only to the law to constitute themselves final judges of the worth of pictorial illustrations, outside of the narrowest and most obvious limits. At the one extreme some works of genius would be sure to miss appreciation. Their very novelty would make them repulsive until the public had learned the new language in which their author spoke. It may be more than doubted, for instance, whether the etchings of Goya or the paintings of Manet would have been sure of protection when seen for the first time. At the other end, copyright would be denied to pictures which appealed to a public less educated than the judge. Yet if they command the interest of any public, they have a commercial value—it would be bold to say that they have not an aesthetic and educational value—and the taste of any public is not to be treated with contempt.

– Justice Oliver Wendell Holmes,
Bleistein v. Donaldson Lithographing Co. (1903)

involved sufficient creative effort to qualify them for copyright protection. The Supreme Court reversed the lower court decisions, and granted protection.

What was left of the higher "fine arts" standard? Not much. So it's not surprising that when Congress recodified copyright in 1909, it dropped the limiting language, and protected all "works of art"—whether "fine" or not.

There may still be a lingering fine arts bias in some court opinions. In a 1959 case, a scale replica of Rodin's *Hand of God* was granted copyright protection, even though the court found no significant variations from Rodin's original work except for the scale and the medium. Yet, in a 1976 case, a plastic model of an antique Uncle Sam mechanical bank was held *not* to be copyrightable, even though the court conceded several distinguishable variations from the original. So what *is* the meaning of originality in this context? Are the cases consistent? Might one of them be "wrong"? Are they

reconcilable on the ground that the Rodin replica is "fine" art and the Uncle Sam bank is "junk" art? These are all questions that law professors love to ask, although we are quick to insist that our purpose is to make students think, not—or at least not only—to confuse them.

Movies, 1912

As we've seen, movies* have been included within the scope of copyright since their inception, and have been specifically enumerated since the copyright amendment of 1912. One interesting case again raised the issue whether an "ordinary" photograph or movie, without particular artistic pretensions, exhibits sufficient "originality" to be protectable under copyright.

In 1963, Abraham Zapruder† took what would have been an ordinary home movie of a presidential motorcade, but for an extraordinary event beyond his control. He happened to have taken the best actual footage of the assassination of President John F. Kennedy. He imme-

The Hand of God.

Here are several different versions of Rodin's *Hand of God.* Although the plaster original was completed by Rodin in 1896, there were several authorized "executions" of the piece in marble and bronze. (This may help explain why the court was willing to find originality even in the making of copies.) At the left is the version in the New York Metropolitan Museum, upon which the defendants claimed they based their work. In the middle is plaintiff's rendition, based upon careful measurements of the version in the Carnegie Museum in Pittsburgh. At the right is the defendants' version.

Although there are clearly elements of the defendants' style that make that version distinctive, the plaintiff claimed that the defendants had taken plaintiff's version, sanded down some of the details, and then added new details. The issue in the case was whether plaintiff's version had sufficient originality to be protectable in its own right. The court held that it did. Another issue is whether defendant's version is "substantially similar" to plaintiff's (see p. 151). The court, in finding for the plaintiff, implicitly held that it was.

*Movies, see p. 57.
†Zapruder film, see p. 202.

Zapruder in the headlines.

Abraham Zapruder is still in the headlines over three decades later. Although he died in 1970, Time, Inc. transferred the copyright in his work to his heirs in 1975. The physical film—a quarter-inch wide and six feet long—has resided in the National Archives. The government acquired ownership of the film in 1992 under a federal law requiring that all materials relating to the Kennedy assassination be transferred to the National Archives for preservation and research. The amount of compensation was ultimately left to arbitration; in 1999, the arbitration panel awarded the Zapruder heirs $16 million for the film. For the difference between ownership of copyright and ownership of the physical copy, see p. 212.

diately realized the value of his film, and sold it to Time, Inc. for $150,000. Clearly, the movie was valued not because of its aesthetic quality, but for the crucial information it happened to contain about an important historical event.

When the issue of originality was raised in a federal district court, the court cited other cases suggesting that all photographs and movies are protectable, no matter how modest their artistry. The court nevertheless felt it necessary to emphasize just how much control Zapruder had over the final product, stating that "The Zapruder pictures in fact have many elements of creativity. Among other things, Zapruder selected the kind of camera (movies, not snapshots), the kind of film (color), the kind of lens (telephoto), the area in which the pictures were to be taken, the time they were to be taken, and (after testing several sites) the spot on which the camera would be operated." In fact, Zapruder tried out several sites before he chose a vantage point overlooking the spot where the motorcade would have to slow down to make a sharp turn.

Computer Programs, 1964, 1976

Computer programs* have been considered protected as "literary works" ever since the Copyright Office† started accepting registration of them in 1964. Whatever doubt may have existed under the prior law, the 1976 Act and its legislative history make the coverage of computer programs clear.

Records and Tapes, 1971

In the 1971 Sound Recording Amendment,‡ records and tapes were given their own separate protection, in addition to the protection already accorded the underlying musical works.

Dance, 1976

Some dance was eligible for copyright under prior law, but only if it told a dramatic story that qualified it under "drama." It was not until the gen-

*Protection of computer programs, see p. 79.
†Copyright Office, see p. 177.
‡Sound recordings, see p. 44.

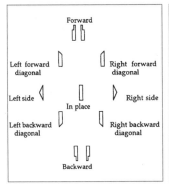

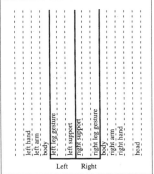

Labanotation.

At bottom left is an example of labanotation, developed by Rudolf von Laban, an early twentieth-century dance teacher and theorist. The notation is read from bottom to top, and the bar lines correspond to the bars of music. In the diagram at left, shapes indicate the direction of movement. At the right, the placement on the staff indicates the part of the body doing the movement. The shading indicates whether the movement is done by the upper, middle, or lower portions of the body or limb.

eral overhaul of copyright in 1976 that a specific category was created for "choreographic works."

Dance is hardly a new art, and it's not clear why earlier Congresses did not see fit to protect it, or what happened in recent years to convince the new Congress that it should. About the only "modern" development is labanotation and Benesh movement notation, systems for transcribing dance steps. However, many new dance works are *not* recorded, either by labanotation or in film, and so don't qualify for federal copyright protection under the separate "fixation" requirement.*

Jump!

The "splash" of movement indicated in measure 577 (left) can be seen in the corresponding movement of the dancers (right). The excerpt and photograph are from Paul Taylor's *Eventide*. As indicated by the measures before and after, the jump is taken from—and returns to—a relatively serene state.

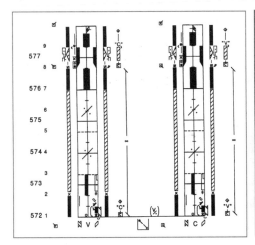

*Fixation, see p. 127.

Architecture, 1990

Doing justice under the earlier law.

Under the prior law, blueprints were protected as drawings, but the buildings depicted in the blueprints were not protected, since they were "works of utility." So, strangely, second comers couldn't copy blueprints, but they could theoretically build the building depicted in the blueprints. Many courts were able to grant indirect protection for buildings by prohibiting the copying of blueprints, without which the second building could not be built. A federal court was able to grant an injunction against the building of the "copycat" home at right because it had been based upon plans traced from those of a luxury home by Chris Demetriades just up the block, at left. Today, a suit could be based upon the copyright in the building itself, whether or not the blueprints were copied.

Works of architecture were added to the list of copyrightable works only in 1990. Later, we'll look at the "works of utility" doctrine.* Under that doctrine, architectural works, like other works of utility, were not generally protected under federal copyright. However, it's easy to understand why architecture was eventually added to the list of copyrightable works. In 1988, the United States ratified the International Berne Copyright Convention,† and under its terms, was required to grant protection to architectural works.

Boat Hull Designs, 1998

Another category of work that was not protected by federal copyright under the "works of utility" doctrine was the design of boat hulls. The problem here was not only the works of utility doctrine, but also another interesting federal principle known as the "preemption" doctrine.

The Supreme Court elaborated upon the scope of preemption of state laws in a series of cases through the 1970s.‡ In 1989, the Court reaffirmed the doctrine in the case of *Bonito Boats, Inc. v. Thunder Craft Boats, Inc.* Florida had passed a statute granting special protection to the design of boat hulls (a valuable regional industry), and the plaintiff had attempted, under that statute, to prevent the defendant from using a "direct molding process" to make a knockoff of its boat design. However, the Supreme Court struck down the state statute under the preemption

*Works of utility, see p. 185.
†Protection of architectural works under Berne, see p. 245.
‡Preemption doctrine, see p. 227.

doctrine. Florida simply did not have the power to protect what Congress had left outside the scope of federal protection.

The boating industry's response to this setback was to lobby Congress to pass a *national* statute to protect boat designs. And in 1998, it was finally successful in getting such a proposal included within the Digital Millennium Copyright Act.* The protection only extends for a maximum of ten years, but the established boating industry finally got the protection it sought.

Characters

Way back in 1930, Judge Learned Hand had suggested that characters, as well as plot, could be copyrighted. Over the past fifty years, however, a lot of ink has been spilled over whether characters may be copyrighted apart from the stories in which they play their parts. The problem arose from a curious case in the Ninth Circuit Court of Appeals, which unfortunately happened to be the circuit court that covered Hollywood, California, and therefore a substantial part of the movie industry.

Dashiell Hammett was a successful mystery writer who created the character Sam Spade in the magazine serial, and then the book, *The Maltese Falcon.* Hammett and Alfred A. Knopf, the publisher, then sold

The Maltese Falcon. Humphrey Bogart (holding the Falcon), Peter Lorre, Mary Astor, and Sydney Greenstreet in the 1941 movie version of the novel.

*Digital Millennium Copyright Act, see p. 112.

Characters, of the cartoon variety, who have been held copyrightable by the courts. (And don't forget Mickey Mouse, pp. 186 and 198, and PAC-MAN, p. 78.)

Spark Plug.
A federal court held that a three-dimensional toy (far right) infringed the character known as "Spark Plug" or "Sparky" from the Barney Google comic strip (right). The defendant in the case had actually applied for a design patent in the doll. Below is a picture of several Sparky dolls in a store window, showing that the dolls were indeed becoming the "sensation of 1923."

Superman.
A federal court held that an all-powerful "Wonderman" infringed upon the character of Superman.

Tarzan, star of over forty movies.

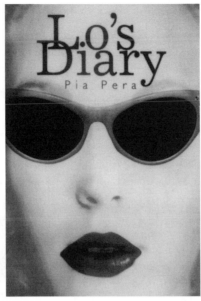

Warner Bros. the exclusive right to the story in movies, radio, and television. Warner Bros. produced a not bad movie version of the story, and then, in 1941, a remake starring Humphrey Bogart as Sam Spade. It was an instant hit and is an all-time movie classic.

Later, Hammett and Knopf sold to CBS the exclusive right to produce additional radio versions of the Sam Spade character. Warner Brothers then sued Hammett, Knopf, and CBS, claiming that they owned the exclusive rights to the Sam Spade character under their prior contract with Hammett.

In 1954, the Ninth Circuit Court held that Hammett had not in fact granted Warner Brothers the exclusive right in the character. And then, in case that reasoning weren't enough, the court went on to state that Hammett could not have done so, because the character was not copyrightable separately from the story. The outcome of the case was the proper one, holding that Dashiell Hammett could not be stopped from producing additional stories using the character that he had created. But the reasoning produced considerable mischief. Characters not protectable? What if it had been Hammett suing someone else? Could the case mean that Hammett had no protectable rights in the Sam Spade character?

Hopalong Cassidy.
William Boyd, the actor who played Hopalong Cassidy in film and on television (far left), bought up the rights in the character from Clarence Mulford, the author, and various other parties (see the diagram on p. 166). Boyd is credited with the first major—incredibly successful—merchandising campaign based upon a television character.

Lolita.
Controversy has surrounded the book publication of Pia Pera's version of *Lolita* told from the viewpoint of Lolita. The press seemed to go out of its way to suggest that there were legitimate legal arguments on both sides. I confess that this looks to me like a clear infringement, based upon the taking of the characters as well as much of the plot of the Nabokov story. Pera was free to take the "idea" of a Lolita-like character, or to develop her own story of an older man's obsession with a young woman; but she was not free to appropriate Nabokov's characters. The case was ultimately settled when Nabokov's son, Dmitri, authorized publication on condition that he receive a commission, and that he be allowed to write a preface, which he did.

For the most part, no one seemed to believe the Ninth Circuit. Hollywood in fact paid handsomely for rights in characters and for sequel rights. Even if copyright did not protect characters, it was possible that state theories of protection* might have filled the gap in the federal statute. But law review writers for the next several decades had lots of fun trying to reconcile the court case with Hollywood reality.

To cut a long story short, the courts eventually conceded what everyone else seemed already to have known: that characters are copyrightable even apart from the stories in which they live. The early cases focused upon cartoon characters, where the visual image of the character represented a protectable drawing. After almost five decades, cases have generally come around to protecting literary characters as well.

CONCLUSION

As you can see, over the 210-year history of copyright, Congress has been constantly expanding the subject matter of protection. The responses to new technologies in the late-twentieth century are only the most recent manifestation of this remarkable growth.

*State theories of protection, see p. 222.

CHAPTER SEVEN

What Rights Does Copyright Grant?

SUBSTANTIAL SIMILARITY

There are several "exclusive rights" of copyright. Within limits, the authors of copyrighted works may prevent other people from copying or distributing their works; from transforming them into what are known as "derivative" works (translations and adaptations); and in some cases from publicly performing or publicly displaying their works. We'll look at each of these and other exclusive rights in more detail later in this chapter. However, overarching all of these exclusive rights is a core concept that is easy to state, but sometimes complex to apply: the concept of "substantial similarity."

It's an infringement of copyright for a user to make a copy of a copyrighted work without the permission of the copyright owner. In Part One, we looked at technological copying in the context of books, sound recordings, videotapes, computer programs, and the Internet. Since much of the copying is of entire works, such unauthorized copying (subject to various exceptions we'll discuss in the next chapter) is usually infringement. The major issue raised by the new technologies is that copying is done by hundreds or thousands or millions of individuals, and the problem is how to adjust the law to take account of such decentralized but massive copying. As we saw, the law has developed considerably in recent years to deal with the problem.

We're now going to focus on a different issue. What if the second work is not an exact duplicate of the original, but rather an independent work that incorporates certain, but not all, aspects of the copyrighted work? For example, a writer incorporates a paragraph of dialogue from a copyrighted book or play, or a songwriter repeats a pattern of six notes of a copyrighted song, or a painter incorporates into a new painting a single figure from someone else's painting. Has the second author infringed the copyright of the first?

The issue in these cases is whether the second work is "substantially similar" to the first. It doesn't have to be an exact duplicate to be an infringement, but it does have to take enough of the copyrighted work that it can be said that the second work was not "independently created." Drawing the line between noninfringement and infringement, between independent creation and substantial similarity, can be frustratingly difficult. The courts have pretty well refused to adopt a simple numerical test to resolve this issue, instead relying upon general statements of policy, and sensitivity to the facts of particular cases. What is clear, however, is that taking even a small portion of a copyrighted work can constitute copyright infringement.

Let's see how the substantial similarity test works in the context of several different types of copyrighted works. We'll see that the test is intimately related to several other key copyright doctrines that are also used to distinguish what infringes from what doesn't.

The Story Lines of Books, Plays, and Motion Pictures

Steven Spielberg has been sued, it seems, for just about every movie he's ever made. Lisa Litchfield wrote a musical about Fudinkle and Lokey, two aliens from Maldemar who are temporarily stranded on Earth and befriended by children who are living with their scientist father at the North Pole. Gary Zambito wrote *Black Rainbow,* a screenplay about the fictional archeologist Zeke Banarro and his expedition in search of pre-Columbian gold artifacts. Geoffrey Williams wrote a children's book about an imaginary zoo containing cloned prehistoric animals. And Barbara Chase-Riboud wrote *Echo of Lions,* a historical novel about a mutiny by slaves aboard the slaveship *Amistad.* All of these authors saw similarities between their own works and Spielberg movies: *E. T. The Extra-Terrestrial, Raiders of the Lost Ark, Jurassic Park,* and *Amistad.* Paul Schrader, who had written an ultimately rejected screenplay of *Close Encounters of the Third Kind,* appealed to the Writers Guild to obtain a screenplay credit. Yet

Spielberg ultimately won each case. (Of the five, Chase-Riboud apparently fared the best. After she lost in her efforts to enjoin the release of *Amistad,* she withdrew the suit and praised Spielberg's production. It was assumed that she received a payment in settlement of her claim.) Of course, the reason people sue Spielberg is not necessarily because he copies, but because his movies are the ones that make money. There's little point in suing people whose movies don't.

The problem with analyzing these or thousands of similar cases is that the plots of stories, books, movies, and plays are quite intricate, and it's not easy to summarize the issues for someone who has not in fact viewed or read both works. The judges typically devote as much as half their opinions to detailed descriptions of the two works. Judge Learned Hand was the author of two of the leading cases. In the first, he considered the claim that a motion picture, *The Cohens and the Kellys,* had infringed on Anne Nichols's popular play, *Abie's Irish Rose* (1922). Judge Hand conceded that "It is of course essential to any protection of literary property . . . that

A piece of buncombe.

Nichols's play is described by Brooks Atkinson as "one of the most naive plays in history . . . a mechanical little piece of buncombe that Anne Nichols wrote in 1922. . . . The comedy bored all the critics except one . . . when it opened, and infuriated them when it settled down to an epochal run" of 2,427 performances.

A Promising Theme.
A still from one of the many movies in the successful *Cohens and Kellys* series from 1926 into the 1930s. Both Anne Nichols and Universal had apparently tapped into a promising theme.

Abie's Irish Rose.
This is the original company among many that played *Abie's Irish Rose.* It was advertised using a life-sized three-dimensional billboard erected next to the West Side Highway in New York. The play was made into a movie in 1929, and again in 1946, and was even adapted into a radio series that lasted for thirty-two months.

A squalidly romantic murder play.
Katharine Cornell as Madeline Cary in *Dishonored Lady*. Ms. Cornell was known as "The First Lady of the American Stage" (until she was joined—or superseded—by Helen Hayes). Brooks Atkinson describes the play as "a squalidly romantic murder play," written by the popular playwright of the day, Edward B. Sheldon (with Margaret Ayer Barnes). Atkinson bemoans the mediocrity that prevailed on Broadway in the early twentieth century, and particularly complains that

> The hacks tainted talented writers who might have accomplished something of permanent significance if the standards of the time had been more discriminating. A case in point was Edward B. Sheldon. . . . Since Sheldon was an educated young man with a genuine understanding of the craft of the theater and cultivated standards of taste in literature, he was qualified to write on a higher level than his contemporaries. But, like them, he thought of plays in terms of craftsmanship. He was not motivated to write by what he saw and experienced in life. He wrote on plausible topics that might produce a hit.

the right cannot be limited literally to the text, else a plagiarist would escape by immaterial variations." Although there were similarities in idea or theme, Hand concluded that "The stories are quite different," and that "A comedy based upon conflicts between Irish and Jews, into which the marriage of their children enters, is no more susceptible of copyright than the outline of *Romeo and Juliet*."

Yet, in the second case, Hand reached the exact opposite result. He found that the movie *Letty Lynton* (1932), produced by Metro-Goldwyn Pictures and starring Joan Crawford and Robert Montgomery, infringed upon Edward Sheldon's play *Dishonored Lady*. After a careful analysis, Hand found "parallelism" of character and incident sufficient to constitute substantial similarity, even though the dialogue of the works was different, and even though both works were based loosely upon an actual murder case in which Madeleine

The padded-shoulder look.
Joan Crawford and Nils Asther in Metro-Goldwyn's *Letty Lynton*. The movie is noted for ushering in Crawford's "padded-shoulder look," developed by the Hollywood costume designer Adrian.

Smith in 1857 poisoned her former lover, but was found by a jury not to be guilty of the crime.

Ever since Hand decided these classic cases, law professors have delighted in assigning them to students, in order to underscore how difficult it can be to reconcile the outcome of complicated cases. In these and later cases (particularly Peter Pan Fabrics, from which the following quote is taken), Judge Hand himself recognized the difficulty of drawing the line between noninfringement and infringement:

> The test for infringement of a copyright is of necessity vague. In the case of verbal "works" it is well settled that although the "proprietor's" monopoly extends beyond an exact reproduction of the words, there can be no copyright in the "ideas" disclosed but only in their "expression."* Obviously, no principle can be stated as to when an imitator has gone beyond copying the "idea," and has borrowed its "expression." Decisions must therefore inevitably be *ad hoc*.

At least one thing is clear, however. If someone *does* copy the exact language of a copyrighted work, then it can be infringement even if it represents only a small portion of that work. In one recent case, *The Nation* magazine printed an article that copied between three hundred and four hundred words from Gerald Ford's as yet unpublished memoirs.† The article focused upon the circumstances surrounding the Nixon pardon, and was designed to "scoop" *Time* magazine's "first serial rights," for which *Time* had paid $25,000. The Supreme Court, by a vote of 6 to 3, held that the taking of as little as three hundred words from the original unpublished manuscript constituted copyright infringement.

Visual Works

The issue of substantial similarity can be better conveyed in the context of visual works, because then you

---

Remind everybody of Watergate.

Here's a portion of the article in *The Nation*, highlighting 138 of the 300–400 words taken verbatim from Gerald Ford's memoirs, *A Time to Heal*, as marked in the appendix to the Supreme Court opinion:

> In justifying the pardon, Ford goes out of his way to assure the reader that "**compassion for Nixon as an individual hadn't prompted my decision at all.**" Rather, he did it because he had "**to get the monkey off my back one way or the other.**" . . .
>
> Ultimately, Ford sums up the philosophy underlying his decision as one he picked up as a student at Yale Law School many years before. "**I learned that public policy often took precedence over a rule of law. Although I respected the tenet that no man should be above the law, public policy demanded that I put Nixon-and Watergate-behind us as quickly as possible.**"
>
> Later, when Ford learned that Nixon's phlebitis had acted up and his health was seriously impaired, he debated whether to pay the ailing former President a visit. "**If I made the trip it would remind everybody of Watergate and the pardon. If I didn't, people would say I lacked compassion.**" Ford went.
>
> **He was stretched out flat on his back. There were tubes in his nose and mouth, and wires led from his arms, chest and legs to machines with orange lights that blinked on and off. His face was ashen, and I thought I had never seen anyone closer to death.**

---

*Idea-expression distinction, see p. 188.
†Fair use in the Ford memoirs case, see p. 203.

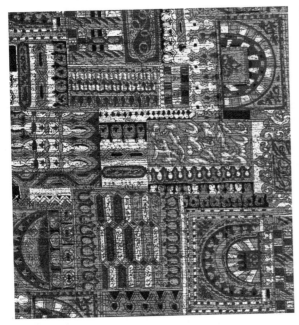

Byzantium.
At left, Peter Pan's fabric design; at right, the infringing design. The case illustrates a common confusion between the standards of copyrightability and infringement. As we saw in the last chapter (p. 127), even a small modicum of originality may be sufficient for copyrightability. It may therefore be the case that the relatively minor variations in the defendant's design would have been sufficient for it to have claimed copyright in those variations. In the case of infringement, the test is *not* how much creative work the defendant adds, but how much it takes from the first work. In this case, that amount made the second work "substantially similar," and therefore infringing.

can see the entirety of each work at a glance, and make your own assessment of the similarity of the two. One of the leading cases was again decided by Judge Learned Hand. It involved fabric designs by Peter Pan Fabrics, Inc., which were allegedly infringed by Martin Weiner Corp.

The Peter Pan fabric was a quiltlike montage of individual squares based upon traditional Turkish designs. Martin Weiner created its fabric by carefully—but only slightly—altering the design of the individual elements, while maintaining the same overall appearance. Judge Hand was not impressed.

No one disputes that the copyright extends beyond a photographic reproduction of the design, but one cannot say how far an imitator must depart from an undeviating reproduction to escape infringement. . . . In the case at bar we must try to estimate how far its overall appearance will determine its aesthetic appeal when the cloth is made into a garment. Both designs have the same general color, and the arches, scrolls, rows of symbols, etc. on one resemble those on the other though they are not identical. Moreover, the patterns in which these figures are distributed to make up the design as a whole are not identical. However, the ordinary observer, unless he set out to detect the disparities, would be disposed to overlook them, and regard their aesthetic appeal as the same. That is enough; and indeed, it is all that can be said, unless protection against infringement is to be denied because of variants irrelevant to the purpose for which the design is intended.

Another leading case is that of Saul Steinberg, a cartoonist for *The New Yorker* magazine. His illustration for a cover of the magazine became an immediate classic, and was afterward distributed in poster form. Later, a movie company incorporated some of the features of this cartoon into an advertisement for one of its movies, *Moscow on the Hudson* (1984). Clearly, the works are not identical: they show different buildings, and they even show views looking in opposite directions from New York.

However, the court focused on numerous similarities, including the general style of the posters, the use of a blue wash across the top to represent the sky and of a red band to represent the horizon, the use of similar typeface, similar perspective and layout, and similar details, such as the water towers, cars, buildings, and other features. Citing the oft-quoted lines that "no plagiarist can excuse the wrong by showing how much of his work he did not pirate," and that "copyright infringement may occur by reason of a substantial similarity that involves only a small portion of each work," the court found that the movie poster infringed Steinberg's artwork.

A recent case from the world of television highlights how difficult and fact-intensive the cases can be. Sid & Marty Krofft created a very successful children's television program in the 1960s, *H. R. Pufnstuf,* that generated a line of unique products and endorsements. McDonald's Corp. decided to develop a series of commercials that used characters obviously inspired by the Krofft creations. Take a look at the pictures and

"That famous poster."
Saul Steinberg's *New Yorker* cover, later adapted to a poster.

Moscow on the Hudson.
The infringing portion of the movie poster.

"Total concept and feel."
Top, Sid & Marty Krofft's Pufnstuf and Witchiepoo. Bottom, Mayor McCheese and Hamburglar, circa 1971. The court held that the substantial similarities were evident in the "total concept and feel" of the Pufnstuf Living Island and the McDonaldland settings, including the other characters and the backgrounds.

decide for yourself whether the characters were "substantially similar." There were certainly differences in details, but the jury in the trial court concluded, and the circuit court on appeal agreed, that the similarities in overall appearance were too great, and that McDonald's had infringed.

The case was very much flavored by two different factors: first, Needham, Harper & Steers, the advertising agency for McDonald's, had been negotiating with the Kroffts to use the Pufnstuf characters in the proposed McDonald's advertising campaign, and, after breaking off the negotiations, proceeded to develop Krofft-like characters anyway. Indeed, Needham even hired former Krofft employees to design and construct the costumes and supply the voices for the McDonaldland characters. Such behavior might have demonstrated a certain bad faith on the part of the agency, which led the court to be less sympathetic to them and McDonald's.

Secondly, the court felt that the intended audience—children—might be unsophisticated and therefore not likely to catch the subtle distinctions between the characters. For example, in response to McDonald's assertion of differences between the Pufnstuf and Mayor McCheese characters, the court stated: "We do not believe that the ordinary reasonable person, let alone a child, viewing these works will even notice that Pufnstuf is wearing a cummerbund while Mayor McCheese is wearing a diplomat's sash." It was also clear that the Kroffts were injured by the infringement; after the McDonald's campaign, the Kroffts began having trouble making or extending their own licensing arrangements. To add insult to injury, the Ice Capades, which had previously licensed the Pufnstuf characters, discontinued their license with the Kroffts and signed on to use the McDonald's characters!

Photographs

Some summers ago, on a family vacation to the Grand Canyon, I took what has become one of my favorite photographs, shown on the next page. Later that same summer, I saw for sale on the sidewalk in Greenwich Village in New York the poster also shown on the

---

Try this at home.

The Pufnstuf case is certainly one where reasonable people can disagree. Each year, I ask my copyright students whether they believe the characters are substantially similar, and there is always a split in opinion. About the relative unsophistication of children, however, I suggest the following experiment: whatever the next doll fad—Barbie, Cabbage Patch Kids dolls, beanie babies, or Pokémon—try slipping your child an inexact look-alike doll and see if they are willing to overlook the subtle differences.

Astounding interpretations.

Ansel Adams apparently would not object to the making of creative prints of his works, provided permission was obtained from his estate or his archive at the University of Arizona.

Trained as a pianist, I am aware that I depended upon the music of the past (Bach through Scriabin) as the source for my musical expressions. As most musicians, I am not a composer. Photographers are, in a sense, composers and the negatives are their scores. They first perform their own works, but I see no reason why they should not be available for others to perform. In the electronic age, I am sure that scanning techniques will be developed to achieve prints of extraordinary subtlety from the original negative scores. If I could return in twenty years or so I would hope to see astounding interpretations of my most expressive images. It is true no one could print my negatives as I did, but they might well get more out of them by electronic means. Image quality is not the product of a machine, but of the person who directs the machine, and there are no limits to imagination and expression.

Ansel Adams (right).
The credit states that this poster was "printed from a copy of an Ansel Adams photograph." As a matter of fact, this particular photograph is in the public domain, since it was originally commissioned as a government work. As such, anyone may make a print of it, and even alter it. (On U.S. government works, see p. 215.) In one recent official-looking book of Adams photographs, the print of this photo is cropped at the top, cutting off the top of the rock formation!

By contrast, Ansel Adams closely controlled his copyrighted prints, personally producing many of them himself, and assigning control of his copyrighted works to the Ansel Adams Publishing Rights Trust.

page: a copy of a photograph by Ansel Adams (in the bargain bin for a mere $5, including the frame). Could my photograph be an infringement of the Ansel Adams photograph?

The answer is clearly no, my photograph does not infringe. I didn't in fact copy Ansel Adams's photograph, and so, no matter how similar the resulting picture may be, mine didn't infringe his. Indeed, when I took my photo, I wasn't even aware there was such an Adams photograph, and so could not possibly have copied it.

The situation illustrates the doctrine of "independent creation." Two authors may independently create similar works, and they may each have a copyright if they did not copy the other. Similarly, neither one infringes the other. I assume that there are thousands of photographs more or less similar to these—taken of the most conspicuous formation in the Grand Canyon looking south from the main visitors' center on the north rim—and that they are each copyrightable, for what it's worth, and each not an infringement of any of the others.

However, let's do what law professors love to do, and change the facts a little. Let's assume that I was an admirer of Ansel Adams, knew about his photograph of the Grand Canyon, and planned my own trip precisely in order to duplicate his photo as best I could. I hiked to the precise location, chose the correct lens and filters, and waited for the precisely correct weather and the precisely correct time of day to get the shadows just right to duplicate Ansel Adams's photograph. Might I thereby infringe the copyright in Adams's work?

Edward Samuels
The Grand Canyon 1993

Ansel Adams
The Mural Project 1941-1942

The Village Vanguard.
Left, the Kisch photograph of a woman sitting at a table at the Village Vanguard nightclub in Manhattan. Right, the Ammirati & Puris photograph of musician John Lurie.

Several cases suggest that I might. In 1982, John Duke Kisch took a photograph of a "woman holding a concertina" under a stylized poster at the Village Vanguard nightclub in New York. In 1985, Perry Ogden took a photograph showing John Lurie, a famous saxophonist, at the same location in the nightclub. Kisch sued Ammirati & Puris, the advertising agency that had hired Ogden to take the photograph for a beverage advertisement. Ammirati moved to dismiss the case, on the ground that the photograph was obviously different. The court refused to dismiss the case, finding that there were sufficient similarities that a jury might find the works "substantially similar" under the law. The court particularly cited the fact that the photos "were taken of the same small corner of the Village Vanguard nightclub," that "the same striking mural appears as the background for each photograph," that the individuals in each photo are seated and holding musical instruments, and that "the lighting, camera angle, and camera position appear to be similar."

Howard Alt took a photograph showing two pens on a grid with a yellow circle. This was not an idle snapshot, but a carefully set up arrangement that was part of a series of photos taken over several days. Joe Morello, a famous photographer, witnessed the photo shoot, and saw the

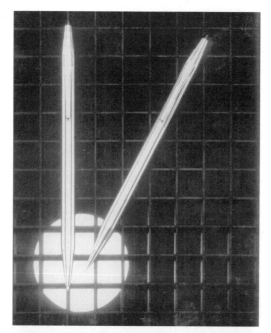

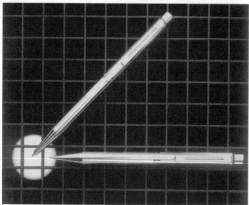

Pens.
Above, Howard Alt's photograph, and below, Joe Morello's copy.

final product in Alt's portfolio. Morello then created a similar photograph. Was Morello's photo an infringement? The court had no difficulty finding that "the composition, backgrounds, colors, lighting, objects photographed and cropping, are substantially similar," and thus a copyright infringement. The case was made particularly appealing because Alt, a beginning photographer, had included the photograph in his portfolio, and was himself accused of copying the work from the more famous Morello, when in fact the copying was the other way around!

What these cases show is that the copyright in a photograph can be infringed not only when it is mechanically and precisely reproduced; it can also be infringed when other people reproduce substantially similar works using their own cameras.

Music

Ronald Mack wrote the song "He's So Fine," which was made popular by the Chiffons in 1962. Several years later, George Harrison wrote "My Sweet Lord," which was first recorded by Billy Preston and then became a hit for Harrison in 1970. The works are very different in their orchestration and mood, but there are some basic similarities. In 1976, a federal court in New York found that the works were substantially similar, and that the Harrison song infringed the Mack song.

The experts and the court ultimately reduced the songs to their essential notes. In each song, there were two motifs: the first consisted of three notes, "sol-mi-re" (G-E-D, or "He's so fine," or "My sweet lord") repeated about four times; followed by "sol-la-do-la-do" (G-A-C-A-C, or "Don't know how I'm gonna' do it," or "I really want to see you"), repeated three or four times. Although almost every repetition involved a different number of beats, the judge found that the "differences essentially stem . . . from the fact that different words and number of syllables were involved. This necessitated modest alterations in the repetitions or the places of beginning of a phrase, which, however, has nothing to do whatsoever with the essential musical kernel that is involved."

The first motif.

There was also an intervening melody in Harrison's song, repetitions of "Hallelujah" or "Hare Krishna," which the court found to be a mere "responsive" interjection that, like the "Dulang-dulang" repetitions in the Mack song, was "used . . . in the same places to fill in and give rhythmic impetus to what would otherwise be somewhat dead spots in the music."

The second motif.

Every year my copyright students listen to the songs, and every year we disagree about whether they are or are not substantially similar. Every year, Marcia, my wife, tells me that she immediately recognized the similarities, and wondered why someone didn't tell Harrison before the work was released. After the case, radio stations around the country played the songs back to back, and it proved to be a tremendous embarrassment for Harrison, whose creativity was bound to look pale when compared to that of Lennon and McCartney. The judge tried to save face for Harrison by concluding that Harrison did not deliberately copy, but that the copying had been "subconscious."

The case is reminiscent of a similar one from an earlier era. "Dardanella" was a popular song of 1910–20. It had a hypnotic bass accompaniment of eight notes, repeated over and over, "with no changes, except the variation of a musical fifth in the scale to accommodate itself harmonically to the changes in the melody." Jerome Kern, one of the great songwriters of the day, then wrote an even more popular song, "Kalua," which allegedly used a similar bass accompaniment. The case was decided by Judge Learned Hand, this time as a district court judge, who seemed to get all the interesting copyright cases in New York. Hand found that Kern's work infringed the earlier song, even though it did so only in the accompaniment and not in the melody. He accepted Kern's assertion that "he was quite unconscious of any plagiarism," but found that "Mr. Kern must have followed, probably unconsciously, what he had certainly often heard only a short time before."

"Dardanella," made up of eighth notes.

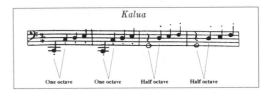

"Kalua," made up of quarter notes.

Although Hand described the bass accompaniments as "ostinatos" that were "exactly alike," it's obvious that

The half-a-million-dollar difference.

There was a major difference between the Harrison and Kern cases. In the Harrison case, the recovery was ultimately $587,000. (This amount was reduced from over $1.6 million, because Allen Klein had purchased from the copyright owner the claim against Harrison. This was described as a gross fiduciary breach, in that Klein was a former manager of the Beatles!) In the Kern case, Hand called the controversy "a trivial pother," "a mere point of honor," and set the damages at the nominal sum of $250–a rather Pyrrhic victory for the plaintiff.

The nominal recovery suggests that Hand was trying to apply the wisdom of Solomon to reach a just result–allowing the plaintiff a technical victory, but not the monetary relief that normally accompanies such a victory. As we'll see later in this chapter, if a copyright owner proves infringement, then, among other things, the owner is entitled to recover the defendant's profits attributable to the infringement. Hand never even seems to have considered the possibility.

they're not identical. The "Dardanella" theme is made up of eighth notes, with a return to the same note (G, and later D) to fill out the second half of every beat. This was said to evoke the beat of a drum or tom-tom, appropriate to the piece. There are no such eighth-note fillers in "Kalua," which results in a less frequent beat that was said to "indicate the booming of the surf upon the beach," appropriate to the "Kalua" theme. If you look closely, you'll also see that in the third and fourth bars of each theme of "Dardanella," the notes on the beat of the ostinato jump a full octave. In "Kalua," in the third and fourth bars, they jump only half an octave.

Thus, in order to conclude that the tunes are "exactly alike," one has to first assume that certain notes simply don't count, and that certain notes have the same tonal impact as others. These are some of the same assumptions that were necessary to conclude that "My Sweet Lord" was the same song as "He's So Fine." (Indeed, even the characterization of Kern's use of the notes as an "ostinato" is a generalization, since the sequence appears in only about half of the bars in the chorus, not continuously throughout it.)

In my copyright class, I suggest that these cases are examples of how the same notes, given a very different orchestration in the Harrison case, or a different melody line in the Kern case, can actually sound quite different. I also suggest that different notes can be made to sound quite similar. By way of example, I play a musical parody created by the fictional musical group The Rutles (actually a Lorne Michaels production starring the British comedian Eric Idle together with several stars from the early *Saturday Night Live*), in parody of the Beatles. The parodies are probably excused by the fair use doctrine.* But the clever parodies also manage to conjure up—arguably sound "substantially similar" to—the originals by the use of different notes. For example, the Beatles song "Get Back" has a repeated sequence of F#–G, F#–G. The parody of it, "Get Up and Go," uses the sequence G–F#–E–G, G–F#–E–G, orchestrated precisely like the Beatles song, to make a tune that after a few repetitions seems like a perfect substitute for the original. The point of the

*Fair use, see p. 190.

exercise is that music cannot be reduced to a simple series of notes. Just as with story lines, visual works, and photographs, musical works can be similar even when there are distinct differences. Whether or not the similarities go as far as to make them "substantially similar" is, obviously, a tough call.

Access

Even if a work is substantially similar to a prior work, it doesn't necessarily prove that the second author in fact copied. In order to win an infringement suit, an author must prove that the alleged infringer had *access* to the copyrighted work, so that copying *could* have taken place. This will be easy to prove if, as in the "He's So Fine" and "Dardanella" examples, the first work was popular and would have been known to the second writer. But access may be hard to prove if the first work was obscure.

To illustrate the point, let's take a look at another recent musical copyright case. Ronald Selle wrote "Let It End" in 1975. He performed the song with his group in Chicago, and sent copies to several record companies; but the song was never a success, and was never sold either in record or sheet music form. In 1978, the Bee Gees wrote "How Deep Is Your Love," which was later featured in the movie *Saturday Night Fever.* Selle sued the Bee Gees, and presented an expert witness who testified that the songs were substantially similar—indeed, so similar "that they could not have been written independent of one another."

At the trial, the jury returned a verdict that the Bee Gees had infringed Selle's song. Nevertheless, the judge granted the Bee Gees what is known as a "judgment notwithstanding the verdict." Basically, the judge concluded that the Bee Gees had no access to Selle's song, and so could not have copied it, no matter how similar the songs may have sounded to the jury. Without access, there is no infringement. This obviously means that successful songwriters, whose works are being

"How Deep Is Your Love?"
Copyright suits are hard on the reputation of defendants. Here's an excerpt from a sixties-style tribute to the Bee Gees, lamenting the suit brought against them.

Not millionaires many times over.

According to the old Tin Pan Alley model, still the basis of much pop and rock songcraft and of our antiquated music copyright laws, a song has a lyric, a melody, and a sequence of chords. In a court of law, you can sue and win if someone writes a song that quotes substantially from the words, the tune, or the chord progression of a song you have previously copyrighted. You cannot sue on the basis of a pirated rhythm pattern or beat, which is one of the main reasons rhythmic innovators like Bo Diddley and James Brown are not millionaires many times over.

–Robert Palmer

I don't agree with Palmer that copyright protects a chord progression–certainly not if the chord progression represents the only similarity between two works.

The complications of copyright licenses.

The primary purpose of copyright is not to bring lawsuits, but to make money from licensing the rights of copyright. This chart, which I produced as a lawyer on the case, shows some of the interlocking licenses and purchases of the television rights in the Hopalong Cassidy character. Clarence Mulford was remarkable for his foresight in reserving television rights before most people yet realized the tremendous potential of the medium. And William Boyd (see p. 149) was equally remarkable for his foresight in buying up the various strands of rights in the television productions.

performed (and heard, and "subconsciously" copied) will be more likely to win infringement suits than unknown songwriters.

WHAT ARE THE EXCLUSIVE RIGHTS OF COPYRIGHT?

Copyright is nothing more nor less than a series of "exclusive rights" that we grant to authors in order to encourage them to create their works. The authors may invoke these rights by bringing lawsuits against others who do any of the things included within the enumerated rights. But of course authors don't generally make money only by bringing lawsuits. The primary value of the copyright is the right to make money by making and selling copies of the work, or by selling to someone else, generally a publisher, the exclusive rights to make and sell copies of the work.

Let's take a closer look at the exclusive rights enumerated in the current Copyright Act. (In the enumerations below, the date represents the date on which the exclusive right was first added to the statute.)

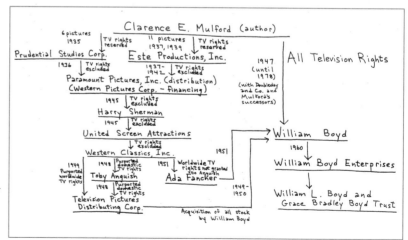

Copying, 1790

The essence of copyright is the exclusive right to "copy." Under the original 1790 act,* this right was subsumed under the "sole right and liberty of printing" or "reprinting" the copyrighted work; but today it is described as the exclusive right "to reproduce the copyrighted work in copies." Obviously, this right is not absolute, as isolated or personal copies will probably be allowed in many circumstances. We'll explore some of the limitations in the next chapter.

Distribution, 1790

The exclusive right to distribute a copyrighted work has been a part of the law since the 1790 act. Originally subsumed under "the sole right and liberty of . . . publishing and vending" the works, the statute now speaks in terms of the "exclusive rights . . . to distribute copies or phonorecords of the copyrighted work to the public by sale or other transfer of ownership, or by rental, lease, or lending." This exclusive right includes the exclusive right to import copies of the work into the United States. In many cases, the distribution right will overlap with the right to copy, since it will be the same person or company that makes and distributes the infringing works. But a manufacturer who doesn't distribute will infringe the first right, and a distributor who doesn't manufacture will infringe the second.

The distribution right is subject to a very important exception, known as the "first sale" doctrine. Under this doctrine, once someone has bought a legitimate copy of a copyrighted work, that person is free to resell that particular copy without copyright liability. Thus, if you buy a book, you may sell or lend only that copy of the book, so long as you don't make additional copies; if you buy a videocassette of a movie, you may sell or rent or lend only that copy to others, so long as you don't make additional copies; or if you buy a painting, you may sell or display that painting to others, so long as you don't make additional copies.

For the most part, then, you're allowed to further distribute individual copies of works that you have legitimately obtained. The copyright owner is supposed to charge enough when the work is first sold to compensate for any additional resales of those particular works; or, to put

*1790 act, see p. 14.

it another way, the exclusive rights in particular copies are exhausted upon the "first sale" of those particular copies. As a result of this doctrine, the exclusive right to distribute is much more limited than it might at first appear. (As we saw earlier, there are exceptions to the first sale doctrine that extend control of copyright owners over the rental, as opposed to the sale, of sound recordings* and computer programs.†)

Derivative Works, 1870 and 1909

The exclusive right to make derivative works covers all ways in which a copyrighted work might be adapted or incorporated into a new work. The exclusive right of translation was added only in 1870, and expanded in 1909 to include the exclusive right "to translate the copyrighted work into other languages or dialects, or make any other version thereof, if it be a literary work; to dramatize it if it be a nondramatic work; to convert it into a novel or other nondramatic work if it be a drama; to arrange or adapt it if it be a musical work; to complete, execute, and finish it if it be a model or design for a work of art."

The current act is even broader, granting the exclusive right to make a "translation, musical arrangement, dramatization, fictionalization, motion picture version, sound recording, art reproduction, abridgment, condensation, or other form in which a work may be recast, transformed, or adapted."

Public Performance, 1856 and 1897

For those works that are normally performed—music, drama, choreography, and motion pictures—the copyright owner of the original work retains the exclusive right to perform the work publicly. This right was only added for dramatic works in 1856, and for musical works in 1897.

The important issue here is what constitutes a *public* performance. If you write a song, I'm free to sing the song in the shower (assuming that I don't take my shower in public), but I'm not free to perform the work publicly without your permission—usually upon paying a licensing fee. There are lots of limitations on this right, particularly excusing many nonprofit performances of a work.‡

*Rental of phonorecords, see p. 47.
†Rental of computer programs, see p. 92.
‡Nonprofit performances, see p. 181.

Prior to 1995, the public performance right did not extend to sound recordings. In that year, however, Congress provided that a limited public performance right would be granted for digital audio transmissions* of sound recordings.

Public Display, 1976

The display right, added only in 1976, gives the copyright owner the exclusive right to display the work in public. Just like the distribution right, the display right is subject to the first sale doctrine: owners who have purchased individual copies of works may display those individual copies "either directly or by the projection of no more than one image at a time, to viewers present at the place where the copy is located." Thus, the public display right is also much more limited than it at first appears.

Attribution and Integrity, 1990

Many foreign countries grant authors certain "moral rights" in their works, and recognition of such rights is required by the Berne Convention,† the major international treaty dealing with copyright. These rights have included, among other things, the right of attribution—that is, the right to have one's name associated with one's works—and the right of integrity—that is, the right to protect against the destruction or mutilation of one's works. In the United States, a handful of states in recent years extended to certain authors such rights in their works. When the United States joined the Berne Convention in 1988, it was debated whether American law was truly in compliance with the international requirement, and whether the American law should be changed.

The response, in 1990, was a very limited federal right of attribution and integrity. The right extends only to authors of "visual art," defined to include paintings or sculptures that exist in only one copy, or in a limited edition of no more than two hundred signed and consecutively numbered copies. For such works, the statute gives the painter or sculptor the right to claim the authorship of works, or to deny the use of one's name for works not created by the author; and the right, with limitations, to prevent intentional distortion of one's work, or to prevent the use of one's name in association with works that have been distorted or mutilated.

*Digital audio transmissions, see p. 51.
†Berne Convention, see p. 242.

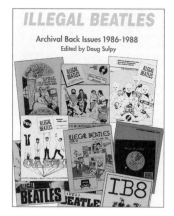

Illegal Beatles.
This is a reprint cover showing issues of *Illegal Beatles,* a magazine devoted to tracking both pirated and bootleg recordings. Complete listings of Beatles covers, pirates, and bootlegs can also be found at various sites on the Internet.

Fixation and Trafficking in Sound Recordings and Music Videos, 1994

In December 1994, as part of its treaty obligations under the World Trade Organization (WTO), Congress added a new section granting performers of live musical performances the exclusive rights to record their performances, or to transmit or distribute unauthorized recordings. Prior to this time, federal copyright existed only in works that were already "fixed in a tangible medium of expression"* (although live performances might be protected under the law of some states). With the adoption of this new amendment, "live" musical performers are now granted special protection under federal law against unauthorized "bootlegging" of their performances. Some commentators have read this new section not only to prohibit future creation of bootleg recordings, but also to prohibit the continued distribution or transmission of previously made unauthorized recordings of live musical performances.

Technological Protection Measures, 1998

The Digital Millennium Copyright Act† granted a new type of protection against the unauthorized circumvention of technological protection measures. Under that act, owners of copyright in digital works may protect them by encoding the works to prevent unauthorized access or copying. If owners so encode their works, users are legally prohibited from circumventing such protection schemes. As we've seen, the 1998 Act, the most complicated in the history of copyright, has lots of exceptions and special limitations.

Copyright Management Information, 1998

The Digital Millennium Copyright Act also added a new type of protection for "copyright management information." Owners of copyright in digital works may put their works in electronic "envelopes," or electronically embed in their works, information that identifies the author and certain other copyright information relating to the work. If an owner does so, then it is now illegal for a user to knowingly alter or remove such copyright management information from copies of the work. This infor-

*Fixation, see p. 127.
†Technological protection measures and copyright management information under the DMCA, see p. 112.

mation will make it easier for copyright owners to notify users about their rights, and to track the posting of copies of their works on-line.

REMEDIES

What if one of the exclusive rights of an author, as described above, is violated? Normally, an attorney for the author calls up the infringer or the attorney for the infringer, and they discuss how the infringer will stop violating such rights, or how much the infringer should pay for the rights. If they can't come to terms, then the author's ultimate weapon is to bring a lawsuit in federal court.

Assuming that the author is able to prove the infringement, and that there are no exceptions or limitations (as described in the next chapter), then the author is entitled to a broad range of remedies. Some of these remedies (like recovery of lost profits and the recovery of costs and attorneys' fees in bringing a lawsuit) are designed to compensate the copyright owner for losses. Some (like fines and injunctions and criminal liability) are designed to deter infringement in the first place. And others (like forfeiture of infringing copies and recovery of the infringer's profits) are designed to prevent the infringer from gaining by the infringement. Let's take a closer look at the specific remedies available to a wronged copyright owner. (Again, the dates indicate the date that the remedy was first enacted by Congress. Most of the remedies, except as noted, continue to be available today.)

Out on the streets in eight days.

In his book *Bootleg*, Clinton Heylin distinguishes between pirated and bootleg records. The former are unauthorized copies of existing records, which were first brought under federal copyright protection with the Sound Recording Amendment of 1971. The latter, bootlegs, are unauthorized recordings or copies of live performances, and were not regulated under the Copyright Act until the 1994 amendment. One bootlegger describes how fast he could do his work:

> Pink Floyd, when they came back in '87, the first show of the world tour was in Ottawa, and a friend of mine drove up there, taped it, bought a concert programme, Fed Ex'd the tape and the programme from Ottawa the next morning to me [in California]. I handed it all in. It was mastered that afternoon. I had plates by the day after on the other side of the continent! We had records, in a double gatefold, on pink vinyl, with four-colour labels, out on the streets in eight days. . . . And we sold 7,000 of those. . . . One of the guys who worked for the Floyd went into It's Only Rock and Roll in the Village [in New York] and he saw this bootleg and they hadn't even played there yet! "Jesus Christ! I work for these guys, let me see that!" He looked at it and was absolutely stunned. He took it back to the hotel and showed it to the band. They were so freaked out they sent him back to buy three more for them. This is a week and a half after the show.

Forfeiture of Infringing Copies, 1790

The English Statute of Anne,* all the way back in 1710, provided that infringers of copyright "shall forfeit" all infringing books "to the . . . Proprietor thereof, who shall forthwith Damask and make Waste Paper of

*Statute of Anne, see p. 11.

them." The first U.S. law in 1790 similarly provided that infringing copies of all copyrighted works would be forfeited to the owners, "who shall forthwith destroy the same." In 1802, this provision was extended to include "the plate or plates on which such print or prints are or shall be copied."

Under the current law, a court may impound infringing works, and ultimately order the destruction of copies or "plates, molds, matrices, masters, tapes, film negatives, or other articles by means of which such copies or phonorecords may be reproduced." This can be a formidable weapon. For example, in one commercial record piracy case, twenty-five thousand illicit tape recordings were seized, in addition to the blank cartridges, labels, machinery, and equipment used, or that might in the future be used, for their manufacture. Except in the most egregious cases, the infringers often agree to the payment of a licensing fee, in order to avoid forfeiture of what might involve a substantial capital investment.

Fixed Fines, 1790–1909

Beginning in 1790, the statute provided for what was essentially a fine for copyright infringement. The amount of the fine was usually split between the owner of copyright and the United States. The 1790 act provided for payment of "fifty cents for every sheet which shall be found" in the possession of the infringer. The 1802 act provided for $1 to be paid for every infringing print; the 1856 act, for violation of the performance right, provided $100 for the first violation and $50 for each subsequent violation; the 1870 act provided for $10 to be paid for every infringement of a painting or statue. The 1895 act provided for a total penalty, in the case of a photograph, of not less than $100 nor more than $5,000; and, in the case of a painting or statue, raised the penalty to not less than $250 nor more than $10,000.

All of these fixed fees were replaced in 1909 by the provisions described below under the headings "Lost Profits" (p. 174) and "Discretionary Remedy" (p. 176).

Injunctions, 1819

Since 1819, the courts have had the power to enforce copyrights by way of injunction. With this power, a court can order an infringer to stop the infringement, and (as specifically provided in 1897) enforce the order, if necessary, by holding the infringer in contempt. Injunctions are granted rather liberally in copyright cases.

Criminal Liability, 1897

Congress first made copyright infringement a crime in 1897, when it made it a misdemeanor, punishable by up to a year in prison, for an infringer willfully and for profit to present an unauthorized public performance of a dramatic or musical work. The criminal provisions were broadened in 1909 to cover *any* copyright infringement undertaken "willfully and for profit."

Criminal proceedings are rarely brought, except in the case of fairly extensive record, videotape, and computer program piracy. In these contexts, however, in order to deter such activity, the penalties have been raised several times over the years. Under current law, you're in serious trouble if you're involved in major piracy of records or disks, videotapes, or computer programs. The really serious stuff is when you're involved in creating or distributing, in any 180-day period, at least ten copies of works with a retail value of more than $2,500. For that you can go to jail for up to five years (up to ten years for a second offense), and pay a fine of up to $250,000 for individuals, or $500,000 for organizations. Even in lesser quantities, the penalty can still be severe.

Under the 1909 statute, criminal infringement required that the infringement be "willfully and for profit"; but in 1976, the language was expanded to include acts done willfully and "for purposes of commercial advantage or private financial gain." In 1997, in the No Electronic Theft (NET) Act, the definition of "financial gain" was extended to include the "receipt, or the expectation of receipt, of anything of value, including the receipt of other copyrighted works." Under that act, the unauthorized reproduction and distribution of even a single copy of a copyrighted work with a retail value of more than $1,000 can subject a person to criminal penalties. Are you scared away yet?

FBI warning.

Here's a typical warning found at the beginning of a home videotape:

FBI WARNING

Federal law provides severe civil and criminal penalties for the unauthorized reproduction, distribution or exhibition of video discs.

Criminal copyright infringement is investigated by the FBI and may constitute a felony with a maximum penalty of up to five years in prison and/or a $250,000 fine.

This warning, as applied to wholesale pirates, is a reasonable one. But as applied to home consumers, it is a bit of bravado. Unless done "for profit or private financial gain," copyright infringement, though giving rise to civil remedies, is not a crime. I suspect the warning scares away a few home tapers, but for most consumers it probably has about the same impact as the warning of criminal penalties for removing the tags from pillows.

Allocation of profits.

The testimony showed quite clearly that in the creation of profits from the exhibition of a motion picture, the talent and popularity of the "motion picture stars" [in this case, Joan Crawford and Robert Montgomery] generally constitutes the main drawing power of the picture, and that this is especially true where the title of the picture is not identified with any well-known play or novel. . . . In addition to the drawing power of the "motion picture stars," other factors in creating the profits were found in the artistic conceptions and in the expert supervision and direction of the various processes which made possible the composite result with its attractiveness to the public.

—Chief Justice Charles Hughes,
Sheldon v. Metro-Goldwyn Pictures

Copyright owners generally plaster their CDs, tapes, and computer programs with warnings of "severe civil and criminal" penalties for copyright infringement.

Lost Profits, 1909

In its major recodification of the Copyright Act in 1909, Congress provided that a copyright owner could generally recover against an infringer for "such damages as the copyright proprietor may have suffered due to the infringement." This usually meant the loss of sales by the copyright owner that were attributable to the infringement. There's plenty of precedent for this type of recovery in other areas of law—for example, for personal injuries or breaches of contract—so the courts have developed lots of rules for figuring out exactly how much "damage" is attributable to particular wrongs. However, it is frequently difficult or impossible to prove such damages with any degree of certainty. So Congress added another remedy, the amount of profits made by the infringer.

Infringer's Profits, 1909

When the copyright owner hasn't suffered much harm, or when it's impossible to prove the amount of the harm, the best recovery may be the infringer's profits from the infringement. If I write a book that's only modestly successful, but then a famous Hollywood producer makes an unauthorized but popular movie of it, which do you think I'd rather recover: the meager sales I might have lost on the book, or the massive profits that the movie producer has made from the movie? Since 1909, the Copyright Act has allowed the copyright owner to recover "profits which the infringer shall have made from such infringement."

The problem in cases like this will be to prove how much of the infringer's profits are attributable to the wrongdoing. The leading case on the subject is the *Letty Lynton* case.* The district court in that case had

Letty Lynton case, see. p. 154.

awarded damages of $587,604.34, Metro-Goldwyn's net profit from the movie. The appellate court had reduced the recovery to only 20 percent of that amount, figuring that about 80 percent of the movie's success was due to factors other than the infringing script. The Supreme Court agreed, and let the figure stand at only 20 percent of profits (plus $33,000 for attorneys' fees). Although that may seem like a small amount for a case that, including appeals, had stretched out over many years, it was certainly more than Sheldon had originally been bargaining for, about $30,000 for the movie rights.

"Costs" of the Lawsuit, 1831; Attorneys' Fees, 1909

Since 1831, parties to copyright lawsuits have been entitled to "costs." This covers the relatively minor costs of filing papers or having transcripts made. The usually much larger attorneys' fees—reimbursement for the fees paid to one's own attorneys to prepare and present the case—have been allowed to the prevailing party, in the discretion of the judge, since 1909. This practice is presumably designed to fully compensate copyright owners who must sue in order to enforce their rights; to encourage infringers to settle, lest they end up paying the copyright owner's attorneys' fees (as well as their own); and to assure that meritorious copyright owners are not denied justice just because they are too poor to afford an attorney.

The provision can sometimes backfire on copyright owners. Courts increasingly make *plaintiffs* pay the attorneys' fees of defendants! The recent trend was set in motion by a Supreme Court case involving the songwriter John Fogerty. Fogerty, as a member of the group Creedence Clearwater Revival, had written the song "Run Through the Jungle," and then sold the copyright in the work. Fogerty, as a solo performer, later wrote and recorded the song "The Old Man Down the Road." Fogerty was then put into the unenviable position of being sued for infringing his own earlier work.

Pitfalls of Hollywood accounting.

The Sheldon *(Letty Lynton)* case illustrates the numerous pitfalls involved in trying to determine profits in the movie industry. The courts had to figure out whether to include, in the calculation of "net" profits, those profits from international distribution and those profits received by Loew's theaters that were subsidiaries of Metro-Goldwyn. The courts also had to determine whether and how to charge the following items, among others, against the "net" profit reported for the film: a portion of profits paid directly by Metro-Goldwyn to the Louis B. Mayer Co., a partnership that had exacted the percentage when they merged with Metro to form MGM; allocation of overhead costs, such as production, advertising, publicity, distribution, and interest; charges for "idle time" during which key employees—directors, producers, stars, and writers—were paid under a yearly salary, even though they were not actually involved in the production of movies; and income taxes. Who said this was easy?

"Run through the Jungle."
At left, Creedence Clearwater Revival's *Chronicle, The 20 Greatest Hits,* including Fogerty's "Run through the Jungle," originally released on the multiplatinum album *Cosmo's Factory* (1970). At right, John Fogerty's *Centerfield* album (1984), containing the hit song "The Old Man down the Road."

The two works were not identical, though they did have thematic similarities, particularly in the repeated chorus and the base accompaniment. The case went to a jury, which found that the works were not substantially similar. The Supreme Court upheld the award of attorneys' fees for defendant Fogerty, even though there was no allegation or proof that the suit had been brought in bad faith or that it was frivolous. Ultimately, Fogerty was awarded over $1.35 million in attorneys' fees, apparently the largest fee ever awarded in a copyright case.

Might such an outcome have a chilling effect upon owners of copyright thinking about bringing infringement suits? Possibly—balanced only by the possibility of *getting* reimbursement of attorneys' fees if they win.

Discretionary Remedy, 1909

In 1909, Congress eliminated the "fixed fines" system described above, and replaced it with a system allowing recovery of any amount by which the copyright owner was injured. Recognizing, however, that there were many cases where damages would be hard to prove, Congress gave copyright owners the option of receiving a special recovery "in lieu" of actual damages or profits. Recovery was available in an amount that "to the court [that is, the judge] shall appear just," within ranges set in the statute for different types of works. The system was basically retained in the 1976 Act, under the heading "statutory damages," with a general range for all copyright infringements. As they currently stand, statutory damages may be set within the discretion of the judge at any amount between $500 and $20,000, with an option to go as high as $100,000 for "willful" infringement, or as low as $200 if the infringer had no reason to know that the acts constituted copyright infringement. The damages may even be reduced to zero for certain innocent educational, library, or public broadcasting uses.

> **Advantages of registering.**
>
> Since 1988 Congress has dispensed with all "formalities," so that notice and registration are not a prerequisite to federal copyright protection. However, there are still advantages to registering copyrighted works. One such advantage is that you cannot recover either the discretionary "statutory damages" or the potentially substantial "attorneys' fees" if you don't register. My advice: if you think there's any chance you'll need to sue to protect your copyright, then register the work with the Copyright Office, as described on p. 209.

Who're You Gonna Sue?

In the Betamax case,* the Supreme Court addressed the issue known as "contributory infringement"—that is, the issue of when one party is liable for the infringing activities of another. Since there were few authoritative cases in the field of copyright, the Court borrowed from patent law, where the doctrine was more developed. The Court concluded that, if the video recorder was capable of "substantial noninfringing" uses, then the manufacturer, Sony, would not be liable for the activities of its customers who might otherwise infringe. That way, the machine remains available for use by those persons who have a legitimate, noninfringing purpose in using it.

One of the major themes of late twentieth-century copyright has been the extent to which the intermediate players have managed to get themselves out of copyright liability. Sony was held not liable for potential infringements by customers using its machines; NYU essentially got itself out of liability for infringing activities of its professors; libraries got a broad statutory exemption; on-line service providers got a limitation on general liability in the Digital Millennium Copyright Act; and even companies that used to find themselves liable for copyright infringement for the activities of their employees have managed to set up systems so that they now comply with their copyright obligations.

In most of these contexts, the price for immunity has been the obligation to assist in the enforcement of rights. The Digital Millennium

*The Betamax case, see p. 66.

Copyright Act provides that manufacturers of video recorders must include copy protection systems in their machines.* NYU,† under its settlement governing photocopying by its professors, must notify its professors of their copyright obligations, and help to enforce against abuse. (The settlement was presumably supposed to be a model for other schools to follow, but, as a settlement, it has no precedential impact, and I doubt that many other schools have as aggressive an enforcement policy as NYU.) Libraries have to implement reasonable standards for preventing widespread infringement by their patrons.‡ On-line service providers,• under the Digital Millennium Copyright Act, are required to cooperate with copyright owners by removing or blocking access to on-line sites that infringe, and, under some circumstances, identifying the primary infringers.

One of the great success stories of recent years has been the extent to which businesses have gone from being the copyright infringers to being the copyright enforcers. The Copyright Clearance Center now has site licenses with many large companies so that they pay for their photo-

Worker Bees, Unite!
This is an ad by the Business Software Alliance (BSA) encouraging "worker bees" to report software piracy at their companies. The BSA claims that the campaign was successful, and resulted in a substantial increase in the reporting of software piracy. Through education, advertising, offering site licenses, and, where necessary, pursuing infringers in court, the Alliance and other software organizations have been successful in getting most major companies to purchase legitimate copies of software for their businesses, and even to police against illegitimate copies brought in by employees.

*VCRs, see p. 114.
†NYU, see p. 27.
‡Libraries, see p. 20.
•On-line service providers, see p. 115.

copying activities.* And various computer software organizations, by bringing test cases and advertising their enforcement efforts, have been successful in getting most large companies to purchase site licenses to cover the multiple copies of their business software, and to police against the installation of unauthorized copies by their employees.

CONCLUSION

Copyright owners are given a broad range of rights, and a broad range of remedies to ensure that their rights are protected. However, these rights are not absolute. In the next chapter, we'll discuss some of the very important limitations on the rights of copyright owners.

*Copyright Clearance Center, see p. 28.

CHAPTER EIGHT

Copyright Limitations, Exclusions, and Compromises

I suspect that most people think of themselves most of the time as copyright users rather than copyright owners. For every book or movie or song we write, we're likely to read or watch or hear hundreds. So I wouldn't be surprised if my general enthusiasm for copyright has struck fear into the hearts of most readers. If copyright is really so powerful, and if so much of our consumer technology impinges upon it in one way or another, how in the world can we be expected to avoid an inevitable confrontation with the "copyright police"?

Well, don't worry. Copyright isn't nearly as absolute as it may sound: it's subject to dozens of limitations and exclusions and compromises that preserve a careful balance between the owners and users of copyrighted works. We've already seen many of these limitations in the preceding chapters, such as the special rules for library photocopying, the limitation to "original" works of authorship, the limitations from the first sale doctrine, and from various compulsory licenses for the making and performing of phonorecords and for cable television.*

In this chapter, we'll take a look at other limitations upon copyright. Some of these limitations are very specific, such as those governing certain nonprofit performances. However, several are general in nature, fundamental in principle, and sometimes fiendishly difficult in explanation and application. Perhaps the most abstract and difficult to apply is the doctrine of fair use, which we'll consider last.

 *Library photocopying, see p. 20; originality, p. 127; first sale doctrine, p. 167; phonorecord compulsory license, p. 38; cable compulsory license, p. 66.

SPECIFIC LIMITATIONS AND EXCLUSIONS

Nonprofit Musical Performances

In 1856, Congress granted copyright owners the exclusive right to perform their works publicly, and in 1897 that exclusive right was extended to musical works.* In the case of musical works, the performance right was limited to public performances "for profit." ASCAP was successful, however, in getting the courts to interpret many performances as "for profit," including "free" musical accompaniments to silent movies, "free" music in bars and restaurants, and "free" radio and television programming on stations that nonetheless were ultimately run for profit.† So users

Cue the music!
The musical accompaniment was an integral part of the silent movie experience—an entertainment open to the public, and certainly for profit. At left is an example of a cuesheet for suggested music for the movie *The King of Kings,* a $2.5 million Cecil B. DeMille extravaganza. It would hardly do to skimp on the music! In 1924, a federal circuit court held that any such copyrighted music had to be licensed for public performance, even though the defendant argued that the musical accompaniment was "free" (for customers who paid to see the movie). Even after the advent of sound movies, ASCAP tried to get the theater owners to pay a fee for the right to perform music on movie soundtracks. That practice was held invalid in 1948; now theatrical performance rights in music are "cleared at the source" by movie producers, through so-called synchronization licenses.

---

*Public performance rights, see p. 168.
†Bars and restaurants, see p. 41; radio, see p. 43.

Girl Scouts making music.
These Girl Scouts of the 1950s would not have been infringing any copyrights in the music they played, because the performances were arguably not public, and in any event not for profit.

had to get licenses for all such public performances. But truly nonprofit musical performances, such as Girl Scouts singing around the campfire, or high school musicians performing for free, were perfectly okay under the existing statute.

In 1976, Congress changed its approach to public performances of music. It dropped the specific "for profit" requirement in the statute, and replaced it with a number of specific exemptions, generally covering specified nonprofit performances of musical, and some dramatic, works. Most of these exceptions were in response to lobbying efforts by the particular nonprofit organizations involved. For example, there are special provisions for the performance of works in "face-to-face teaching activities" or in television broadcasts for use in "a nonprofit educational institution"; for certain performances as part of religious services at a house of worship; for certain performances for educational, religious, or charitable purposes; and for works prepared for the blind or other handicapped persons. There are special exemptions for performances at "a nonprofit agricultural or horticultural fair or exhibition," or a "nonprofit veterans' organization or a nonprofit fraternal organization" fund-raising event.

Radio Musical Performances in Restaurants and Small Businesses

One of the specific exemptions in the 1976 Act allowed for a public performance by means of turning on a radio or television in a public place "on a single receiving apparatus of a kind commonly used in private homes." This section led to an inordinate amount of litigation and some contentious lobbying in Congress. Cases involved such commercial establishments as the Gap, Claire's Boutiques, and Plaza Roller Dome, Inc., of Laurinburg, North Carolina, all of which provided radio music to their customers, some using elaborate radio systems that arguably went beyond what was "commonly used in private homes."

A coalition of businesses generally opposed to paying ASCAP licenses fought for legislation to exempt from the licensing requirement "small" businesses that merely provided radio music to their customers. In 1998, the coalition won a major victory against the performing rights organizations, the so-called Fairness in Music Licensing Act. That act limited the licensing powers of ASCAP, BMI, and other music licensing organizations in several ways. Most importantly, it created an exemption for restaurants and certain small businesses (based upon square footage of the establishment) that previously had to pay the licensing organizations for the privilege of playing the radio on their premises. The immediate effect of the amendments was that these restaurants and businesses did not have to pay the few hundred dollars per year in licenses that the performing rights organizations had been charging them; and the licensing rights organizations immediately saw their expenses increase and their revenues decrease.

There are several reasons why the small businesses succeeded in getting their victory. For one thing, the advocates were able to convince Congress that the fees they had to pay were a nuisance, and something of a double recovery, since the copyright owners were already paid substantial royalties from the radio and television stations and networks whose music was made available to customers. The advocates of the amendment were also able to make it the price that copyright owners had to pay for getting the 1998 extension of the length of copyright from life of the author plus fifty years to life of the author plus seventy years;* it was clear that the term extension would not pass without some relief to the small business establishments. (In theory, by linking music "fairness" to the extension of the copyright term, musical copyright owners' decrease in revenues per year would be offset by the longer period they had to receive those revenues.) The advocates of the amendment also got some very good press from some overexuberance by ASCAP in trying to enforce its licensing rights (see sidebar).

I'm hard-pressed to think of a single other example in the 210-year history of copyright in which Congress has cut back on already established rights of copyright owners. The closest analogy is a 1948 court decision that ASCAP could not charge movie theaters for playing the music recorded on movie soundtracks, but instead had to rely on "synchronization" licenses with the movie producers. The rationale for

A fit of overexuberance.

In a fit of overexuberance to collect public performance licensing fees, ASCAP recently asked several summer camping organizations, including the Girl Scouts, to pay a modest ASCAP fee for music performed at the camps. Although the Girl Scouts are nonprofit, many summer camps are not, and it is at least arguable that some of their musical performances are "public." After a flurry of newspaper articles critical of ASCAP, the embarrassed music organization quickly retreated from any efforts to require licenses. The episode indicates, however, that the exceptions are not automatic, and that it is best for an organization to have a specific exemption in the statute.

*Extension of copyright term, see p. 205.

such an outcome is the same: you get one licensing opportunity at the source, but not multiple licenses with everyone else down the distribution chain.

Compulsory Licenses

In several instances involving the challenge of new technologies, Congress has come up with "compulsory licenses" that allow users to "take" works upon payment of predetermined fees. The first such compulsory license, the phonorecord compulsory license, was introduced in 1909.* It provided that, once a music copyright owner made a recording of the work, anyone else could make and distribute recordings of the same work for a set fee.

The next set of compulsory licenses was introduced in the Copyright Act of 1976. The cable television issue had held up copyright revision for many years. The ultimate resolution of the problem was to adopt a compulsory license that allowed cable systems to import distant television signals upon payment of a statutory fee.† Also in 1976, Congress adopted a compulsory license for the playing of music in jukeboxes for the payment of a set fee, originally set at $8 per jukebox, and gradually increased to $63 and upward per jukebox. (This particular compulsory license has been repealed, in favor of industry-negotiated arrangements for payments of fees. The current agreed-upon fees are $275 per year for an operator's first jukebox; $55 per year for each of the second through tenth jukeboxes; and $48 per year for each additional jukebox thereafter.) The third new compulsory license in the 1976 Act provided for licensing of music and certain pictorial works for noncommercial television and radio broadcasts.

Each of these compulsory arrangements represented congressional compromises between granting an exemption and holding copyright users fully accountable for their uses of copyrighted works. Each of these arrangements also resulted in a complicated payment scheme that was less than satisfactory, but perhaps the best that could be done in the circumstances.

Right after the 1976 Act, it was unclear whether the compulsory licenses were solutions for an isolated set of problems, or whether they were the wave of the future. Since 1976, it appears that they were the wave

*Phonorecord compulsory license, see p. 38.
†Cable compulsory license, see p. 66.

of the future. Congress has adopted a compulsory licensing scheme to handle satellite television systems that work similarly to cable systems; to handle digital audio home recorders;* and to handle subscription digital audio transmissions.† And there are other limited situations in which people or companies that would otherwise be infringers will be allowed to continue using copyrighted works upon payment of a reasonable fee—essentially, a compulsory license. Whether one loves or hates these arrangements, they do indicate that there are options available in the copyright scheme that steer a middle course between full liability and no liability at all.

GENERAL LIMITATIONS

Works of Utility

A copyright in a work that combines decorative and functional elements does not prevent others from either using or copying the functional elements. In the somewhat cryptic words of the statute,

> "Pictorial, graphic, and sculptural works" . . . shall include works of artistic craftsmanship insofar as their form but not their mechanical or utilitarian aspects are concerned; the design of a useful article, as defined in this section, shall be considered a pictorial, graphic, or sculptural work only if, and only to the extent that, such design incorporates pictorial, graphic, or sculptural features that can be identified separately from, and are capable of existing independently of, the utilitarian aspects of the article.

What in the world does this mean? A sculpture is generally copyrightable. If the sculpture is in the shape of a chair, then it's *not* copyrightable as a chair, because the "sculptural" features of the chair don't exist independently of the chair.

The distinction helps to elucidate what copyright law is and what it is not. Copyright is directed primarily at the aesthetic, but cannot be used to create monopolies in functional aspects of works. To some extent, the "works of utility" doctrine is explained by bearing in mind the distinction between copyrights and patents. It's primarily the role of patent law to grant exclusive rights in the functional aspects of works, and there's even a special category of "design patents" to cover the design aspects of

Take away the design.
The pedestal chair designed by Eero Saarinen was revolutionary in the 1950s, and has been much imitated since then. The chair, while innovatively and pleasingly designed, is not copyrightable as such, because it has no features that can be said to exist separately from the functional aspects of the chair. Take away the "sculptural features," and there's nothing left: you fall on the floor!

"If it's for me, I'm a-sleepin'!"

$99 Goofy Phone

Mickey Mouse.
These Mickey and Goofy telephones, though utilitarian, would be protectable under copyright, because their character designs can be separated from their utilitarian function.

certain utilitarian products. The problem is that most works don't meet the higher standard of "novelty"* required by the patent statute, so most designs of useful articles don't qualify for design patent protection. In recent years, there have been some cases suggesting an expansion of trademark and unfair competition law† to cover the "trade dress" of certain products, but there are still gaps in effective protection.

Perhaps the strangest application of the doctrine is in the area of two-dimensional depictions of three-dimensional works of utility. If you draw a fashion or car design, for example, it's an infringement of copyright for someone to copy your drawing to make their own drawing (since there is nothing utilitarian about the drawing); but it is not an infringement for someone to make the dress or car depicted in your drawing (since that *is* utilitarian). The same rule used to apply to architectural plans, until architectural works were given their own separate protection in 1990.‡

Withholding protection of pleasingly designed works of utility is said to be necessary in order to assure that designers don't use copyright to gain an effective monopoly of functional elements. But some critics argue that in recent years, American designers have been losing out to European and other foreign designers of useful articles, partly because the U.S. law is not as protective of designs as is some foreign law. Critics also argue that the works of utility doctrine discriminates against modern design, where form is supposed to follow function. Some of the designers perennially go to Congress asking for some new form of protective legislation to cover their industrial designs, but such efforts have generally failed. However, designers have had two notable victories in recent years. In 1990, architectural works were granted copyright protection for the first time; and in 1998, boat hull designs• were granted a special limited form of protection. What this means is that these special works are protected by copyright even if their artistic elements cannot be separated from their functional elements. Can the car and dress and industrial designers be far behind?

*Higher patent standard, see p. 128.
†Expansion of unfair competition, see p. 224.
‡Architectural works, see p. 146
•Boat hull designs, see p. 146.

The New Look in Arkansas

Three months after Dior presented a New Look creation at $450 in France, wholesale dress manufacturers in New York began cranking out copies like those shown here. Using rayon instead of silk, four elegant flounces instead of eight—and high-speed electric cutters—the mass-production geniuses sewed up a million dresses within weeks. Then, as fast as a garment-district schlock meister could say "100,000 yards of taffeta—by Thursday, Morris," any woman who wanted the look of Paris, France, could get it in Paris, Arkansas, for $20 or less.

Straight from Paris—via New York—are the gently sloping shoulders, the curving waist of a classic $19.95 suit dress in royal blue flannel (1). A $14.95 afternoon dress of blue and white tie silk has a neckline new for now—the deep, deep plunge (2). Slipping off the shoulders is the taffeta of a chic $17.95 cocktail dress (3). For evening hours, an ensemble for $16.90: a frothy white organdy blouse blossoms from its peg-top velveteen skirt (4).

The New Look in Arkansas.

The two-dimensional pattern of a fabric or the picture of a dress might be protectable under copyright as two-dimensional images (see the Peter Pan Fabrics case at p. 156). But the three-dimensional design of a dress is not protectable, because it is a work of utility as well as function. Time-Life Books describes the new postwar look that took the world by storm:

> In late 1945, less than a year after the last German had decamped, a middle-aged Parisian named Christian Dior sat down and sketched out a handful of outrageously luxuriant dresses. With their swirling skirts twelve inches from the floor, shoulders definitely without padding and bosoms definitely with, they changed every wartime fashion notion that America had so conscientiously observed. . . .

It then describes the ease and speed with which cheap copies were made:

> Three months after Dior presented a New Look creation at $450 in France, wholesale dress manufacturers in New York began cranking out copies like those shown here. Using rayon instead of silk, four elegant flounces instead of eight—and high-speed electric cutters—the mass-production geniuses sewed up a million dresses within weeks. . . . [A]ny woman who wanted the look of Paris, France, could get it in Paris, Arkansas, for $20 or less.

Neither the law nor the practice has changed much in the intervening fifty-five years.

The Fact-Expression Distinction

Facts, like functional aspects of works, are not protected by copyright. The fact-expression distinction is rooted in the requirement that authors may only copyright what they create, what is original to them. For example, in the Feist case,* the entries in a telephone directory were not protected by copyright, because they represented facts that did not owe their origin to the telephone company.

While facts are not protected as such, compilations of facts can be protected, if their selection and arrangement are the result of sufficient originality. The Supreme Court made clear in the *Feist* case that the alphabetical listing of telephone subscribers and numbers was not such an original compilation, and so could not be protected against duplica-

*The Feist case, see p. 129.

The discovery of facts.

[T]he first person to find and report a particular fact has not created the fact; he or she has merely discovered its existence. . . . Census-takers, for example, do not "create" the population figures that emerge from their efforts; in a sense, they copy these figures from the world around them. . . . Census data therefore do not trigger copyright because these data are not "original" in the constitutional sense.

—Justice Sandra Day O'Connor,
*Feist Publications, Inc. v. Rural
Telephone Service*

Patterns of generality.

As Judge Hand explained in the Nichols case:

If *Twelfth Night* were copyrighted, it is quite possible that a second comer might so closely imitate Sir Toby Belch or Malvolio as to infringe, but it would not be enough that for one of his characters he cast a riotous knight who kept wassail to the discomfort of the household, or a vain and foppish steward who became amorous of his mistress. These would be no more than Shakespeare's "ideas" in the play, as little capable of monopoly as Einstein's Doctrine of Relativity, or Darwin's theory of the Origin of Species.

Upon any work, and especially upon a play, a great number of patterns of increasing generality will fit equally well, as more and more of the incident is left out. The last may perhaps be no more than the most general statement of what the play is about, and at times might consist only of its title; but there is a point in this series of abstractions where they are no longer protected, since otherwise the playwright could prevent the use of his "ideas," to which, apart from their expression, his property is never extended.

tion. That case, which held that "originality" could not be found merely in the labor or expense of acquiring and organizing data, raises a serious hurdle to the copyright protection of databases, such as databases of financial or geographical information.

In 1996, a European Community directive extended special protection to databases in countries of the European Union. But so far, similar efforts in the United States have failed. Since such a database protection gap puts American database companies at a competitive disadvantage, we can expect pressure on Congress to change the law to protect databases.

The Idea-Expression Distinction

Let's go to the statute: "In no case does copyright protection for an original work of authorship extend to any idea, procedure, process, system, method of operation, concept, principle, or discovery, regardless of the form in which it is described, explained, illustrated, or embodied in such work."

Many of the traditional examples are actually more properly viewed as examples of the works of utility doctrine just discussed. For example, if someone "discovers" a previously obscure medicine or medical treatment, or invents a previously unknown medicine or technique, and writes a treatise explaining the discovery, the author is protected in the particular words used to explain the process; but the book creates no specific rights in their use. That right may be granted if the process is novel, and the author applies for and receives a patent; but the book itself doesn't protect the substance of the "discovery." Similarly, a treatise on relativity or perspective or accounting creates rights in the words used to explain the principles, but doesn't give any exclusive rights in the use of the principles themselves. These examples could all be explained either because the principles are to some extent "functional," and therefore not protected under the works of utility doctrine, or because they are "ideas," separate and apart from any description of the principles.

However, the idea-expression distinction goes beyond just the functional. It also bars copyright of abstract ideas and concepts. Earlier, we looked at the *Abie's Irish Rose* case* to illustrate the concept of "substantial similarity." In that case, Judge Hand concluded that *The Cohens and the Kellys,* a movie about the love between young Jewish and Catholic lovers, was not substantially similar to the successful Anne Nichols play on the same theme. Another way of reaching the same conclusion is to find that, even though the "idea" or "theme" of the first work may have been copied, the elements taken by the second work were no more than the copyright law allowed.

The idea-expression distinction is most firmly entrenched in the context of factual works, where the doctrine obviously overlaps with the fact-expression distinction. It is quite clear that we don't want an author to be able to monopolize the "idea" or theory or interpretation of historical events. A. A. Hoehling, for example, developed the theory that the airship *Hindenburg,* which caught fire and crashed in 1937, was destroyed by a saboteur. He sued Universal City Studios for making a movie that incorporated some of the same elements as his book. The court found, however, that he could not stop the movie.

Of course, the trick for all of these general principles limiting copyright is to come up with a test for distinguishing between protectable expression on the one hand, and unprotectable function, fact, or idea, on the other. While the principles are theoretically clear, the distinctions can be frustratingly complex in particular cases. A sense of the law can be derived by looking at how the courts have decided particular cases, but summarizing the range of factors can be frustrating for both teachers and students of the law.

The Hindenburg disaster.

[T]he hypothesis that Eric Spehl destroyed the *Hindenburg* is based entirely on the interpretation of historical facts, including Spehl's life, his girlfriend's anti-Nazi connections, the explosion's origin in Gas Cell 4, Spehl's duty station, discovery of a dry-cell battery among the wreckage, and rumors about Spehl's involvement dating from a 1938 Gestapo investigation. Such an historical interpretation, whether or not it originated with Mr. Hoehling, is not protected by his copyright and can be freely used by subsequent authors.

    —The Second Circuit Court of Appeals in the *Hindenburg* case.

The *Hindenburg* disaster, described on live radio by Herb Morrison on May 6, 1937, brought an end to the luxury zeppelin travel of the day.

Abie's Irish Rose, see p. 153.

The Dillinger Dossier.

In a series of books, the writer Jay Nash developed the hypothesis that John Dillinger was not the man shot in front of the Biograph Theater in Chicago in 1934. In 1984, CBS broadcast an episode of *Simon & Simon* that was based upon this same hypothesis. Nash sued CBS for copyright infringement. The Seventh Circuit Court of Appeals found that there was no infringement, saying:

> Nash does not portray *The Dillinger Dossier* and its companion works as fiction, however, which makes all the difference. The inventor of Sherlock Holmes controls that character's fate while the copyright lasts; the first person to conclude that Dillinger survived does not get dibs on history. If Dillinger survived, that fact is available to all. Nash's rights lie in his expression; in his words, in his arrangement of facts (his deployment of narration interspersed with interviews, for example), but not in the naked "truth." The Dillinger Print does not use any words from *The Dillinger Dossier* or Nash's other books; it does not take over any of Nash's presentation but instead employs a setting of its own invention with new exposition and development. Physical differences between Dillinger and the corpse, planted fingerprints, photographs of Dillinger and other gangsters in the 1930s, these and all the rest are facts as Nash depicts them.

Cartoon by Bion Smalley.

FAIR USE

Even if a work meets the tests of copyrightability ("originality" and "fixation," for a category of work entitled to protection under the statute),* and even if it's found that someone has apparently infringed (by violating one of the exclusive rights with a "substantially similar" copy),† and even if it's found that the use is not within one of the other exceptions or limitations on copyright (functionality, facts, idea, or any of the other specific limitations), there's still one final hurdle that the copyright owner must pass before enforcing rights against someone who copies. This hurdle is the "fair use" defense. This flexible defense protects users for what might otherwise be considered relatively minor or technical violations, or violations that for policy reasons we don't think should lead to copyright liability.

"What is 'fair use'?"

*Copyrightability, see chapter 6.
†Infringement, see chapter 7.

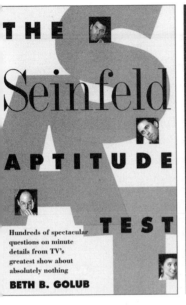

What's the difference?
The difficulties of predicting exactly how cases will come out under the "substantial similarity" test of the last chapter, or the "fair use" test of this chapter, is illustrated by two *Seinfeld* books. The first was found to be infringing on the *Seinfeld* program; the second was published a few years later by the same publisher, but apparently would not be considered infringing. What's the difference? The court concluded that, in the first book, "every question and correct answer has as its source a fictional moment in a Seinfeld episode." A recognizable portion of dialogue was repeated verbatim. (The nature of the book was given away in the cover description of the "minute details" to be found inside.) According to the court, the book simply took too much, and was not excused as fair use because the purpose was not to comment on or to parody the original, but simply to cash in on the popularity of the series.

First developed by judges to decide individual cases, the defense is now authorized by the copyright statute itself. Although the term "fair use" is not defined, it is fleshed out by the following statutory "factors:"

[T]he fair use of a copyrighted work, including such use by reproduction in copies or phonorecords or by any other means . . . for purposes such as criticism, comment, news reporting, teaching (including multiple copies for classroom use), scholarship, or research, is not an infringement of copyright. In determining whether the use made of a work in any particular case is a fair use factors to be considered shall include—

(1) the purpose and character of the use, including whether such use is of a commercial nature or is for nonprofit educational purposes;
(2) the nature of the copyrighted work;
(3) the amount and substantiality of the portion used in relation to the copyrighted work as a whole; and
(4) the effect of the use upon the potential market for or value of the copyrighted work.

The fact that a work is unpublished shall not itself bar a finding of fair use if such finding is made upon consideration of all the above factors.

Examples of fair use.

The House Report to the Copyright Act cites the following examples to "give some idea of the sort of activities the courts might regard as fair use under the circumstances":

> quotation of excerpts in a review or criticism for purposes of illustration or comment; quotation of short passages in a scholarly or technical work, for illustration or clarification of the author's observations . . . summary of an address or article, with brief quotations, in a news report; reproduction by a library of a portion of a work to replace part of a damaged copy; reproduction by a teacher or student of a small part of a work to illustrate a lesson; reproduction of a work in legislative or judicial proceedings or reports; incidental and fortuitous reproduction, in a newsreel or broadcast, of a work located in the scene of an event being reported.

These examples may suggest a rather limited role for fair use.

This is not to say that the fair use analysis is straightforward. In fact, of the cases that have made it to the Supreme Court, the typical pattern is a district court decision reversed by an appellate court reversed again by the Supreme Court, usually by a split decision, frequently 5 to 4. Reasonable people may certainly, maybe even inevitably, disagree in many of the cases where fair use has been called upon to distinguish between permissible use and copyright infringement.

A few examples will illustrate the range of what might be considered fair use.

Parody

There's a long tradition protecting parody as a fair use, even though it's not specifically mentioned in the statute, if the parody otherwise seems reasonable under the four statutory factors. Here are some examples of what has been found to be within the ambit of fair use: *From Here to Obscurity,* a Sid Caesar television takeoff of the movie *From Here to Eternity*; *MAD* Magazine parody lyrics to be sung to the tunes of famous songs (such as "The First Time I Saw Maris," sung to the tune of "The Last Time I Saw Paris"); "I Love Sodom," a *Saturday Night Live* spoof of the New York jingle, "I Love New York"; and an advertising poster for *Naked Gun 33-1/3,* showing Leslie Nielson in a pregnant spoof of the Annie Leibovitz photograph of Demi Moore on the cover of *Vanity Fair.*

Not all examples of parody qualify for the exemption. In some cases, courts have found that purported parodies did not qualify for protection under the fair use doctrine, and thus constituted copyright infringement. Among these are *Autolight,* a Jack Benny television takeoff of the movie *Gaslight*; *Air Pirates Funnies,* a 1970s counterculture spoof of Walt Disney comic books; Jeff Koons's *String of Puppies,* a sculpture

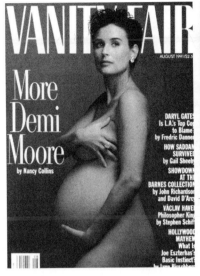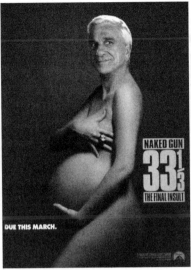

lifted from an Art Rogers photograph of Jim Scanlon and his wife with their eight German shepherd puppies; and a book using Dr. Seuss characters and style to tell a purportedly humorous version of the O. J. Simpson story.

Why do some parodies qualify for protection and others not? To the frustration of some observers, the courts generally refuse to articulate any clear dividing lines, instead emphasizing that fair use is an "equitable" doctrine to be decided on a case-by-case basis with a detailed weighing of all of the statutory fair use factors. In fact, the appellate courts reverse lower courts if they conclude that the lower courts have allowed one factor to be given too much weight over the others.

Judge James Carter, who decided both the Jack Benny and the Sid Caesar cases in the district court, felt that the important distinguishing feature in those cases was in the amount taken. Jack Benny simply took too much from the original movie—the locale and period, the main setting, the characters, the story points, the development of the story, the incidents and sequence of events, the points of suspense, the climax, and much of the dialogue, although the story was of course a burlesque of the original, with gags added throughout. Sid Caesar's spoof, on the other hand, had parallels to the original movie, but transformed it substantially. The judge found that "There is no substantial similarity between said

Everybody's getting into the act!
Left, the Annie Leibovitz photograph of a pregnant Demi Moore for the cover of *Vanity Fair* magazine. Center, the spoof photo of Leslie Nielsen in an advertisement for the movie *Naked Gun 33-1/3*. A court held the spoof to be a fair use. At right, yet another spoof, on the cover of *Spy* magazine, in which Bruce Willis (at the time Demi Moore's husband) was at least allowed to keep his own arms and hands. The Leslie Nielsen ad arguably took more from the original than was necessary to "conjure up" the original—the image was not scanned from the Demi Moore image exactly, but the part of the photo taken from an actually pregnant woman was digitally processed to make it pretty much identical to the Annie Leibovitz original.

Appropriation art.
Above left, Art Rogers's 1980 photograph, which had been exhibited in museums and distributed on a 1984 notecard. Above right, a sculpture by the "appropriation artist"(!) Jeff Koons, which the court held was not a fair use, but a copyright infringement. Koons did not execute the sculpture himself, but instead gave detailed instructions to his European studios to copy the photograph. Three of the sculptures were sold to collectors for a total of $367,000, and a fourth was retained by Koons. Koons has lost other copyright suits as well, including one for the copyright in "Odie," from the Garfield comic strip. Right, the infringing Koons sculpture, *Wild Boy and Puppy.*

burlesque and said motion picture as to theme, characterizations, general story line, detailed sequence of incidents, dialogue, points of suspense, subclimax or climax." If you want to make an informed judgment on your own, I suggest that you see the movie and the spoof, both of which are available on videotape.

While the courts generally allow a parodist to copy as much as is necessary to "conjure up" the target of the spoof, I'm impressed with how little actually has to be taken in order to create a clever parody. Watch just about any episode of the Animaniacs, the Muppets, or *The Simpsons,* and you'll see clever spoofs—cultural references—to great movies like

In this wickedly clever and hilariously funny rendition of the O.J. Simpson trial, Dr. Juice recounts in rhyming verse the highlights of the case and the personalities involved. Beginning in Brentwood, the "happy town inside L.A., where rich folks play the day away," it moves on to the Bronco chase with "A pal named Al," and Kato Kaelin, "a house guest [who] is faithful one hundred percent." From the cases presented by Marcia Clark and the Dream Team, to the witnesses and jury "Injury. Perjury. His jury. Her Jury," and the verdict that decrees "The Cat goes free..." *The Cat NOT in the Hat* is pure poetry, a fresh new look at a much told tale that trial watchers everywhere will enjoy.

Dr. Seuss?

At left, excerpts from Dr. Seuss; at right, a so-called parody making fun of the O. J. Simpson case. One of the points made by the court in finding that this was not a fair use was the fact that it parodied the O. J. Simpson case, not really Dr. Seuss. Thus, there was less need to "take" the Dr. Seuss original. The printing of the book was enjoined; but the words, if not the images, survive on the Internet. Do a search on "Simpson" and "Seuss" and see how many people seem to think this parody is funny or otherwise worth distributing on their Web sites.

The Great Escape or *The Godfather* or hundreds of other movies, television programs, or commercials. The references go over the heads of the younger viewers, but help the shows appeal to an older audience that "gets" and appreciates the references.

Maybe the cartoonists who made the "Air Pirates" (p. 198) went too far precisely in their lack of subtlety. In that case, the appellate court disallowed the fair use defense, emphasizing that "given the widespread public recognition of the major characters involved here . . . very little would have been necessary to place Mickey Mouse and his image in the minds of the readers" to "conjure up" the original being spoofed. The court also

From Here to Obscurity.
Above, Montgomery Clift played a former boxer who wanted to bugle, not fight, opposite Frank Sinatra in the Oscar-winning movie *From Here to Eternity.* Below, Sid Caesar played a humorous version, *From Here to Obscurity,* with Carl Reiner and Howard Morris (and, not shown, Imogene Coca). The skit has been described as "one of the best remembered skits" from *Your Show of Shows.* The courts held that the spoof was not a copyright infringement.

Gaslight **and** ***Autolight.***
Above, Charles Boyer and Ingrid Bergman in the classic movie *Gaslight.* Below, Jack Benny and Barbara Stanwyck in the spoof, *Autolight.* The court made it sound as if the spoof was just silly, and not very funny. (Calling a parody not funny is the kiss of death for a parody defense.) But the plot is about a man trying to drive his wife insane, and it's possible that silly things can do that, or that the Benny parody was making fun of how illogical and silly the things were that Boyer was doing to drive his wife mad. (Note the upside-down picture in the background.)

concluded that "when the medium involved is a comic book, a recognizable caricature is not difficult to draw, so that an alternative that involves less copying is more likely to be available than if a speech, for instance, is parodied."

Yet the degree of similarity, the "amount taken," cannot be the only factor here. There have been other instances in which Mickey has been spoofed just as graphically as in the "Air Pirates" case. For example, *MAD* Magazine has spoofed Disney characters, as well as just about every other cultural icon around. And yet *MAD* generally is not sued, or wins lawsuits brought against it. How does *MAD* Magazine get away with it?

It's all in the setting. The *MAD* spoof is contained in a publication that is obviously a parody, and that, for all its pretensions at being outra-

---

More *MAD*.

Here's an example of the *MAD* Magazine parody lyrics that were held to be a fair use: the words to the original, "The Last Time I Saw Paris," are at the left, and the words to *MAD*'s parody, "The First Time I Saw Maris," on the right. The beauty of the parody is that *MAD* Magazine never actually copied any copyrighted work: the words were different, and although the reader was invited to sing the parody to the original tune, the tune was not copied by the magazine.

The last time I saw Paris	The first time I saw Maris
Her heart was warm and gay,	He'd signed up with the A's!
I heard the laughter of her heart	He slugged the ball but never found
In ev'ry street cafe.	How big league baseball pays!
The last time I saw Paris,	The next time I saw Maris
Her trees were dressed for spring,	A Yankee he'd become!
And lovers walked beneath those trees,	And now endorsements earn for him
And birds found songs to sing.	A most substantial sum!
I dodged the same old taxicabs	He signed a contract with Gillette
That I had dodged for years;	To plug their razor blades!
The chorus of their squeaky horns	And when he found he cut himself,
Was music to my ears.	He went and plugged Band-Aids!
The last time I saw Paris	The last time I saw Maris
Her heart was warm and gay.	He plugged six brands of beer!
No matter how they change her	The Democrats should pay him
I'll remember her that way.	To plug the New Frontier!

Pirates!

Although not emphasized in the case, the "Air Pirates" comics not only "took" the Disney characters; some of the story lines and even frames were duplicated almost precisely. The cover of the first "Air Pirates" issue (above) was lifted from a particular Disney "Big Little Book" cover (1933) (above right); and the name "Air Pirates" would be recognized, by those who remembered it, as a variation on the "Mail Pilot" comic strip, book, and movie short.

This side of parodies.

Right, the Bill Elder *MAD* Magazine spoof of Mickey. In defense of such parodies, Harvey Kurtzman of *MAD* stated, "Will understood parody. Of course what it is, is mimicry. Willy was just so good at it. He understood that you had to have an exact duplicate of what you're parodying." A similar argument in the "Air Pirates" case was rejected by the court.

geous, is fairly gentle in its style. Many copyright owners think it's a compliment to be parodied by *MAD*. The "Air Pirates" comics, on the other hand, were underground comic books depicting Disney characters in bawdy or drug-related activities. The covers of the first two comics were deceptive, in that they might even be mistaken for legitimate Disney publications (Mickey's "real" name was used). The "Air Pirates" announced their intention to continue publishing their comics, so that they were an ongoing threat to Disney. No wonder, then, that Disney asked for, and got, impoundment and destruction of all of the comics still in the defendant's possession.

But how can you capture all of these elements in a precise definition of fair use? No formulation of the rule can anticipate the wide range of potentially legitimate activities, and yet adequately capture the fine distinctions. Fair use "factors" are about all that we can expect, plus a sensitivity of the courts to the nuances of the particular cases.

As clean as they wanna be?

Left, the 2 Live Crew album cover. This album is about the only 2 Live Crew album that *doesn't* contain explicit lyrics; and the banner announcing that fact covered the barer parts that were more explicitly displayed in their *Dirty As They Wanna Be* album. This particular copy was bought some time after the circuit court had held 2 Live Crew's version of "Pretty Woman" to be an infringement, and before the Supreme Court reversed that decision. During this period, the "Pretty Woman" track was removed from the album, but the credits on the back cover, shown below right, still curiously listed Roy Orbison, William Dees, and Acuff-Rose with an asterisk. Pity the poor fan trying to figure out what that referred to—or the poor law professor who couldn't find the infringing track. And if Orbison and his estate didn't approve of 2 Live Crew, imagine the embarrassment at the implication that Orbison had been involved in the writing and publishing of the album!

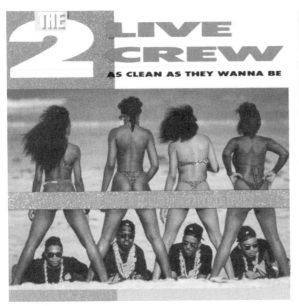

It may be that the pendulum in this area is currently swinging in favor of parodists. A recent Supreme Court case considered 2 Live Crew's rap version of Roy Orbison's musical hit *Pretty Woman*. The Court emphasized the "transformative" nature of parody, and implied that the work in that case was sufficiently transformative to meet the test. Interestingly, the Court did *not* find that the spoof was a fair use, instead remanding the case for the lower courts to make their own determination. In a bit of overstatement, the press's general description of the case was that it "found" the 2 Live Crew song to be a fair use. In any event, the language of the opinion makes clear the Court's tolerance for parodies, and it would be a bold lower court or law professor who would ignore the Court's language about the wide berth to be given to parodies under the fair use doctrine.

Compromise on Public Policy Grounds

The fair use doctrine is also available as a tool for deciding difficult cases involving new situations and raising major policy concerns that have not otherwise been specifically addressed by Congress. It can serve as something of an "escape valve" when literal application of the law would otherwise lead to undesirable results. For example, we've already seen how fair use has been used to analyze the difficult issues raised by the educational photocopying* of copyrighted materials.

In the Betamax case, the Supreme Court invoked the doctrine to hold that the Sony Corporation, makers of the Betamax video recorder, was not liable for copyright infringement when users of its machines made unauthorized copies of copyrighted works.† As part of its decision, the Court held that the home recording of television programs, which were otherwise delivered to homes for free over the public airwaves, for the purpose of "time-shifting"—viewing at another time, after which the copy is erased—did not constitute copyright infringement because it qualified as a fair use. The Court did not say that *all* copying of programs in the home—particularly the "librarying" of programs to be viewed more than once—was a fair use; but since the Court found that there was at least some legitimate, noninfringing use for video recorders, Sony wouldn't be held liable for the potentially infringing actions that others might undertake.

*Library photocopying, see p. 20; classroom photocopying, p. 25.
†The Betamax case, see p. 66.

Another fascinating technology case involved the copying of a Sega game cartridge by Accolade, Inc. Here's what happened: Sega made the popular Genesis game system, which together with Nintendo and later Sony systems accounted for the vast majority of game systems bought by millions of kids throughout the world. Selling the game machines was only half the road to success, however; the real money was in selling the game cartridges to run on the system. In order to assure that only it or its licensees sold such cartridges, Sega built into its console a system that would check to see if cartridges contained the appropriate code indicating that the cartridge was authorized to run on the system.

In order to produce compatible programs, Accolade did the following. First, it "reverse-engineered" several existing Sega cartridges. It copied the programs contained on the cartridges, and "disassembled" the object code to produce printouts of the source code. It studied the source code of the different game cartridges to see what parts of the code were present on all of the cartridges. It was thus able to determine the appropriate short code that had to be on any cartridge to make it run on a Sega Genesis console. Accolade did not copy any of Sega's actual games, but it did copy the short code—about 20–25 bytes—which was necessary to trick the Sega Genesis console into "thinking" that the Accolade cartridges were licensed, and therefore run the Accolade programs— Ishido, Star Control, Hardball, Onslaught, Turrican, and Mike Ditkas Power Football—on the Sega console.

Sega sued for copyright infringement. Because the amount of actual code taken, the 20–25 bytes, was arguably minimal, and arguably entirely functional, Sega chose in its suit to focus upon Accolade's "intermediate" copying, arguing that the intermediate copies that Accolade had admittedly made were infringing copies of Sega's copyrighted game cartridges. Accolade raised several defenses, most of which were rejected. However, the appellate court accepted Accolade's fair use argument. The court held that "disassembly of copyrighted object code is, as a matter of law, a fair use of the copyrighted work if such disassembly provides the only means of access to those elements of the code that are not protected by copyright and the copier has a legitimate reason for seeking such access." Accordingly, the court dissolved the preliminary injunction that had been granted by the lower court, and allowed Accolade to continue selling its Sega-compatible game cartridges.

Implicit in the court's holding is the assessment that Accolade's goal of creating Sega-compatible cartridges was a valid one, supported by public policy. The court pointed out that

> Accolade's identification of the functional requirements for Genesis compatibility has led to an increase in the number of independently designed video game programs offered for use with the Genesis console. It is precisely this growth in creative expression, based on the dissemination of other creative works and the unprotected ideas contained in those works, that the Copyright Act was intended to promote. . . . [Sega's] attempt to monopolize the market by making it impossible for others to compete runs counter to the statutory purpose of promoting creative expression and cannot constitute a strong equitable basis for resisting the invocation of the fair use doctrine. . . . Because Sega's video game programs contain unprotected aspects that cannot be examined without copying, we afford them a lower degree of protection than more traditional literary works.

The case did not hold Sega's copyright in its cartridges invalid. Sega could clearly prevent any other company from pirating and selling copies of its game cartridges. But Accolade produced its own original games, which did not copy Sega's. Under the unique facts of the case, the *intermediate* copying that Accolade had to do in order to make Sega-compatible games, and the minimal amount of code that it actually had to take in order to make its cartridges work on the Sega console, were excused under the fair use doctrine.

In addition to the technology setting, the "public interest" occasionally excuses what would otherwise be a copyright infringement. Perhaps the best example is the case involving the Zapruder movie* of the Kennedy assassination—the most explicit movie footage of that important historical event. The movie was copyrighted by Abraham Zapruder and immediately sold to Time, Inc. Josiah Thompson made unauthorized drawings of many of the frames in order to illustrate his analysis in the book *Six Seconds in Dallas*. When Time, Inc. sued for copyright infringement, the court identified the public interest as overriding the rights of the copyright owner, in the context of a complete analysis under the standards of fair use.

*The Zapruder case, see p. 143.

Six Seconds in Dallas.
Above, a frame from the Zapruder film, reprinted in *Life* magazine, October 2, 1964. Below, a sketch of Zapruder frame 237, about five frames later in the sequence, reprinted in Josiah Thompson's book, *Six Seconds in Dallas.* In the book, the author and the publisher made clear that they had sought permission to use the actual Zapruder frames, but had been refused. They apparently felt that the use of sketches instead of actual film footage avoided their liability under the Copyright Act. That's clearly not true, is it? But the court did ultimately find in their favor on the basis of the fair use doctrine and the strong public interest in allowing this limited use of the work.

There is a public interest in having the fullest information available on the murder of President Kennedy. Thompson did serious work on the subject and has a theory entitled to public consideration. While doubtless the theory could be explained with sketches . . . the explanation actually made in the Book [*Six Seconds in Dallas*] with copies is easier to understand. The Book is not bought because it contained the Zapruder pictures; the Book is bought because of the theory of Thompson and its explanation, supported by Zapruder pictures.

This does not mean that every work on a matter of public interest should get a fair use free ride. For example, in the Harper & Row case,*

*Harper and Row, see p. 155.

The Nation had argued that fair use gave it the right to publish excerpts from former President Ford's *A Time to Heal* prior to its authorized "first serialization" in an exclusive *Time* magazine article. The Supreme Court held that the lifting of three to four hundred words was not excused by fair use, but instead constituted an infringement of the author's and Harper & Row's copyright. The public interest did not require the taking, since Ford and Harper & Row were already in the process of trying to get the work to the public. As Justice Sandra Day O'Connor stated in that case, "[I]t should not be forgotten that the Framers [of the Constitution] intended copyright itself to be the engine of free expression. By establishing a marketable right to the use of one's expression, copyright supplies the economic incentive to create and disseminate ideas. . . ."

Justice O'Connor cites Lionel Sobel for the proposition that "If every volume that was in the public interest could be pirated away by a competing publisher, . . . the public [soon] would have nothing worth reading."

CONCLUSION

We've now seen so many doctrines limiting copyright that it's hard to believe copyright owners ever win lawsuits at all. Between the difficulties of discovering violations highlighted in chapter 5, and the limitations on enforcing rights highlighted here, there are certainly a lot of hurdles along the way. Maybe that's the reason Congress grants such broad rights (outlined in chapter 7) to those copyright owners who are successful in navigating the hurdles—to compensate successful copyright owners for the difficulties in enforcing their rights.

CHAPTER NINE

Other Major Copyright Principles

There are other copyright principles that are just as important as those already discussed in this book, but that don't fit neatly into the categories of earlier chapters. In this chapter, we'll look at some basic questions: How long does copyright last? What formalities are required? How do you determine who owns a copyright? And what about other theories for protecting creative works?

HOW LONG DOES COPYRIGHT LAST?

Nothing illustrates the tremendous expansion of copyright over the years more clearly than the extension of copyright protection to cover ever-longer periods of time.

14 to 28 years, 1790

As we have seen, the initial American copyright act,* modeled after the British Statute of Anne, granted copyright protection for 14 years, with an option to renew for another 14 years, for a maximum of 28 years.

28 to 42 years, 1831

In 1831, the first term was extended to 28 years, to create a maximum period of 42 years.

28 to 56 years, 1909

In the recodification of copyright in 1909, the second term was also extended to 28 years, making the maximum period of protection 56 years. Thus, over a period of 120 years, the term of copyright was exactly doubled.

*1790 copyright act, see p. 14.

Only a bathtub-full of books.

Here's a fun quote from Mark Twain: "[P]erhaps no important American or English statutes are uncompromisingly and hopelessly idiotic except the copyright statutes of these two countries." The quote, taken out of context, might seem to imply that Twain (Samuel Clemens) was not a fan of copyright. But actually his frustration was with the fact that these countries placed *any* restriction on the duration of copyright. He argued that most creative works were not of much value for very long anyway, so that it would not be a great burden upon society to allow the successful works protection virtually in perpetuity. It's of course more fun to look at Twain's own words, from his autobiography:

> If you could prove that only twenty idiots are born in a century and that each of them, by special genius, was able to make an article of commerce which no one else could make; and which was able to furnish the idiot and his descendants after him an income sufficient for the modest and economical support of half a dozen persons, there is no Congress and no Parliament in all Christendom that would dream of descending to the shabbiness of limiting that trifling income to a term of years, in order that it might be enjoyed thereafter by persons who had no sort of claim upon it. I know that this would happen because all Congresses and Parliaments have a kindly feeling for idiots and a compassion for them, on account of personal experience and heredity. Neither England nor America has been able to produce in a century any more than twenty authors whose books have been able to outlive the copyright limit of forty-two years [the applicable term at the time], yet the Congresses and the Parliaments stick

Even by 1909, most of the rest of the world had expanded their protection to the life of the author plus 50 years, and that term was seriously considered in the congressional debates of 1909. But Congress, in its wisdom, chose to retain the renewal system, and to limit protection to 56 years.

Life of the author plus 50 years, 1976

Throughout the twentieth century, authors complained that 56 years was too short. Unlike other forms of property, copyrights might not survive long enough to allow authors to provide for their children. Life expectancy was lengthening, and many authors lived long enough to see their own works go into the public domain. Or some less conventional writers weren't "discovered" by the public until years after they created their works, sometimes after their copyrights had expired. America had fallen behind the rest of the world in the period of protection it granted authors; and, since the Berne Convention* required life plus 50 years as a minimum period of protection, the 56-year term prevented the United States from joining the premier international copyright convention.

After fending off authors for most of the twentieth century, the United States in 1976 finally adopted the period of protection that prevailed throughout the rest of the world: the life of the author plus 50 years. After another dozen years, it joined the Berne Union, and everyone pretty much assumed that was the end of the process.

Life of the author plus 70 years, 1998

But a curious thing happened. Many other countries, particularly in Europe, extended their copyright to life of the author plus 70 years. For foreign authors, however, they conditioned the extension upon reciprocity: that is, they would protect the rights of foreign

*Berne Convention, see p. 241.

authors only if the foreign authors' own countries also extended protection to life of the author plus 70 years. So, American authors couldn't participate in the extension of copyright in these countries. It didn't take the authors very long to figure out that they should get Congress to extend the term of protection in this country; and it didn't take Congress long to figure out that, as a copyright exporting country, we stood to gain by the reciprocal extension of the copyright term.

There was considerable opposition to the term extension. For one thing, the Constitution provides that Congress may grant copyright protection "for limited times." It was thought by some observers that the life of the author plus 70 years—which could in some circumstances extend copyright for over a century—somehow violated the spirit of the "limited times" provision. (Though, to be sure, life plus 70 is still a limited time.) Several critics argued that the term extension was a ploy by existing copyright owners—or, worse, their "freeloading" heirs—to simply gouge every last dollar out of their copyrights.

Ultimately, the term extension argument won, with the passage of the Sonny Bono Copyright Term Extension Act of 1998. There was a price, however, that some of the copyright holders had to pay. A coalition of music licensees convinced Congress to condition the term extension upon passage of the Fairness in Music Licensing Act,* also of 1998. The result was that, while all copyrights were extended for an additional 20 years, the value of the music copyrights was decreased by limitations imposed upon the music licensing organizations. But the net result was that we now have a copyright term of life of the author plus 70 years—a substantial increase over the original copyright maximum of 28 years.

to the forty-two-year limit greedily, intensely, pathetically, and do seem to believe by some kind of insane reasoning that somebody is in some way benefited by this trivial robbery inflicted upon the families of twenty authors in the course of a hundred years. . . .

In a century we have produced two hundred and twenty thousand books; not a bathtub-full of them are still alive and marketable. The case would have been the same if the copyright limit had been a thousand years. It would be entirely safe to make it a thousand years and it would also be properly respectable and courteous to do it.

Plucky Panda unplucked.
A cartoon warning of the dangers of public domain status to cartoon characters, and advocating—or showing cartoon characters advocating—copyright extension.

  *Fairness in Music Licensing Act, see p. 182.

Mark Twain.
This photograph of Mark Twain (center, with friends George Alfred Townsend and David Gray) was taken by Mathew Brady in 1871.

Works created as of these dates	Duration of copyright	Explanation
Published before 1923.	Already in public domain.	These works originally received at most 56 years of protection, extended to 75 years in 1976; but they went into the public domain before they could be extended by the 1998 amendment.
Published 1923-1977.	If published with notice, and renewed in 28th year, copyright lasts for 95 years from date of publication.	These works originally received 28 year term, renewable for 28 more years; extended to total of 75 years in 1976; extended again to 95 years in 1998.
Created after January 1, 1978.	Life of author plus 70 years.	These works originally received life plus 50, extended to life plus 70 in 1998.
Created before 1978, but not yet published.	Life plus seventy years, or until 2002, whichever is later. If published by 2002, extended to 2047.	These works, as unpublished works, would have gone on forever, but were given the listed terms by the 1976 and 1998 acts.

Different rules for existing copyrights.
When Congress extended copyright protection in 1976 and in 1998, it also extended the term for already existing copyrights. In 1976, previously existing copyrights were given a 19-year "gift," to extend them from 56 years to 75 years. In 1998, previously existing copyrights were given another 20-year "gift," to extend them to a total of 95 years. It is therefore necessary to do a little historical analysis to figure out the copyright term of works that were created or published under prior copyright laws.

WHAT FORMALITIES ARE REQUIRED? NONE!

One of the questions I'm most often asked about copyright goes something like this: "If a copyright is so great, how do I get one? What do I have to do to copyright my book/play/sculpture/song/ photograph?" The simple answer is, you don't have to do anything. Or, to be more precise, all you have to do is "fix" it* "in a tangible medium of expression"—that is, make some sort of physical copy of it—write it down, make a video of it, or audiotape it. That's it. Copyright protection is automatic.

Some of the apparent confusion may arise from the fact that under prior copyright acts, a copyright owner had to register the claim with the Copyright Office and

*Fixation, see p. 127.

place a copyright "notice" on all published copies. The notice was a simple and conspicuous statement including all of the following elements: (1) the word "Copyright" or the abbreviation "Copyr." or the symbol of a "c" in a circle—©; (2) the year of first publication of the work; and (3) the name of the copyright owner. In the 1976 statute, the registration, deposit, and notice requirements were eased somewhat, but not totally abandoned.

However, in 1988, as a condition to joining the international Berne Copyright Convention,* the United States was forced to abandon the copyright formalities it had previously required. What this means is that, while works may have gone into the public domain prior to 1988 because of a failure to comply with technicalities, since 1988 there are virtually no technical prerequisites to federal copyright.

Better Protection for $30

If you're an author or composer or artist, I still recommend that you fill out and send in the appropriate copyright registration forms, pay the $30 fee (as of 2000), deposit the recommended copies, and receive a copyright registration certificate. You should also place the copyright notice described above on all published copies of your work. Although a copyright will be valid whether or not you do these things, there are advantages in taking such actions, such as entitling you to recover more money in the event someone infringes the copyright.†

Prior to 1988, the United States was the last major industrial country to still impose copyright formalities. By joining the rest of the world and eliminating these formalities, we've made copyright simpler and easier for copyright owners. This is important, because many of the people most affected by copyright don't seem to know a lot about it. It's said that an invention is great only if it's capable of being used by people who don't know how it works. (If we all had to know how to make and main-

Copyright notice.

This is what a copyright notice looks like:

Copyright © 2000 by Edward Samuels

You should find it at the beginning of this and most other books. Under prior acts, the existence and proper placement of the copyright notice were critical to the continued viability of copyright protection—even slight slip-ups could result in loss of all rights!

The symbol ©, while not the only option for notice, was the preferred symbol because it also triggered international rights under the Universal Copyright Convention. Many notices also contained the words "All rights reserved," because those words triggered rights under other international copyright treaties.

Works under prior law.

The copyright status of a work published prior to 1988 depends on the applicable law at the time. For works published prior to 1978, copyright notice requirements were strict, and lack of notice very likely meant that the work went into the public domain. Between 1978 and 1988, there were relaxed standards, and copyright might even be "rescued" for works that were inadvertently published without notice. Since 1988, notice is encouraged, but not required.

  *Berne Convention and copyright formalities, see p. 242.
†Better remedies, see p. 176.

More et cetera, et cetera.

Charles A. Goodrum in 1980 pointed out that many of the claims about the collection of the Library of Congress are exaggerated:

> But the superlatives that *are* true boggle the mind: It *is* the largest collection of stored knowledge in the world. It does have more maps, globes, charts, and atlases than any other place on earth. It *has* accumulated more books from England and America than anywhere else–but, *mirabile dictu,* barely one-fourth of its collections are in English! It does have–almost–every phonograph record ever made in the United States, the largest collection of motion pictures in America, more Civil War photographs, more personal letters in Sigmund Freud's handwriting, more Stradivari violins, more flutes, more handwritten copies of the Gettysburg Address in Lincoln's own hand, more . . . et cetera, et cetera, than any other institution in the world.

Obviously, not all of these items come from copyright deposits. The Library also benefits from exchange programs with other countries and other libraries, and from gifts.

tain an internal combustion engine before we could drive a car, we'd probably still be using the horse and buggy.) Well, copyright becomes a great invention when it can be used even by people who aren't lawyers. That's the beauty of copyright simplification.

The Library of Congress

One of the primary benefits of copyright has been the requirement that authors register their works, and also deposit copies with the Copyright Office. Many, but by no means all, of these works are chosen for retention by the Library of Congress. As a result, the Library of

The Library of Congress main reading room, circa 1890.

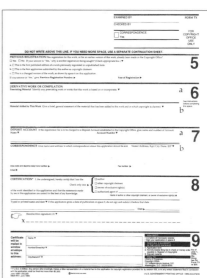

Congress now represents the "largest collection of stored knowledge in the world."

The Library of Congress was first established in 1800, when the United States capital was moved to Washington, D.C. It was completely destroyed in 1814, when the British burned down almost all government buildings in the new capital. (The British action in burning Washington was nominally in retaliation for the American burning of the Parliament Building in York, now Toronto, Upper Canada, and the destruction of its archives and library.) In a grand gesture, Thomas Jefferson replenished the Library with his own private collection from Monticello, making it still the most complete collection in the country. It was not until 1870 that the federal copyright law was amended to make the Library of Congress the official depository of all works registered for copyright. In 1897, the Copyright Office was established as a separate office within the Library of Congress.

Now that copyright registration and deposit have been made voluntary rather than mandatory, might the Library of Congress's acquisition program suffer? Only time will tell. But it appears that most publishers still take advantage of copyright registration in order to provide maximum protection of their works, and are eager to supply copies to the Copyright Office for ultimate retention in the Library of Congress.

Forms and other goodies from the Copyright Office.
A wealth of information, including registration forms, can be accessed on-line through the Internet (home page, above left, at http://lcweb.loc.gov/copyright). I particularly recommend Circular 1, Copyright Basics.

Application forms can also be obtained by mail from the Register of Copyrights, Library of Congress, Washington, D.C. 20559. Above center and right is a copy of one copyright application form, Form TX for a literary work. There are similar application forms for works of visual art (VA), performing art (PA), sound recordings (SR), and other works or collections of works. Informative publications and forms can also be ordered twenty-four hours a day by leaving a recorded request on a telephone "hotline" at 202-707-9100.

Beyond his wildest dreams.

There had been copyright legislation since 1790 with the law calling for deposit to the State Department and then to the Interior Department and then to the Patent Office, but few people gave it much attention. What books were deposited (after paying a dollar to the clerk of your nearest district court) were stacked in damp basements all over Washington. [Librarian Ainsworth] Spofford saw the concept as a gold mine. It took him four years of brisk lobbying, amendments, and general legislative exercises but by 1870 he had a law that read: "All records and other things relating to copyrights and required by law to be preserved, shall be under the control of the librarian of Congress." Anyone claiming a copyright on any book, map, chart, dramatic or musical composition, engraving, cut, print, or photograph or negative thereof must send two copies to the Librarian within ten days of its publication. Penalties were spelled out, and the Librarian could demand compliance.

It worked beyond Spofford's wildest dreams. In the next 25 years the Library received 371,636 books, 257,153 magazines, 289,617 pieces of music, 73,817 photographs, 95,249 prints, and 48,048 maps. . . . While the stuff was pouring in, [Spofford] carried on complicated negotiations with the Departments of State and the Interior to recover all the deposits he'd missed back to 1790!

–Charles A. Goodrum

WHO OWNS THE COPYRIGHT?

The Medium Is Not the Message!

As a basic premise, the author of a work—its creator—owns all the rights of copyright. But what if the author of the work gives a copy of it—perhaps the only copy—to someone else? A painter sells a painting, an author sends a letter, a musician gives away a master recording of a song. Who owns the copies, and who owns the copyrights? The law is clear: the recipient owns the physical copy of the work, and the original author retains the exclusive reproduction and other rights. For example, J. D. Salinger may own the right to control the making and distribution of copies of his private letters to Joyce Maynard, but she was clearly given the physical letters themselves, and had the right to sell them to whomever she wished.

To make the distinction clear, different terms are used to describe the metaphysical concept of a copyrightable work, and the more concrete material object in which it is embodied. On the one hand, the listed copyrightable works include "literary," "musical," "dramatic," "pictorial," and "audiovisual" works. These works are embodied in "copies" (such as books) or "phonorecords," the physical objects that exist in the material world. It is technically imprecise to talk about the copyright in a book; the copyright is in the literary work contained in the book.

In order to protect against the inadvertent transfer of copyrights, the Act generally requires that, to legally give away the copyright (as opposed to the physical object), the owner of the copyright must sign a written "instrument of conveyance." This will usually be in the form of a written contract or a will or other formal document. Think of it this way: the Copyright Act creates property rights in creative works, but it's the law of contracts and transfers that will often determine who ends up with the rights. There is also a system for recording in the Copyright Office the transfers of copyrighted works, in order to determine priority among competing interests (in the event two or more parties acquire overlapping rights) and to provide a public record of who owns particular copyrights.

The Giant Corporations

Some critics suggest that it's the giant corporations, not individual authors, that end up owning most of the copyrights. A handful of giant publishing, music, movie, television, and software companies, we're told, buy up all of the major creative works, and use copyright to control the flow of works in their industries and keep the poor, starving artists and creators from sharing in the bounty.

Even if true, this situation doesn't imply that we should abandon the copyright system. The fact of the matter is that copyrighted works are generally expensive to publish, and particularly risky as investments. It's estimated that fewer than one in ten books, records, movies, or other creative works ever make much of a profit. Movies and other high-tech productions cost millions or hundreds of millions of dollars to produce, and require the cooperation of many thousands of individuals. In such an environment, it is only logical that corporations should subsidize the production and distribution of creative works, and end up owning many of the rights of copyright. If there were no copyrights, then the corporations would not be able to protect their investments, and would not be in a position to pay the authors who create the works.

The Work-for-Hire Doctrine

Traditionally, if an employee creates a work within the scope of the employee's job, then any resulting copyrights belong to the employer. So if a *New York Times*

The Library's collection.

But, you ask, doesn't everything that's copyrighted become a part of the Library's collections? Not at all. Each year about five hundred thousand items are deposited for copyright; about three hundred thousand of these will be transferred to the Library and made available to the visiting public. Of these, the first third are trade books, the kind you see in bookstores; the second third are magazines; and the final third are tens of thousands of pieces of sheet music. . . . (In addition to the three thirds, just to keep it from being too neat, there are three or four percentage points of such things as maps, motion picture reels, telephone directories, fashion photographs, computer programs, phonograph records, and phonograph album jackets.)

The remaining two hundred thousand are put into storage and kept indefinitely, simply arranged by registration number.

–Charles A. Goodrum

Contrary to popular belief, the Copyright Office is not required to retain copies of materials not retained by the Library of Congress, and periodically disposes of some materials.

The 1976 Act provides.

Ownership of a copyright . . . is distinct from ownership of any material object in which the work is embodied. Transfer of ownership of any material object, including the copy or phonorecord in which the work is first fixed, does not of itself convey any rights in the copyrighted work embodied in the object; nor, in the absence of an agreement, does transfer of ownership of a copyright . . . convey property rights in any material object.

There's work for hire and there's work for hire.

The statute provides two categories of work for hire. The first is the traditional employee who in fact works for the company. The second covers independent contractors who are not employees of the company. In order for a work by such an independent contractor to be considered a work for hire, two conditions must be met. The contract must specifically provide that the work is considered a work for hire; and the work must be within one of ten specific categories of works. These categories are a contribution to a collective work, a motion picture or other audiovisual work, a translation, a supplementary work, a compilation, an instructional text, a test, answer material for a test, or an atlas; or, in a controversial 1999 amendment that may yet be further amended, a sound recording. Several of these terms are separately defined in the statute.

Third World America.

In the leading Supreme Court case on work for hire, sculptor James Earl Reid was hired by the Community for Creative Non-Violence (CCNV) to produce the sculpture *Third World America.* The contract provided that the work was made for hire, but the Supreme Court held that Reid was an independent contractor, who did not qualify under any of the special categories of work for hire. The Court left open the possibility, however, that CCNV and Reid were joint authors. The parties ultimately settled the issue by agreeing that CCNV owned the sculpture itself, while Reid owned the right to make three-dimensional reproductions. The parties agreed to share the right to make two-dimensional reproductions.

reporter or photographer is paid to cover a story, the story and the photos belong to the *Times*; if a Universal Studios employee works on a movie, the copyright in any resulting movie belongs to Universal.

The doctrine works well enough in the case of true employees, but it has led to some problems in the case of so-called independent contractors. What if the reporter and the photographer don't work for the *Times,* but are freelancers who supply a story or a photograph to the *Times*? What if the contributors to a Universal movie are not employees of Universal, but independent writers or composers or special effects specialists who are paid just for the one project? What if a musician-composer is not an employee of a record company, but independently creates works and sells them to the company?

In 1976, Congress tightened up the definition of works for hire to make it harder for companies to claim the copyright in works under that doctrine. For the most part, the courts seem to be getting the message, and closely scrutinizing "work-for-hire" contracts to assure that they qualify under the statute. My advice to independent contractors who sell copyrights to compa-

AND STILL THERE IS NO
ROOM AT THE INN

nies: have a lawyer review the contract, to make sure you don't give away more rights than you intend.

Government Works

Under the federal statute, U.S. government works do not qualify for copyright protection. This is easy to apply when government employees create works within the scope of their employment (analogous to the work-for-hire doctrine just discussed). Such government works are not copyrightable, but are in the public domain, and may be reproduced by anyone.

The problem gets trickier when a government employee prepares a work outside the normal scope of employment. If a government official prepares a speech expressing the official's own views, then it is possible that the official can claim copyright in the work. Also, if an individual obtains a copyright in a work, the individual may subsequently convey the copyright to the United States, which can then itself enforce the copyright. The trickiest problem is when the United States pays an individual to prepare a work for the government. In that case, it's usually up to the administrative agency to determine whether the individual may hold the copyright, or the individual should convey the copyright to the United States, or the work is unprotected by copyright because it is essentially a U.S. government work.*

The statute does not make clear the status of state government works. However, it's generally considered that state statutes and court opinions, at least, are not protected by copyright, but are free for all to use.

Some official-looking documents may be copyrightable. The American Law Institute and the National Conference of Commissioners on Uniform State Laws, for example, publish the Uniform Commercial Code, for the purpose of encouraging its

William Clark's private notes.

The maps produced by the Lewis and Clark expedition were quite clearly government works, in which no one, including Lewis, had a copyright. Jefferson's formal instructions to Meriwether Lewis were quite clear:

> Your observations are to be taken with great pains & accuracy, to be entered distinctly, & intelligibly for others as well as yourself, to comprehend all the elements necessary, with the aid of the usual tables, to fix the latitude and longitude of the places at which they were taken, & are to be rendered to the war office, for the purpose of having the calculations made concurrently by proper persons within the U.S. Several copies of these, as well as your other notes, should be made at leisure times & put into the care of the most trustworthy of your attendants, to guard by multiplying them, against the accidental losses to which they will be exposed. a further guard would be that one of these copies be written on the paper of the birch, as less liable to injury from damp than common paper.

But what about the private papers of William Clark, discovered in an attic in 1952? These he had prepared on his own during the famous expedition, and he was not subject to the particular instructions made to Lewis. In a fascinating case, it was held that these physical papers were owned by Clark: the claim of title by the U.S. government was set aside. Though not decided in that case, the copyright in the previously unpublished work would presumably belong to Clark's heirs.

*Ansel Adams's governmental work, see p. 160.

States are free to infringe.

The Eleventh Amendment provides that states may not be sued (at least without their consent) in the federal courts. In 1989, the Supreme Court suggested that a specific grant of power to the federal government (such as the copyright power) might trump the state's immunity, at least if the federal statute specifically so provided. In response to this suggestion, Congress in 1990 added a provision specifically making states liable for copyright infringement, on the same terms as applied to other entities. In a series of recent cases, however, the Supreme Court has held that such a provision (or, to be precise, similar provisions in other laws) is beyond the power of Congress. It appears that the federal government cannot enforce copyright laws against states, and that states are thus free to infringe copyrights, patents, trademarks, or a number of other federal rights with impunity.

The implications of this outcome are staggering. I doubt that states are going to start getting into the business of mass-producing commercial movies or books. But if you were in charge of acquiring millions of dollars worth of computer programs to run essential operations for a state, and you knew that you could just take copyrighted works with impunity, what would stop you? I assume that if the copyright industries scream loudly enough, the states will refrain from outrageous behavior. (After all, the copyright industries are major contributors to political campaigns, both in donations and in providing services.) But I also expect that there will be some interesting future developments in the range where reasonable people may disagree.

adoption by the state legislatures. As my colleague, Jim Brook, was surprised to learn when he wrote a series of books on the Uniform Commercial Code, those nongovernmental bodies consider their work copyrighted, and ask a modest fee for publication of excerpts of their version of the work (though it is presumably not copyrighted as specifically enacted in any particular state).

Give Me Back My Copyright!

Read this closely, because it's rather incredible, and you may not believe it the first time around. Authors generally have the right, between thirty-five and forty years after making a grant of copyright, to "terminate" any such license or grant. For example, if I write a book or a play or a song, and sell the copyright to someone else—even if I say that I grant the copyright forever—thirty-five years later, I may terminate the grant. I may then either renegotiate with the original buyer (presumably for a higher price), or I may convey the right to someone else entirely (again, presumably for a higher price). (This provision is quite complicated, but I think you can get the general idea without going into all the technicalities.)

Is there any other form of property that allows you to take back rights decades after you've conveyed them? I don't think so.

In order to understand why Congress created such a special right in copyright, we have to look back to the statute prior to 1976. Under the prior act, copyright existed in two separate "terms"—an initial term of twenty-eight years from the date of first publication, and a renewal term of twenty-eight additional years (if the copyright owner properly filed for renewal*). If an author died before the renewal term, then the renewal term would pass to the author's heirs.

*Renewal terms, see p. 205.

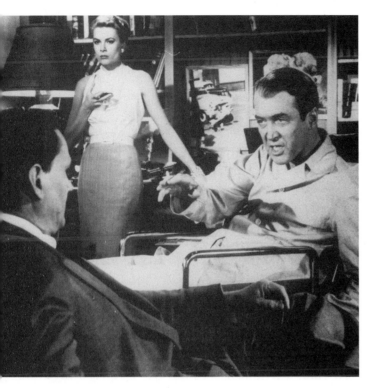

In an incredible series of cases, the courts held that the renewal term did not "exist" until the twenty-eighth year after publication of the work. If an author sold the renewal rights, and died before the twenty-eighth year, then the author's heirs were not bound by the assignment, even if the contract said that they were.

The court interpretations produced some pretty odd results. Suppose an author conveyed away the renewal rights, and lived to the twenty-eighth year; then the assignment of the renewal rights was effective. But if the author died, then the renewal rights could be claimed by the author's heirs, independently of any contract the author may have made. If you were an author who sold your copyrights, and you wanted to leave something of value to your children, you might be better off dead!

Rear Window.

The *Rear Window* case arose under the prior law's tricky renewal provisions. Cornell Woolrich had written a story, "It Had to Be Murder," for *Dime Detective* magazine in 1942. In 1953–54, Alfred Hitchcock obtained the rights to make a movie based upon the story, and produced the now classic *Rear Window* (starring Grace Kelly and Jimmy Stewart). Woolrich died in 1968, just two years before the renewal of his story; the renewal was ultimately obtained by a trust, set up in Woolrich's will, for the benefit of Columbia University.

In the 1980s, MCA, which had acquired the rights to the movie, re-released it in theaters, on television, and on videocassette and videodisc. Sheldon Abend, who acquired rights from the trust, sued various parties, including Jimmy Stewart, who owned a part interest in the production company that initially bought rights in the story.

The Supreme Court, in the case known on appeal as *Stewart v. Abend,* held that MCA could not continue to distribute the movie without the agreement of Abend, who now controlled the renewal rights in the story. As a result of this case, *Rear Window* and hundreds of other movies were held off the market for years, and were absent from television screens, because the motion picture producers were unable to come to terms with the owners of the renewals in the underlying stories.

In setting up the new termination rights under the 1976 statute, Congress was concerned that works, such as movies, that required the investment of millions of dollars should not be held up in this fashion. So they built into the termination rights an important exception that hadn't existed for the old renewal scheme: a copyright owner who has granted someone else the right to make a derivative work (including, most importantly, a movie adaptation of a book or story) cannot terminate the right to continue distributing that version of the derivative work (movie) on the terms originally negotiated. That way, the copyright owners will not be able to "hold up" the continued distribution of movies based upon their stories, for which they have been paid. Copyright owners who have terminated rights can, however, renegotiate the rights to make a *new* version of the underlying work.

Justification for termination provisions.

As is usually the case when Congress is inspired by prior laws, it nevertheless gave specific policy reasons why it should continue to grant termination rights to copyright owners. The House Report explained that "A provision of this sort is needed because of the unequal bargaining position of authors, resulting in part from the impossibility of determining a work's value until it has been exploited." However, I doubt that Congress would have come up with such a provision had it not worked its way gradually into the interstices of the law.

A Moon for the Misbegotten.

The complicated renewal rules that protected heirs did not always work out the way authors might have wanted. For example, Eugene O'Neill disapproved of the marriage of his daughter, Oona (then eighteen), to Charlie Chaplin (then fifty-four), and subsequently (though not necessarily for that reason) disinherited her. Yet Oona Chaplin was able to establish her rights to works that came up for renewal after her father's death, including *A Moon for the Misbegotten,* which at the time (1973) was having a successful Broadway revival. A similar result can be expected under the new termination rights of the 1976 Act.

Hearing of the success of Ms. Chaplin, two estranged children of William Saroyan were able to assert their rights to his works that came up for renewal after his death. Although Saroyan in his will left "all copyrights" in his play *The Cave Dwellers* (1958) to the William Saroyan Foundation, a court held that the children, not the foundation, held the renewal rights directly under the statute. Such a result will not occur under the new termination provision of the 1976 Act, because that provision specifically allows termination only of transfers "otherwise than by will."

I'm not at all convinced that Congress really intended this result when it first adopted the two-term copyright system. But Congress basically allowed the interpretation to stand, by not changing the language of the statute even after the definitive court interpretations.

Congress finally eliminated the two separate terms of copyright when it passed the 1976 Act. But Congress liked some of the features of the two-term system, particularly the "second bite of the apple" enjoyed by some copyright owners or their heirs. Indeed, Congress liked it so much that it passed the termination provisions, and made sure that they were available not only to heirs but also to copyright owners who were lucky enough to live thirty-five years after conveying rights in their works.

The upshot of all this is that most purchasers of rights in copyrighted works are only sure to get the exclusive right for the first thirty-five years. Thereafter, the rights are terminable by the copyright owner. Does this dampen the prices that purchasers are willing to pay for copyrighted works? Not by much. As Mark Twain observed, only "a bathtub-full of works"* are of any real value decades after they are created. The vast majority of copyrights will not be terminated precisely because they're not of much value anyway.

Remember our discussion of works for hire.† What is the difference between an author's creating a work, on the one hand, as a work for hire; and, on the other hand, as an independent contractor, and then simply conveying the copyright in the work to the "employer"? For the most part, there is no difference, since the "employer" in either case will own the copyright. But it makes a big difference thirty-five years later! If the work is a work for hire, then the "employer" is the copyright owner, and a specific exception provides that there is no termination right. But if the work is by an independent contractor, subsequently

*Mark Twain's bathtub, see p. 206.
†Works for hire, see p. 213.

conveyed to the "employer," then the grant of copyright may be terminated thirty-five years later. Now maybe you can understand why companies try so hard to treat their copyrights as works for hire.

OTHER THEORIES FOR PROTECTING CREATIVE WORKS

There are dozens of other federal and state rights that overlap copyright in one way or another. It would take another book to catalogue all of them completely; but I will at least briefly review some of the related rights that lawyers and lawmakers have come up with over the years.

Patents

We've already seen a brief description of patents,* which have been covered by federal statute since 1790, the same year as the first federal copyright statute. Patents generally protect new and useful inventions and improvements of inventions, including mechanical, chemical, biological, and electronic works and processes. While copyright is granted almost as a matter of course if an author has created the work without copying it from someone else, a patent applicant has the high burden of convincing a patent examiner that the invention is new, useful, and nonobvious. The patent is much more powerful while it lasts, because it protects against even the independent creation of similar works and processes. On the other hand, while a copyright is generally good for the life of the author plus seventy years, a patent is only good for twenty years from the date of the patent application.

A special category of patent is the *design patent*,† which is good for fourteen years from the date it is granted. It protects the design of functional works, but has to meet the high standard of novelty and nonobviousness.

Other termination rights.

Congress added other termination rights to the copyright law as well. In 1976, when it extended existing copyrights from 56 years from publication to 75 years from publication, it granted the owners of copyright a special privilege to "capture back" the benefit of the added 19 years, instead of giving the gift to the licensees. When Congress in 1998 again extended existing copyrights to a total of 95 years, it granted the same "capture back" privilege to copyright owners for the extra 20 years.

Trademark notice.

The most effective trademark notice is the symbol that indicates that the trademark has been registered for federal trademark. This notice consists of an R in a circle—®—or the words "Registered U.S. Patent and Trademark Office," or "Reg. U.S. Pat. & Tm. Off." Interestingly, the symbols ™ (for trademark) or ˢᴹ (for service mark) are only "informal" notice of a state trademark claim, with a possible intention to register a federal trademark in the future.

*Patents, see p. 128.
†Design patent, see p. 185.

A Night in Casablanca.

In 1942, Warner Bros. produced *Casablanca,* starring Humphrey Bogart and Ingrid Bergman. Several years later, their lawyers notified the Marx Brothers that they objected to the name of their upcoming film, *A Night in Casablanca.* Here aresome excerpts from Groucho Marx's famous response:

> Apparently there is more than one way of conquering a city and holding it as your own. For example, up to the time that we contemplated making this picture, I had no idea that the city of Casablanca belonged exclusively to Warner Brothers. However, it was only a few days after our announcement appeared that we received your long, ominous legal document warning us not to use the name Casablanca. . . .
>
> I just don't understand your attitude. Even if you plan on re-releasing your picture, I am sure that the average movie fan could learn in time to distinguish between Ingrid Bergman and Harpo. I don't know whether I could, but I certainly would like to try.
>
> You claim you own Casablanca and that no one else can use that name without your permission. What about "Warner Brothers"? Do you own that, too? You probably have the right to use the name Warner, but what about Brothers? Professionally, we were brothers long before you were. We were touring the sticks as The Marx Brothers when Vitaphone was still a gleam in the inventor's eye. . . .

There were further exchanges, as described by Andrew Carroll:

> Unamused, Warner Bros. requested that the Marx Brothers at least outline the premise of their film. Groucho responded with an utterly ridiculous storyline, and, sure enough, received another stern letter requesting clarification. He obliged and went on to describe a plot more preposterous than the first, claiming that he, Groucho, would be playing "Bordello, the sweetheart of Humphrey Bogart." No doubt exasperated, Warner Bros. did not respond. *A Night in Casablanca* was released in 1946.

Trademarks

What are trademarks? They are names, phrases, designs, or marks that identify the source of products. Once a manufacturer has registered a trademark, or begun using it in commerce, then other manufacturers are not allowed to use the mark in such a way as to confuse the public about the source of the product. For example, once the Coca-Cola Company registered the names "Coca-Cola" and "Coke" as trademarks for their brand of beverage, no one else could sell similar products using those names.

The federal trademark law effectively dates only from 1946. The primary function of the federal law

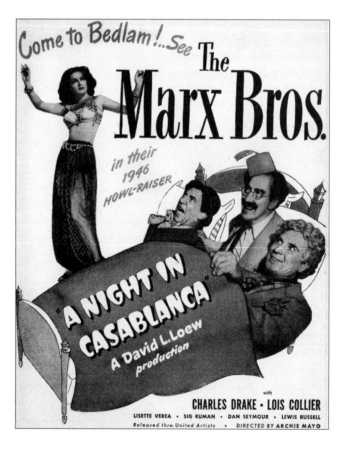

is to provide a federal registry for trademarks, and a federal forum for enforcing trademarks. Otherwise, the federal law works as a supplement to state law, which still governs many of the substantive rights of trademarks.

While copyrights require originality, trademarks need not be original, but can be words or symbols adopted by a company to identify its products. Thus, Microsoft Corporation did not create the word or concept of "Windows," but once the company adopted the word and used it to describe their particular operating system, and the public came to associate the word with Microsoft's product, then others could not use the term to describe their products in a way that would make customers think that they came from Microsoft.

There are many special rules for determining the scope of trademarks. Trademarks are generally not granted for words that merely describe a product. Nabisco, Inc., was not able to get a trademark in the term "Shredded Wheat," because that phrase simply described wheat that was shredded, and it was thought that (once the patent on the process expired) other manufacturers of similar products should be able to describe their wheat as shredded. A related doctrine is that if a word, once distinctive, comes to be used as a generic term to describe a whole category of products, then a trademark owner may lose the trademark. Some famous trademarks that have been lost through "genericide" are aspirin, trampoline, cellophane, and thermos. That's why companies that own trademarks in danger of turning generic will go to great lengths to remind the public that, for example, "Sanka" is the trademark of a particular brand of decaffeinated coffee, and "Xerox" is the trademark of a particular brand of photocopying and document processing equipment.

Patents, copyrights, and trademarks are the three federal forms of protection frequently lumped together under the rubric "intellectual property." They are each distinct, and governed by their own statutes,

Don't ask Pat Riley!

Words and short phrases are generally not copyrightable. But a few years ago, whenever I would explain this aspect of copyright, students would argue with me that they knew this wasn't true. They had read that Pat Riley had copyrighted the word "three-peat" to describe the act of getting a national basketball championship for a third consecutive year, and that he was suing to prevent anyone else from using the word.

For several weeks, I simply said that that was wrong. But then I did some research on sports columns across the country, and discovered many references to Pat Riley's allegedly copyrighting the word "three-peat." Knowing that a word couldn't be copyrighted, and following a hunch, I looked up the trademark registrations, and discovered what was going on. Riley had registered the word as a trademark, to be used in conjunction with the sale of sports-related products such as T-shirts and jerseys. Under trademark law, Riley is allowed to control the use of the word to identify the source of such specific products, but he is certainly not allowed to prevent other people from using the word generally, even if he did "invent" it.

If you want to know about basketball, don't ask me, I don't know a thing. But if you want to know about copyright, don't ask Pat Riley or sports reporters!

The Cadillac of trademarks.

Under traditional trademark law, marks were protected only if they were used on competitive products. For example, Cadillac dog food did not infringe on Cadillac automobiles, because the products were sufficiently dissimilar that customers would not be likely to confuse one company as the source of the other's product. However, this strict approach has been changing in recent years. Many states adopted "anti-dilution" laws to protect against the erosion of so-called strong marks. In 1995, the federal statute was amended to provide for the first time that strong marks would be entitled to federal protection against such dilution.

Although decided before that amendment, exemplary of the expanding trend is a suit by McDonald's Corp., in which they were able to block Quality Inns' development of a line of hotels under the name "McSleep." McDonald's was able to demonstrate that the "Mc" prefix—hardly their novel creation—had become so associated with products of their company that consumers believed that McSleep must have some association with McDonald's, even though McDonald's was not in the hotel business. The court granted a permanent injunction against the use of the "Mc" prefix by Quality Inns.

though it is sometimes useful to think of intellectual property rights generally in the context of licensing such rights from one company or person to another.

Antitrust Law

Antitrust is the law against monopolies. Primarily covered by federal statute, it prohibits a range of predatory business activities, providing remedies for the government and for individuals and companies that have been injured. Since a copyright (or patent or trademark) is, in a sense, a legal monopoly, it's not unusual that copyright and antitrust issues are raised in the same cases. If a monopoly results from a valid copyright, then the copyright may be a defense to an antitrust claim; conversely, a defense to a copyright claim may include the allegation that the copyright owner has exceeded the boundaries of copyright, and has illegally used the copyright to gain a foothold in other markets. For example, a major issue in the Microsoft antitrust case is whether its monopoly position is the natural consequence of its valid patents, copyrights, and trademarks, or results from predatory business behavior that goes beyond the scope of its intellectual property. Since antitrust law is extremely complicated, I won't attempt a fuller explanation here.

STATE THEORIES OF PROTECTION

The rest of the legal areas we'll look at are state laws, and therefore may vary considerably from state to state.

Common Law Copyright

States may have a very narrow range of law generally described under the term *common law copyright*. At one time, this included all unpublished works. Since 1978, however, even unpublished works are picked up under the federal statute, so long as they are "fixed"*—written or record-

*Fixation, see p. 127.

Women and Cafés.
On the left is a painting in a popular series, *Women and Cafés,* by Itzchak Tarkay. Below it is a painting by Patricia Govezensky that captures some of the same elements as the Tarkay. In a remarkable lawsuit, a federal court found that the Govezensky paintings infringed the "trade dress" of the Tarkay, even though the works may not have been substantially similar enough to find a copyright infringement. The remedy was a preliminary injunction against the further sale of the Govezensky works. Reasonable people can, and have, disagreed about the appropriateness of using this legal approach to find an infringement in this case.

ed. Since 1994, live musical performances are also covered by the federal Act.* What this leaves for the states are unrecorded live conversations and other live nonmusical performances. There are only a handful of relevant cases.

Unfair Competition

There's a broad range of state law described generally under the term *unfair competition*. The essence of unfair competition is fraud, misleading the public; but it frequently includes unfair injury to competitors. This generally involves what is known as "passing off" a

Coca-Cola's secret formula.

Coca-Cola decided that it didn't want to patent its formula for beverages, which would have required disclosing how the beverage was made and losing the rights to the public domain after only a couple of decades. Instead, Coke chose to keep the formula a secret, so that it could be protected indefinitely. If any employee violates the nondisclosure agreement, Coke may seek remedy in a court of law. However, if rivals can do a chemical analysis of Coke, and replicate it without violating any patents, then they are free to do so (so long as they don't use the trademark "Coke" or "Coca-Cola" to describe their product).

 *Live performances, see p. 170.

The Lanham Act.

Section 43(a) of the Lanham Act provides that

Any person [which includes a corporation]
who . . . uses in commerce any word,
term, name, symbol, or device or any combination thereof, or any false designation
of origin, false or misleading description
of fact, or false or misleading representation of fact, which—

(A) is likely to cause confusion, or to
cause mistake, or to deceive as to the
affiliation, connection, or association of
such person with another person, or as to
the origin, sponsorship, or approval of his
or her goods, services, or commercial
activities by another person, or

(B) in commercial advertising or promotion, misrepresents the nature, charac-
teristics, qualities, or geographic origin of
his or her or another person's goods, services, or commercial activities,

shall be liable in a civil action by any person who believes that he or she is or is
likely to be damaged by such act.

company's products as those of another, but it applies in such a variety of settings that it is difficult to summarize easily. Historically, trademark is an offshoot of unfair competition, in which the fraud is based upon the taking of specific words or symbols. But under unfair competition, the fraud may be found in the imitation of design or appearance or trade dress that falls short of trademark status, in the use of a title that is not otherwise subject to copyright protection or registered as a trademark, or in the making of other false claims.

The federal trademark law, the Lanham Act, also contains a general provision on unfair competition. When first passed in 1946, that section was rarely used; but in recent years, the courts have expanded the section greatly, so that some of the law of unfair competition is now being brought within the scope of the federal statute. Many critics believe that the trend has gone too far; the exact parameters of unfair competition are still being worked out by the courts.

Trade Secrets

Trade secret law may be thought of as the state analog to federal patent law, with one important distinction: state trade secret law depends on keeping the information secret, while federal patent law requires its disclosure.

Trade secret law allows entities who have business or technological secrets to make contracts with their employees and business relations to protect those secrets. The law does not protect against "reverse-engineering" of the product, however, to figure out how it's made and to duplicate it if it's not protected by patent. Companies must strategically decide whether it's better to go the trade secret route, or obtain a patent. The decision may depend upon whether the nature of the technology, in normal use, would be revealed to others.

Obviously, one of the purposes of patent law is to encourage the disclosure of technology to the public, by allowing companies to exploit their technologies without having to keep them secret. Under the copyright law prior to 1978, it might also have been said that one of the purposes of copyright law was to encourage disclosure, since federal copyright was generally only granted upon publication of a work. However, since 1978 the federal law protects unpublished as well as published works, so that disclosure to the public is no longer a prerequisite for federal copyright protection.

Contracts

Contract is the general body of law, mainly state law, that allows companies and individuals to make mutually binding agreements that they can enforce in a court of law. Parties set up contracts to govern all sorts of business practices, including those dealing with the transfer of intellectual property. If I write a book, my rights are initially governed by copyright; but I can make a contract with a publisher, and set up in the agreement the terms by which they will be allowed to publish my work and I will get paid for it. Contracts are essentially a way of making "private law" between parties who are willing to work together or pay to obtain the right to use otherwise protected information.

Most contracts are explicit, but there are also rules that recognize contracts as "implied in fact" or "implied in law." For example, many story "ideas"* are not protectable under copyright because they are too general to constitute copyrightable expression. Nevertheless, if you're a successful screenwriter, Hollywood might still pay you handsomely to develop a general movie concept or television pilot. The rights of the parties are then determined not by copyright law, but by contract law. If you don't have an established track record, however, most movie or television producers won't even listen to your suggested plots for *Saturday Night Live* or *Star Trek*, unless you sign a waiver making clear that you are giving them the concept for free, and without the expectation of payment. Most studios hire their own writers, and don't want to

Monty Python's Flying Circus.

Here's an example of how lawyers were able to use the Lanham Act in a new setting. In the 1970s, Monty Python had a contract to produce its comedy series, *Monty Python's Flying Circus,* for BBC Television. The contract was carefully written to assure that the work, once written, accepted, and recorded by the BBC, would not be altered. The BBC licensed Time-Life, which licensed ABC to show six programs on American television. The problem was that ABC made substantial cuts from the original; in twice showing three 30-minute episodes, they cut approximately 24 out of 90 minutes for insertion of commercials. ABC claimed that some of the cuts were necessary to adapt the programs for American sensibilities. The problem was that the cuts undermined the continuity of the programs.

The federal courts found that the omissions were a violation of the contract between Monty Python and the BBC, which could not license Time-Life or ABC to do anything that it was not allowed to do under the contract. In addition, the court said, the presentation of the Monty Python program in an altered state constituted a violation of the Lanham Act. The reasoning was that the final programs were attributed to Monty Python, but that the alterations made the products no longer the work of Monty Python. The alteration essentially resulted in a false description of the work.

*Ideas vs. expression, see p. 188.

Publicity rights.
Successful claimants under the new publicity right were Hugo Zacchini, for his cannonball act (left); the estate of Elvis Presley, for posters and other memorabilia (an infringing poster is shown, center); and the Beatles, for the use of their personae in the musical stage show and film *Beatlemania* (program cover, right).

Coming to America.

Only a handful of people win lawsuits based upon the submission of ideas for works. Art Buchwald won a lawsuit against Paramount Pictures for the concept of *Coming to America* (1988). The court held that there was no copyright in the general idea for the movie, but that Buchwald was entitled to be paid under a specific contract he had with the studio to submit movie treatments. The case is an instructive one for revealing the vagaries of "Hollywood accounting." Paramount had claimed that, while the movie grossed over $300 million at the box office, it had not produced a net profit. Since Buchwald's contract was only for a percentage of the net profits, Paramount claimed Buchwald was entitled to nothing. The court ultimately held the contract formula unconscionable. Buchwald got a judgment for $900,000; Paramount appealed, but then ultimately settled for over $1 million, either because it was unsure of its legal position or because it didn't want its accounting methods too closely scrutinized.

accept any suggestions under circumstances that might imply that they're under a duty to pay for them.

Defamation, Right of Privacy, and Right of Publicity

The common law recognizes the right of individuals to prevent others from injuring their reputation by telling lies about them. These rights are recognized by the law of defamation. In a fascinating expansion of these principles in the early twentieth century, the courts of many states came to recognize the right of individuals to protect their privacy against unwarranted public disclosure.

In the last few decades, the law has again been expanded in many states to recognize a related right of "publicity." The doctrine was literally catapulted onto the scene when the Supreme Court in 1977 recognized the right of Hugo Zacchini, the "human cannonball," to prevent a local television station from televising his act without his consent. Shortly thereafter, a large number of states adopted such a right, either by legislation or by action of the courts.

Federal Preemption of State Laws

A paramount issue for all of the above as well as other state theories of protection is the extent to which the states may legislate in this area at all. To understand the problem, we have to go back to 1964. In that year, two cases worked their way up from the Illinois state courts to the Supreme Court of the United States. They both involved lighting fixtures—in one case, Stiffel Company's design of a "pole lamp" popular in the 1950s and 1960s, and in the other case Day-Brite Lighting Company's design of a "cross-ribbed reflector" for a fluorescent fixture. The Illinois courts had held that these lamp designs were not protected under either the federal patent or copyright laws, but they nevertheless extended a more limited form of state protection to these works. However, the Supreme Court held that the states could not do this, because the subject matter of patent or copyrightlike protection was "preempted" by Congress's power to protect—or choose not to protect—such works. The Illinois law was struck down; Sears, Roebuck & Co. was allowed to make a knockoff of the Stiffel lamp, and Compco Corp. a knockoff of the Day-Brite lamp.

It's still debatable to what extent the federal laws supersede state laws in this area. In a major retreat from the so-called *Sears-Compco* doctrine,

"Do You Want to Dance?"

In 1985, Ford Motor Co. ran a series of television commercials identified as "The Yuppie Campaign." The nineteen commercials used songs from the 1960s to remind "yuppies" of their college days. For some of the songs, Young & Rubicam, the advertising agency, got the original performers to sing; for others, the agency hired "sound-alikes" who would sing the songs in the style of the original performers.

When the agency asked Bette Midler (left) to sing her version of "Do You Want to Dance?" she declined. Instead, the agency hired Ula Hedwig (third from left) to imitate Bette Midler's voice. Hedwig, one of the "Harlettes" who worked with Midler in several of her stage productions, was instructed to "sound as much as possible like the Bette Midler record."

Young & Rubicam apparently believed that they could use sound-alikes, since there were some cases at the time suggesting that performers had no rights in the songs or other materials they performed. Nancy Sinatra, for example, had lost in a lawsuit against Goodyear Tire & Rubber Company for a commercial imitating her voice singing "These Boots Are Made for Walkin'," and Shirley Booth had lost in a lawsuit to protect against someone imitating her voice as the television character Hazel. By the time Midler brought her suit, however, the courts were more sympathetic to such claims. The court held that "when a distinctive voice of a professional singer is widely known and is deliberately imitated in order to sell a product, the sellers have appropriated what is not theirs." Bette Midler won the suit under state law.

Have Claim, Will Sue.

During the period when the *Sears-Compco* preemption doctrine was interpreted most broadly, several plaintiffs lost out on what might otherwise have been meritorious actions under state law. Perhaps the plaintiff most whipsawed by the changing law was Victor DeCosta (top, right), a mechanic from Cranston, Rhode Island. DeCosta invented the character Paladin, fitted with black cowboy suit, mustache, derringer, and a card with a chess symbol proclaiming "Have Gun Will Travel, Wire Paladin, N. Court St., Cranston, R.I." CBS took the character for its television series *Paladin* (starring Richard Boone, bottom right). Over a period of twenty years, DeCosta won three lawsuits for substantial sums against CBS, only to see the verdicts overturned each time on appeal to the federal circuit court.

The first time, in 1967, the court held that his state-based claim was preempted by federal law under the *Sears-Compco* doctrine. The second time, in 1975, the court held that he didn't qualify under the state theories of trademark or unfair competition, because his appearances at local functions were not for profit, and the viewing public was not ultimately confused by CBS's taking of the Paladin character. Although the court conceded that in the earlier case they "were, in our interpretation of the preemptive reach of the Copyright Clause, overinclusive," they refused to overrule that part of the case on the ground that it had already been decided, and was thus binding on the parties. The same reasoning led the court in 1992 to reverse the third verdict in DeCosta's favor.

DeCosta, who died a few years ago, was buried in his Paladin suit.

the Supreme Court in 1973 held that states could pass statutes that created rights in sound recordings prior to the 1971 federal protection of sound recordings. The Court held that states were free to enter the field of protection where Congress "had not acted" (or, in this case, prior to the time Congress acted to protect sound recordings).

The 1976 statute purported to make the matter clearer, but may only have succeeded in making it more complicated. Under the Copyright Act, states are not preempted from passing statutes that protect "subject matter that does not come within the subject matter of copyright" or "activities violating legal or equitable rights that are not equivalent to any of the exclusive rights within the general scope of copyright." Needless to say, given these abstract concepts, the proper adjustment between federal and state theories of protection can be complicated in particular cases.

CONCLUSION

Even in the miscellaneous copyright principles reviewed in this chapter, the major theme of copyright at the end of the twentieth century is evident: copyright is an expanding doctrine. It has been expanded in terms of duration. It has been expanded by eliminating the formalities that sometimes resulted in the loss of copyright. The rights of original authors have been expanded by the creation of termination rights in their favor, and by rules of conveyance that limit the work-for-hire doctrine that might otherwise deprive them of rights. And the peripheral principles surrounding copyright, for better or for worse, have been expanded by courts' willingness to explore new rights, and by a preemption doctrine that has at least in recent years allowed such a development of state laws.

CHAPTER TEN

International Copyright Relations

From outlaw to champion.

Barbara Ringer, then assistant register of copyrights, later register of copyrights, described the American role in international copyright in 1968:

> Until the Second World War the United States had little reason to take pride in its international copyright relations; in fact, it had a great deal to be ashamed of. With few exceptions its role in international copyright was marked by intellectual shortsightedness, political isolationism, and narrow economic self-interest. . . .
>
> After a century as a virtual outlaw, a half century as an outsider, and 15 years as a stranger at the feast, the United States suddenly finds itself cast as a leading champion of literary property. . . . In view of our dubious past performance we are hardly in a position to adopt a tone of moral indignation . . .

1790–1891: COPYRIGHT OUTLAWS

The role of the United States in the international copyright community has gone from that of outlaws to outsiders to "strangers at the feast" to leading members of the club. When we finally decided, in recent years, to fully join in the feast, we pushed ourselves to the front of the line with all the moral bravado of newcomers. All in all, it's a pretty embarrassing history. What has happened in the intervening two centuries, however, is that we have gone from a position in which the domestic concerns limited our international vision to one in which the international agenda has driven most recent domestic copyright reforms.

The first copyright act of 1790* specifically protected only American authors. It provided protection to "the author and authors . . . being a citizen or citizens of these United States, or resident therein." And the treatment was not inadvertent; the statute specifically went on to clarify the limitation:

nothing in this act shall be construed to extend to prohibit the importation or vending, reprinting or publishing within the United States, of any map, chart, book or books, written, printed, or published by any person not a citizen of the United States, in foreign parts or places without the jurisdiction of the United States. . . .

*Copyright act of 1790, see p. 14.

To be sure, the copyright law of many other countries at that time was not any more protective of the rights of foreign authors. For example, England didn't generally grant copyrights to American authors, either. But which way do you suppose the traffic of creative works was flowing in 1790? While any American library would consist primarily of English-language works created abroad, there were very few American authors who were accorded serious attention in England.

Of course, that situation began to change during the nineteenth century. Among others, Washington Irving, James Fenimore Cooper, Ralph Waldo Emerson, Nathaniel Hawthorne, Henry Wadsworth Longfellow, Edgar Allan Poe, Harriet Beecher Stowe, Henry David Thoreau, Herman Melville, and Walt Whitman began to carve out a distinctly American literature, of which even the British took note.

In 1837, several prominent British authors submitted to Congress an address and petition for passage of a copyright amendment to protect foreign authors in the United States. The petition made several major points. The British authors were "exposed to injury in their reputation and property," both monetarily and because their reputations suffered when "mutilated and altered" versions of their works were published with impunity. The British authors were particularly hurt because, "from the circumstance of the English language being common to both nations, the works of British authors are extensively read throughout the United States." The petition also appealed to the national interests of American authors. Without effective protection, foreign works were published extremely cheaply in the United States; but it then became difficult for American authors to compete against the unauthorized and uncompensated cheap imports.

The address of the British authors, presented to the Senate by Henry Clay, was unsuccessful in getting the

In few nations have artists been more rare.

The early output of American literature, art, and science was so meager that de Tocqueville thought it necessary to explain that "The Example of the Americans Does Not Prove That a Democratic People Can Have No Aptitude and No Taste for Science, Literature, or Art." In making his argument, he conceded that

> It must be acknowledged that in few of the civilized nations of our time have the higher sciences made less progress than in the United States; and in few have great artists, distinguished poets, or celebrated writers, been more rare. Many Europeans, struck by this fact, have looked upon it as a natural and inevitable result of equality; and they have thought that, if a democratic state of society and democratic institutions were ever to prevail over the whole earth, the human mind would gradually find its beacon-lights grow dim, and men would relapse into a period of darkness.

Robert Spiller confirms de Tocqueville's assessment, referring to the 1790s as a "false literary dawn" in America, and the following years as the literary "dark ages."

Walter Scott.

While the address of the British authors claimed that Walter Scott "received no remuneration from the American public," recent research indicates that he was paid for the advance sheets of some of his novels. As concluded by James Barnes, "Although Scott's income from the sale of advance sheets was modest, it is certainly inaccurate to say, as the *Knickerbocker* did in 1835, that Walter Scott never received a cent on the sale of his works in America."

I thrust it down their throats.
In 1842, Charles Dickens visited the United States, and sat for this photograph by Mathew Brady. Of his trip, he made the following report:

I spoke, as you know, of international copyright, at Boston; and I spoke of it again at Hartford. My friends were paralysed with wonder at such audacious daring. The notion that I, a man alone by himself, in America, should venture to suggest to the Americans that there was one point on which they were neither just to their own countrymen nor to us, actually struck the boldest dumb! It is nothing that of all men living I am the greatest loser by it. It is nothing that I have to claim to speak and be heard. The wonder is that a breathing man can be found with temerity enough to suggest to the Americans the possibility of their having done wrong. I wish you could have seen the faces that I saw, down both sides of the table at Hartford, when I began to talk about Scott. I wish you could have heard how I gave it out. My blood so boiled as I thought of the monstrous injustice that I felt as if I were twelve feet high when I thrust it down their throats.

United States to change its law. The following year, England passed the International Copyright Acts, and so began the road to recognizing the copyrights of foreign authors. But since the English law was made conditional upon reciprocity in other countries, American authors continued to be denied their rights under British law just as the British were denied rights under the U.S. law.

Notwithstanding the pleas, the American law, protecting only American authors, was renewed several times from 1831 through the 1880s, almost without change in this respect. It was apparently possible under the existing laws for particularly resourceful Americans to obtain protection in England by simultaneous publication there, or for resourceful British citizens to obtain protection in the United States by simultaneous publication here, but protection apparently required that the author travel to the other country and reside there at the time of publication. Or an author might be able to convey the publication rights to a citizen of the other country before publication; but that rarely led to a very reasonable payment. Samuel Clemens claimed that he was able to navigate the technicalities of the British law, but most authors were not as fortunate.

Particularly hard hit were W. S. Gilbert and Arthur Sullivan, whose delightful operettas were performed throughout the United States in the last decades of the nineteenth century. Having gotten burned on their productions of *H.M.S. Pinafore* and *The Pirates of Penzance,* they tried various schemes to try to beat the American system. For *Iolanthe,* they published the libretto and basic piano accompaniment, but withheld publication of the full Sullivan score, on the assumption that it would be better protected as an unpublished work. They then assigned the American performance rights to D'Oyly Carte, whose company specialized in the production of Gilbert and Sullivan operettas, and arranged for a simultaneous opening of the work in

London and at the Standard Theater in New York. Notwithstanding their efforts, an American producer hired John Philip Sousa, leader of the Marine Band in Washington, to arrange his own orchestral accompaniment to *Iolanthe*. When Carte tried to stop the competing American performances, the circuit court in Maryland, in the *Iolanthe* case, found that the work, having been effectively published in England, was not protected under existing American copyright law. Commenting upon the unique orchestration, the court observed that, "as enjoyed by the vast majority of these [thousands of] persons, the musical niceties of the orchestration are quite subordinate to the wit of the libretto and the airs and harmonies of the voice parts,— the orchestration being indeed a subordinate accessory." (Had the judge never seen and heard an authentic Gilbert and Sullivan performance?)

For *The Mikado,* Gilbert and Sullivan not only withheld publication of the Sullivan orchestration, but they hired George Lowell Tracy, a Boston composer, to come to England and create a piano accompaniment; they then assigned the American performance rights to Tracy. To thwart the "*Mikado*-mania" in anticipation of their new production, Gilbert and Sullivan kept everything about their new production a secret; Carte and his company sailed to the United States under assumed names.

Needless to say, a competing *Mikado* performance was organized, and Carte, in charge of the authorized performance, sued to stop it. In 1885, the circuit court in New York called Gilbert and Sullivan's plan "an ingenious one." However, the court found that the American copyright in the libretto had been lost upon publication in England, and that the piano accompaniment, rewritten by the defendant, was not an infringement of the original score. Responding to the case, Sullivan wrote that "every miserable thieving penniless scoundrel in the States" could produce *The Mikado* to his own orchestration, and

The explosion of all Yankee-Doodle-dum.
Daniel J. Boorstin describes how Dickens set out to get even:

Instead of making *Chuzzlewit* a weekly serial, Dickens found another way to heighten interests. He would have Chuzzlewit "go to America." . . . In the United States he had been lionized by readers, and formed warm personal friendships with Longfellow and others, but he was vilified by the press. Slavery in America, which Dickens loudly opposed, they said was none of his business. His plea for an American copyright law to protect authors from pirating they called purely mercenary, a motive that Americans found suspect in foreigners. In 1843, he believed, British readers would eagerly buy anything that Dickens had to say about America, especially if it was unfavorable. His American mail continued to bring scurrilous letters and contemptuous articles. . . . He would use the next numbers of *Chuzzlewit*, still unwritten, to embroider the most offensive points of his *American Notes* and get even with his American assailants. . . . The predictable American reaction was explosive. "Martin has made them all stark raving mad across the water," Dickens reported to Forster with glee. Carlyle also seemed pleased to note that "All Yankee-Doodle-dum" had exploded "like one universal soda bottle."

Less inclined to read the novels of Cooper or Hawthorne.

Max Kempelman has made the same point as the British authors in their 1837 address:

> This practice hurt American authors too for their works had to meet the unfair competition of British books which were cheaper because they were not paid for. American readers were less inclined to read the novels of Cooper or Hawthorne for a dollar when they could buy a novel of Scott or Dickens for a quarter. The same American writers also . . . were similarly not protected in England. Longfellow asserted a few years before his death that he had twenty-two publishers in England and Scotland, but that "only four of them took the slightest notice of my existence, even so far as to send me a copy of the book." Harriet Beecher Stowe too is reported to have received no return whatever for her *Uncle Tom's Cabin,* even though it sold more than 1/2 million copies in Great Britain during its first year alone.
>
> American men of letters were, therefore, apart from any other considerations, unable to rely on literature for a livelihood. Longfellow and Lowell were college professors; Hawthorne was in the government service; Emerson engaged in lecturing. And American readers were weaned on a literature not their own.

Stowe apparently learned her lesson. William Charvat reported that "[S]hrewd writers like Mrs. Stowe [eventually] made better bargains with English publishers than Irving, Cooper, Prescott, and Melville in earlier days."

"there is a chorus of fiendish exultant glee in all the newspapers at our defeat."

To be fair, Gilbert and Sullivan's copyright problems were not limited to the United States. Even in their home country, they were thwarted by a copyright law that, like earlier American copyright laws, failed to adequately protect either performance or adaptation rights. Gilbert even helped to organize a new Association to Protect the Rights of Authors at home and abroad.

In 1878, authors and artists, publishers, academics, and other interested parties, led by Victor Hugo, formed the Association Littéraire et Artistique Internationale, to sponsor conferences and begin drafting proposed international copyright treaties. That effort culminated in 1886 in the Berne Union for the Protection of Literary and Artistic Works, an international treaty that provided for so-called national treatment. Each participating country committed to amend its own copyright law to treat foreign authors from other Berne countries just as favorably as their own. England signed the treaty, as did most western European and many other countries. The United States sent a representative to the proceedings, but did not sign the treaty, claiming that it would be premature to commit to international standards before Congress had determined the appropriate American role in protecting foreign works.

1891–1955:
COPYRIGHT OUTSIDERS

In 1891, 101 years after first adopting federal copyright, the United States finally gave in to the international and domestic pressure, and passed an amendment granting copyright protection to foreign authors. As we shall see, however, such protection proved to be to some extent illusory.

When Gilbert and Sullivan attacked the "Pirates"

When Gilbert and Sullivan attacked the "Pirates."
This 1944 ad by Magnavox was part of a series commemorating the lives of immortal composers. Part of the ad describes Gilbert and Sullivan's difficulties with copyright.

The entire English-speaking world surrendered to *H.M.S. Pinafore*. In 1879 an American newspaper reported, "At present, there are forty-two companies playing *Pinafore* about the country. Companies formed after 6 P.M. yesterday are not included."

Yet from this unprecedented American success, not one penny of profit came to Gilbert and Sullivan. In the absence of an international copyright law, any unscrupulous producer could "pirate" the words and music.

To overcome this situation, the famous partners came to the United States and staged an "Authorized Version." With Sir Arthur Sullivan conducting the orchestra, and William Gilbert directing the performance, the official *Pinafore* received an ovation from music lovers of old New York. . . .

First, let's contemplate why it was that many major American publishers opposed such foreign protection in the first place. To be sure, American publishers of unauthorized foreign works benefited under the old system, by which they could produce cheap foreign works without having to pay for them. But over the years, many American publishers had begun publishing the works of American authors, and wouldn't these publishers, just like the American authors, feel the unfairness of the foreign competition? Wouldn't they want a more level playing field for their editions of American works? Of course they would, and that is part of what explains the

The superiority of Sullivan.

Gerald Bordman notes that Sousa had also orchestrated *Pinafore* for an American audience, and even conducted one of its numerous companies. Later, however,

Sousa discovered Sullivan's orchestrations and instantly recognized their superiority. From then on, Sousa placed Sullivan and Offenbach side by side in his private pantheon, and they would provide his melodic and orchestral models when he was ready to embark on his great works.

Annexing the brain property of others.
Sullivan conducted the American premiere of *The Mikado* (though Gilbert was unable to attend), and made an unusual statement at the close of the performance, including the following:

> The talented ladies and gentlemen who form this company have worked with an enthusiasm and good-will impossible to praise too highly and difficult to acknowledge as we would wish. We should have been grieved indeed, had you received your first impressions of our opera from a spurious imitation . . . , in which the music from having been made up from a pianoforte arrangement must necessarily be mutilated and be a misrepresentation of the meaning of the composer. . . . It may be that some day the legislators of this magnificent country, which I have lately traversed from East to West, may see fit to afford the same protection to a man who employs his brains in literature and art that they do to one who invents a new beer tap or who accidentally gives an extra turn to a screw, doing away with the necessity of boring a hole first. In that day those unfortunate managers and publishers who, having no brains of their own, are content to live by—well, annexing the brain property of others, will be in an embarrassing and pitiable condition, and I for one will promise them my warmest sympathy. But even when that day comes, as I hope and believe it will come, we, the authors and creators, shall still, as we do now, trust mainly to the unerring instinct of the great public for what is good, right,

change in American sentiment from 1790, when there were hardly any American authors, to 1891, when there were many.

But the American publishers' fears went further. What they were really afraid of was that the foreign, primarily British, publishers, would "ride the coattails" of the foreign authors' rights. Once a British edition of a book had been printed, the British publishers would export that edition to the United States, and, under power of the newly granted rights, would extend the monopoly that the British publishers had obtained from their British authors. And since the net flow of works was still from England to the United States, the threat to the powerful American publishing interests was great.

The cleverness of the 1891 amendment was in the discovery of a compromise that granted the foreign *authors* the rights that they demanded, while still denying foreign *publishers* any rights. This result was achieved in the 1891 amendment by the so-called manufacturing clause. This clause simply provided that, as a condition of copyright protection, any foreign "book, photograph, chromo or lithograph" had to be "printed from type set within the limits of the United States." In addition, the foreign authors had to register their works and deposit copies in the United States on or before the date of publication anywhere in the world. Needless to say, it was the rare foreign author who was able to meet these rigid requirements.

As might be expected, there were plenty of objections to the new manufacturing clause, and, over the next several decades, Congress adopted several amendments liberalizing it. For example, instead of having to register and deposit copies immediately, works first published abroad were given a "grace period" before the authors would have to comply with U.S. formalities. And the law was amended to make the manufacturing clause apply only to works in the English language.

(Sales of foreign-language works were presumably not great enough in the United States to warrant a new printing, or to yield enough profits for the publishers to worry about.) But even after the amendments, the fundamental requirement remained: most works had to be printed in the United States. This was quite impracticable, particularly for time-sensitive works, such as periodicals and newspapers. The *Chicago Graphic*, for example, was able to publish weekly articles taken directly from British periodicals without any permission or compensation. And, of course, U.S. law still required the appropriate copyright notice and deposit, which seemed onerous to many foreign authors, since such requirements were eliminated in the Berne countries beginning in 1908.

Americans also discovered a neat ploy that came to be known as the "back door" to Berne. Under the provisions of the Berne Convention, if a work was first published simultaneously in a Berne country, it would be protected in all Berne countries, even if the author of the work came from a country that was not itself a member. So it quickly became standard publishing practice to first publish major American works simultaneously in the United States and in a Berne country—typically England or Canada. In this way, American authors got the privileges of Berne, yet the United States had none of the obligations.

This, of course, didn't fool many people. Canada, particularly sensitive at the possibility that it would be used as the back door to Berne, declared that it would not extend protection to works published simultaneously in Berne countries by authors from non-Berne countries. The members of the Berne Union then unanimously agreed to a protocol that allowed its members to refuse protection under such circumstances, if the author's own country did not grant adequate copyright protection to foreign authors. Although many foreigners

and honest, and we shall still be deeply grateful, as I am to-night to you, ladies and gentlemen, for your cordial appreciation, your quick sympathy, and your generous recognition of our efforts to interest and entertain you.

The *New York Times* responded as follows:

The effect of Sir Arthur's remarks would have been happier had he confined himself to returning thanks for the public's reception of the work just performed, and to expressing his gratification that the "authorized version" of "The Mikado" had met with the success it merited. The first part of the address . . . was in the right vein, and was as graceful in form as it was becoming in spirit. Its second half was less felicitous, and, its tone, which recalled the cry of the proverbial fowl on its proverbial platform, and its setting, in which the hope was uttered that art works should have the same protection as newly invented "beer taps," together with an assumed indignation at the proceedings of other persons, the indignation finding relief in hasty substitutions of civil words for intended vigorous terms, wrought a rather unpleasant impression. Mr. W. S. Gilbert no doubt harbors the same opinions as his colaborer, but his literary judgment would have counseled him to defer their publication until a more suitable opportunity, and, above all, to avoid the inelegant comparisons resorted to by Sir Arthur. Perhaps, however, if Mr. Gilbert were let loose in the orchestra he would play greater havoc than Sir Arthur Sullivan on the rostrum.

Book-selling leviathans.

In 1868, Trollope, who had worked much of his life as an employee in the Post Office in England, visited the United States to negotiate a mail treaty. He also managed to obtain a commission from the British Foreign Office to lobby on behalf of an international copyright treaty between the United States and Great Britain. In his autobiography, he states his own optimism that the Americans might be persuaded to change their minds, and describes a discussion with Charles Dickens in which Dickens "strongly declared his conviction that nothing would induce an American to give up the power he possesses of pirating British literature." Trollope himself did not blame the American people generally, whom he conceded to be generous; rather, he placed the blame squarely upon "the book-selling leviathans, and . . . those politicians whom the leviathans are able to attach to their interests. . . . It is the large speculator who becomes powerful in the lobbies of the House, and understands how wise it may be to incur a great expenditure either in the creation of a great business, or in protecting that which he has created from competition."

Having utterly failed on the copyright front, how did Trollope do on the postal front? Trollope, in his autobiography, boasted of a victory of sorts—though with some irony:

> The treaty . . . was at last made,—the purport of which was, that everything possible should be done, at a heavy expenditure on the part of England, to expedite the mails from England to America, and that nothing should be done by America to expedite the mails from thence to us. . . . This was a state of things which may probably have appeared to American politicians to be exactly that which they should try to obtain.

grumbled about the back door to Berne, few countries had the audacity actually to refuse protection to American works simultaneously published in Berne countries. Barbara Ringer notes that the resentment against the American practice was "surprising only in its relative mildness."

The United States did declare that it would protect the rights of authors from certain countries under the 1891 act, and did later enter into bilateral agreements with several countries, and two multilateral "Pan American" agreements. But the American formalities, and the manufacturing clause, continued to limit the rights of most foreign authors under U.S. law.

1955–1988: COPYRIGHT "STRANGERS AT THE FEAST"

Although there were several efforts at reform, they seem to have been dwarfed during the first half of the twentieth century by two world wars and a world depression. After World War II, however, the United States, a victor on the battlefield, found itself also to be an exporter of copyrighted works, from books to music to movies. It was unseemly that we should remain isolated in the international copyright community.

But what to do? In the intervening sixty-five years, the Berne countries had actually developed the international regime in a direction that the United States was unwilling to follow. The Berne countries had extended the minimal term of international copyright to the life of the author plus fifty years; but the United States still only recognized copyright for a maximum of fifty-six years.* The Berne countries had dispensed with all formalities as a prerequisite to copyright protection; but the United States still required copyright notice and deposit,† and still retained the burdensome manufac-

*Duration of copyright, see p. 205.
†Notice and other formalities, see p. 208.

A memorial of American Authors.

THE undersigned American citizens who earn their living in whole or in part by their pen, and who are put at disadvantage in their own country by the publication of foreign books without payment to the author, so that American books are undersold in the American market, to the detriment of American literature, urge the passage by Congress of an International Copyright Law, which will protect the rights of authors, and will enable American writers to ask from foreign nations the justice we shall then no longer deny on our own part.

Louisa May Alcott

Edward Bellamy

S. L. Clemens (Mark Twain)

Joel Chandler Harris

Oliver Wendell Holmes.

Walt Whitman

Not one shilling.
Anthony Trollope, in his autobiography, explains his own plight.

> [T]he American readers are more numerous than the English, and taking them all through, are probably more wealthy. If I can get £1000 for a book here (exclusive of their market), I ought to be able to get as much there.
>
> I . . . received a copy of my own novel in the American form, and found that it was published for 7-1/2d. . . . Many thousand copies must have been sold. But from these the author received not one shilling.

Trollope recited a boast "on behalf of the American publishers, that though there is no international copyright, they deal so liberally with English authors as to make it unnecessary that the English author should be so protected." His response was to tell of his own experience with "a certain American publisher—he who usually reprinted my works." That publisher

> promised me that *if any other American publisher republished my work in America before he had done so,* he would not bring out a competing edition, though there would be no law to hinder him. I then entered into an agreement with another American publisher, stipulating to supply him with early sheets; and he stipulating to pay me a certain royalty on his sales, and to supply me with accounts half-yearly. I sent the sheets with energetic punctuality, and the work was brought out with equal energy and precision—by my old American publishers. The gentleman who made the promise had not broken his word. No other American edition had come out before his. I never got any account, and, of course, never received a dollar.

A memorial signed by American authors urging passage of an international copyright law. Only 6 of the 145 signatures in the original have been reproduced here.

Piracy was a sophisticated operation.

Piracy of foreign works was not simply a matter of sneaking a few illegitimate copies into the United States, but was a sophisticated operation on the scale of modern tape piracy. As Robert Spiller explained, speaking of the early 1800s:

> John Miller, a hack publisher of London, acted as agent for his most successful American counterpart, Mathew Carey in Philadelphia. It was his task to see that the sheets, or even the proofs if he could get them, of any potential British success were in Carey's hands by fast packet (about thirty days) almost before the bound volumes had appeared in the London bookshops and well before any of them could be imported. Carey paid Miller, not the British author or publisher, for this service. . . .
>
> When the sheets of a new book were received, they were at once divided among three or four typesetters who worked night and day in shifts and sometimes produced a reprint in twenty-four hours. Even one or two days' priority assured financial success. It is perhaps significant that when this traffic was at its height, about 1815, popular books of American authorship were virtually nonexistent. . . . It is also significant that almost all the prominent early American printers of books . . . were violently opposed to any form of international copyright.

turing clause. The Berne countries had added certain "moral rights" to the international regime, granting authors the right to claim authorship of their works and to prevent mutilation of their works, whether or not they had parted with the "economic" rights under copyright; but the United States didn't generally recognize such moral rights.* In our absence, the rules of the game had been tightened, and we simply no longer met the entry requirements.

So did we capitulate, and raise our standards to the international level of Berne? No way. Instead, we came up with an incredible scheme. After World War II, the United States was able to push through the so-called Universal Copyright Convention (UCC). Although negotiated under the auspices of the newly created United Nations Educational, Scientific, and Cultural Organization (UNESCO), the treaty was clearly designed with the United States in mind. After all, most of the rest of the world already belonged to Berne, and relations between Berne countries would continue to be governed by that agreement. The role of the UCC was to accommodate the United States, by setting a lower threshold of protection. The treaty was ratified in 1952, and went into effect in 1955.

The main feature of the Universal Copyright Convention was "national treatment," just like the Berne Convention. But the minimal period of protection was set at twenty-five years from date of first publication, which the United States met (since the first term of copyright in the United States was then twenty-eight years from publication). And there was no mention of "moral rights" that the United States might have trouble with. The major concession that the United States did have to make was in theoretically dispensing with copyright formalities. Even here, we seem to have achieved a limited victory, because the dispensing of formalities was conditioned upon the copyright owners' putting on their works the copyright symbol (©) and the name of the copyright owner and year of

*Moral rights, see p. 169.

first publication. That is, the formality of notice would be waived if there was a copyright notice! The more important effect of our concession was that the United States really did waive any requirement that foreign works be registered in the United States, and we really did dispense with the rigors of the manufacturing clause for UCC works. This was the carrot that got other countries to agree to the idea of a second international copyright system to parallel the one that was already in place for most of the world.

The Universal Copyright Convention remained the major international copyright treaty of the United States for thirty-three years. Under it, Americans were able to get authors all over the world to use the UCC copyright notice on their works, primarily in order to assure copyright protection in the United States.

1988:
MEMBERS OF THE CLUB

In the years after the major copyright law revision in 1976, the United States became more and more aware that it was a copyright exporting nation. The world read American books, listened to American music, watched American movies, and ran American computer programs. And as the technologies for electronically reproducing copyrighted works made it possible for users around the world to make unauthorized copies of U.S. works, we began lobbying around the world for other countries to tighten their copyright protection to regulate record, movie, and computer software piracy. The problem was that America had no real moral leverage in foreign countries. When we complained that their copyright laws were too lax, they just laughed and pointed out that we were the country whose copyright standards didn't even meet the international standards set by Berne. Our trade negotiators came back to the United States and reported that we really just had to do whatever we could to remedy the problem.

And then, in 1988, over a hundred years after the birth of Berne, we finally joined. Congress passed the Berne Implementation Act, and rati-

A proper compensation in money and fame.
One of the supporters in favor of recognizing international copyright was Joseph Henry, inventor of the telegraph (see p. 98). He felt his reputation suffered because of a lack of such protection. Here's how his argument went: because foreign textbooks were free for the printing, there was no financing to produce original textbooks by American authors.

You can readily see how this effects the science of the country, take for example my own case—it is true that I have done but little but that little I think you will say is more than any one else has done in this country in the way of original research yet I have scarcely any popular reputation. . . . the want of an international copy right prevents my furnishing for my class and the classes of other colleges a text book in which I might set fourth my own claims and thus receive a proper compensation in money and fame for my labours.

Salutary effects.

[B]y the end of 1892, nineteen thousand copyrights had been granted to foreign authors and composers. . . . Among salutary effects [of international protection] was the decrease in the reprinting of the trashiest English fiction, the publication of the good British works in reliable texts, and a general reduction in the price of standard foreign works. The most significant result for the author was that in 1894, for the first time, more American than foreign novels were published in the United States. That British titles continued to be well represented in our best-seller lists after 1891 is evidence that lack of copyright was not the only factor in Anglo-American competition in the nineteenth century; but the fact that American titles soon won and kept a majority of these lists shows how quickly our production of commercial literature was able to develop once fair conditions were established.

—William Charvat

I do wonder that the extension of copyright to British authors is said to have *reduced* the price of standard foreign works.

fied the international treaty that the United States had so long avoided. What did it require? The major concession was that the United States finally, reluctantly, did away with copyright formalities. The manufacturing clause had died in 1986; and in 1988, we agreed that copyright notice and registration would no longer be required for copyright protection.

Perhaps the most remarkable thing about the United States's finally dispensing with formalities and joining Berne was how quietly it was ultimately achieved. After all the struggles and compromises that led to the 1976 copyright revision, there was a lot of trade and press coverage describing the new law, and its effect in the library, educational, and other special communities. But after the 1988 act, there was hardly a whimper. One might have expected that there would be newspaper headlines, or at least trade journal articles, announcing that copyright notice was no longer required for copyright protection. But, aside from copyright law journals, hardly an article was to be found. It was almost as if there were a conspiracy to keep the news quiet, so that copyright owners would in fact continue to use "voluntary" copyright notice, and "voluntarily" register their works. Americans still liked public notice of copyright ownership, and a central registry of copyright owners, and they weren't about to go around suggesting that authors and publishers should change their habits.

Pushing to the Head of the Line

Just about as soon as we became members of the club, we started to realize that the club wasn't good enough. Sure, Berne required that member countries pass laws that granted protection to copyright owners. But just try suing under those laws! In many less litigious countries, the court systems were simply not receptive to the needs of copyright owners—or, in some countries, to any foreign plaintiffs; or, in some countries, to any

Sporadic attacks on American copyrights.
Some Dutch publishers launched their own little war on the American "back door to Berne." For example, they published Dutch translations of such major works as Marjorie Kinnan Rawlings's *The Yearling* and Margaret Mitchell's *Gone With the Wind*. At the trial, the publishers claimed that "the only way to compel the United States to accede to the Bern[e] Convention is to disregard, in the countries which have acceded to that Convention, the copyrights of the citizens of that country." At left is Ms. Mitchell, with dozens of translations of her book.

plaintiffs whatsoever. And if the court systems were not quick to enforce rights, then copyright piracy was bound to flourish.

So the United States, along with Japan and European copyright exporting countries, began to explore a new paradigm of protection known as "trade-based" protection. The international regime known as the General Agreement on Tariffs and Trade (GATT) already existed. Under that regime, GATT countries were supposed to maintain free trade with member countries, and not impose unauthorized tariffs or other barriers. More importantly, GATT had an elaborate enforcement mechanism. If France, for example, set up unauthorized barriers to the impor-

U.S. discrimination against U.S. authors.
Ironically, after endorsing the Universal Copyright Convention, the U.S. copyright law actually discriminated against American authors. While foreigners were excused from complying with the manufacturing clause, U.S. authors were not, so they couldn't take advantage of cheap labor costs to publish their English-language works abroad. There was a major effort to eliminate the now hobbled manufacturing clause in the 1976 major copyright revision, but in 1976 it was extended through 1984. In 1984, President Ronald Reagan vetoed an attempt to extend the manufacturing clause through 1986, but the veto was overridden by Congress. In 1986, the manufacturing clause finally died, and American authors were allowed to print their works abroad, just as foreign authors could under the Universal Copyright Convention.

tation of American products, then the United States could bring an action in an international forum, and obtain the right to set up retaliatory barriers to certain French goods coming into the United States. The problem with GATT was that it dealt only with "goods," tangible products. But patents and copyrights were intangible rights, outside the scope of GATT. So if France discriminated against American copyrights in music or movies, there was no remedy under the existing GATT. Wouldn't it be great if the United States could retaliate by putting a tariff on, for example, French wine?

In 1994, the United States and other copyright exporting countries were successful in getting GATT members to accept the TRIPS agreement, expanding GATT to include the Trade Related Aspects of Intellectual Property Rights. (As part of the change in thinking, the international system was renamed the World Trade Organization, or WTO.) What this provided was that intellectual property rights—patents, copyrights, and trademarks—would be brought into the international trade regime; if France failed to adequately enforce the copyrights of authors from the United States, then the United States would have a remedy in the international forum. In addition, the minimal level of protection provided by Berne, which the United States had only recently met, was raised, primarily in those areas in which American law was already more expansive. For example, the TRIPS agreement required that member countries protect computer programs* under their copyright laws, something that the United States had long done and long lobbied foreign countries to do. Also, the TRIPS agreement required that member countries give adequate protection against the commercial rental of phonorecords† and computer programs,‡ protection that had already been provided by amendments to the U.S. law. The TRIPS agreement even went beyond American law in providing that the rental of movies should also be protected*—although there was an escape clause that would arguably allow countries such as the United States not to change their law with respect to movies. Protection for the rental of movies was not required "unless such rental has led to widespread copying of such works

*Computer programs, see p. 81.
†Record and CD rentals, see p. 47.
‡Computer software rentals, see p. 92.
*Video rentals, see p. 69.

which is materially impairing the exclusive right of reproduction," a test that would be hard to prove.

In 1998, the United States was instrumental in promoting two treaties adopted by the World Intellectual Property Organization (WIPO). These treaties, among other things, created a whole new level of protection for digital works. Member countries are obligated to pass laws making it illegal to circumvent electronically protected digital works, or to alter copyright maintenance information embedded in digital works. These treaties then led the United States to pass the comprehensive Digital Millennium Copyright Act.*

International Law Pushing the Domestic Agenda

In the dozen years it has been a member of Berne, the United States has been at the forefront in shaping the international copyright agenda. But the influence has been anything but one-way; in important respects, it is the international concerns that have defined the domestic agenda. For example, it was the carrot of Berne that got the United States first to extend the duration of protection to the life of the author plus fifty years,† and then finally to drop the copyright formalities of notice and registration.‡ Berne also expressly provides that member countries should recognize copyright in architectural works and certain moral rights of attribution and integrity. Although Congress in 1988 had insisted that U.S. laws were protective enough in these contexts, and required no amendments to bring them into compliance with Berne, such a position was dubious. Two years later, in 1990, Congress felt compelled to pay more than lip service to these treaty obligations, by specifically adding architectural works* to those protected by copyright, and by adopting at least a limited moral right for authors of visual works.**

As part of the price for getting the TRIPS agreement creating the World Trade Organization, the United States agreed to do something that

Can we join Berne yet?

Between the 1950s and the 1970s, American copyright underwent the most prolonged revision process in its history. After over twenty years of study and negotiation, the 1976 Copyright Act represented a thoroughgoing overhaul of the entire copyright system. One of its major changes was the adoption of a term of copyright—life of the author plus fifty years—that finally brought the United States into line with the Berne standard. The manufacturing clause was slated for retirement in 1984 (though it was not ultimately retired until 1986). That left only a few hurdles to our joining Berne—primarily the recognition of moral rights, and the dispensing of the notice requirement.

As a young copyright professor in 1977, I attended a meeting of copyright professors and lawyers to discuss the new copyright revision. At one session, I asked one of the speakers if we could perhaps finish the final steps so that we could join Berne. The speaker noted my relative youth, and suggested that I could not possibly have been part of the twenty-year revision process, or I would understand how impossible that was. My recollection is that just about everyone in the room turned around to see who this naive young professor could be. I was humbled and embarrassed at the time, but I do take some comfort in the fact that only a dozen years later, we did the unthinkable, and changed our law to allow us to join Berne.

*Digital Millennium Copyright Act, see p. 112.
†Duration of copyright, see p. 205.
‡Formalities, see p. 208.
*Architectural works, see p. 147.
**Moral rights, see p. 169.

Still encouraging copyright formalities.

The United States still liked the idea of copyright registration, since it provided a public record of copyright owners, making it easier for copyright users to find and clear rights. So we left a bit of an incentive. If a copyright owner, foreign or domestic, does not register a copyrighted work, then the remedies available to the owner will be affected: without registration, the copyright owner cannot recover either attorneys' fees or statutory damages (see p. 175). But even without registration, the copyright owner can still recover actual damages suffered, or actual profits gained by the infringer, and can still get an injunction in proper circumstances. So, my advice is, use the copyright notice (it costs nothing), and register the work (it costs only $30, compared to the loss of statutory damages and attorneys' fees). But if you don't, you at least don't lose your copyright.

it had never before done. Under TRIPS, the United States had to restore the copyright in foreign works that had gone into the public domain because of a prior failure to meet American formalities. This massive restoration of foreign public domain works would never have come about except that it was deemed necessary in the international context: we wanted to get retroactive protection of works—especially sound recordings and computer programs—that hadn't qualified for protection under the prior law in some foreign countries, and we could only get retroactive treatment if we were willing to grant retroactive treatment.

The United States also, for the first time, had to extend copyright protection to cover "live" musical performances. (Prior to that time, federal copyright protection only covered creative works that had been "fixed in a tangible medium of expression" by the copyright owner.) Under the TRIPS enabling legislation in 1994, it became illegal to make or sell "bootleg" sound recordings or music videos of live musical performances.*

In some contexts, it's hard to tell whether it's the domestic agenda driving the international agenda, or the other way around. In the case of the Digital Millennium Copyright Act,† the initial push came from the administration's White Paper. When the proposals from the White Paper foundered in Congress, the matter was diverted to the international WIPO arena, passed there, and then brought back to Congress as part of the international treaty. As a result of the internationalization of copyright, it would seem that the domestic and international agendas have merged considerably.

IT'S A TWO-WAY STREET

I may have created the impression that American copyright has until recently been churlish in comparison with that of the rest of the world. However, there are ways in which the United States has been more hospitable to creativity than its European counterparts.

*Bootleg music performances, see p. 170.
†Digital Millennium Copyright Act, see p. 112.

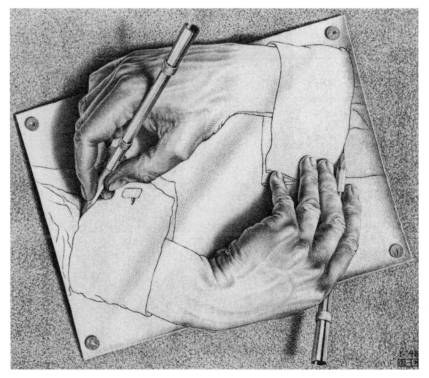

Drawing Hands.
Foreign copyrights have been "restored" since the international amendments became effective in 1996. Notice of many of the restored works has been printed in the *Federal Register,* the publication of federal rules and regulations. In one early case, a court upheld the copyright in many of the works of M. C. Escher, of which prints had been published without the requisite notice. Even if the court was wrong on that issue (which it probably was), the court held that the copyrights were saved because they were restored under the new federal provisions. Left, Escher's *Drawing Hands,* in which copyright was restored.

It has long been perceived that there are two different "cultures" of copyright. One, deriving from the civil law of France and most of the rest of Europe, emphasizes the "moral right," or natural right, of authors; the other, deriving from the common law of England and the United States, emphasizes the economic arguments for copyright. The latter, American approach sometimes reduces copyright from a "natural" or "property" right to a right derived entirely from statute. Copyright is characterized as a "monopoly," to be tolerated only so far as necessary to encourage authors to create their works.

But in some ways, the American approach has been more protective of authors, particularly where the new technologies are concerned. The "natural rights" approach, for example, does not work well for technologically produced copies of works—from photographs to sound recordings to computer programs. Under American law, once these works were accepted under copyright, the full range of protection was made available for them. But under the civil law approach, such mechanical reproduc-

The purpose of copyright.

In another context, I have commented upon the purpose of copyright in this country:

> Many protectionists have tried to justify copyright law as based upon (1) natural rights or (2) moral rights or (3) property rights. Critics have tried to limit this approach by (1) gleefully citing the embarrassing early history of copyright law in England, which was intended as much to regulate publication as to promote it; (2) emphasizing the "social utility" theory of copyright, by which the only or main justification for allowing what is basically a "monopoly" is the ultimate good that is achieved for society by an increase in the number, maybe even the quality, of works destined for the public domain; and (3) in recent years, subjecting copyright protection to a strict economic analysis that would limit any benefit to the copyright owner that was not clearly justified by a concomitant increase in the public good (read "public domain"). These arguments might be bolstered by (4) an explicit or implicit reference to principles, even constitutional standards, from outside the copyright clause, particularly the first amendment's guarantee of free speech.

–Edward Samuels

tions were protected more narrowly—with photographs receiving protection for a much more limited period, typically ten years, or sound recordings being relegated to a lesser range of protection under the rubric of "neighboring rights." It was the American law that led the international push to bring computer programs within the scope of copyright protection generally.

With the internationalization of copyright under Berne, TRIPS, and the other treaties, most of the countries of the world seem to be converging in their copyright doctrine. Whatever differences there may have been in the theoretical underpinnings of their domestic law have become pretty much irrelevant. Indeed, I would argue that our accession to Berne and the later treaties marks an acceptance of a broader natural rights justification for American copyright than Congress or the courts were previously willing to articulate. The law we have now embraced can only be explained by an expansive understanding of the role of copyright in society.

CONCLUSION

With the transnational technologies of radio, television, and the Internet, copyright has become a truly international challenge. Not surprisingly, the expansion of copyright that has typified American law is evident pretty much around the world. Even countries that have balked at property rights generally, such as the Soviet Union in the 1970s, ultimately came to embrace copyright principles. And even China, still hesitant and suspicious about adopting capitalism generally, has joined the Berne international copyright community and lobbied for admission to the World Trade Organization. Copyright will continue to be important in the international legal community for as long as we still want to encourage the making of creative works. I hope that will be forever.

Creativity Wants to Be Paid

Are we finished yet? I doubt it. But we should take a breather here at the beginning of the new millennium to absorb all that has happened in recent years.

In presenting this history of copyright, I've tried to avoid playing the role of the "copyright goon" or the "copyright police." I'm not going to tell you that you can't copy the works of others (though I would appreciate it if you don't make unauthorized copies of this particular book). However, you've probably already figured out that my general sympathy is with copyright owners and the protection of their rights, and I hope you've come away with some appreciation of the remarkable role that copyright has played in promoting creativity and the arts.

There's a saying on the Internet that "Information wants to be free." I doubt that information really cares what happens to it, but if by the saying we mean that *we* want information to be free, then that may be true most of the time. That's even true under copyright, which provides that facts* are not the proper subject of copyright protection. However, creativity is a different matter. Under the principles of copyright, *we* want creative works to be compensated; that's how we pay the creators for creating their works. So, I assert, "Creativity wants to be paid."

When I first became interested in copyright over twenty-five years ago, I felt that the scales were tipped too heavily against copyright owners. Violating rights was just too easy, and enforcing rights was just too costly and time-consuming in most cases. My sense is that the copyright owners have been pretty vocal, have come to understand and appreciate their rights, and have been successful in getting support from the administra-

*Facts, see p. 161.

More on the purpose of copyright.

American copyright law has suffered for two hundred years from the absence of a clearly articulated theoretical basis. Some might see this as some sort of oversight or conspiracy. I don't think so. I think that Congress and the courts have thereby maintained flexibility in the development of the law.

Physicists for years debated the nature of light, whether it was made up of waves or particles. Finally, it came to be understood that light did not neatly fit into either theoretical framework, but that it evinced certain properties that could only be described by wave theory, and certain properties that could only be described by particle theory. It was neither, and it was both. Just so, the different theories represent different ways of looking at copyright law that can be used to explain different aspects of it, but none of which is adequate to explain the whole, and none of which trumps the others.

Although others may of course disagree, I think I detect a shift from a more regulatory framework to a more natural rights framework. Congress has in fact been aggressive in expanding copyright law throughout the past two hundred years. While the early English or American laws might have been described as a minimal, maybe even begrudging, recognition of statutory rights, the early justifications could hardly explain the broad scope of copyright today. Current law protects sound recordings and computer programs, grants performance rights and rights to make derivative works, and even incorporates some modest moral rights protec-

tion, legislature, and the courts, in this country and around the world. It's possible that the scales have tipped the other way, and that it's the copyright owners who now have the upper hand. If in fifteen years the copyright owners again come asking for an extension of their copyrights before they expire, or another technological fix to secure their rights, I doubt I'll be convinced that they need it. But preserve what we've got? Absolutely. Educate the public to understand and appreciate what a remarkable system we have? Of course.

Back in 1997 when I was starting to write this book, the President's Committee on the Arts and Humanities issued a report, entitled *Creative America.* The committee was charged with "articulating the fundamental and intrinsic values of the arts and the humanities," and describing the "cultural sector" and its contributions to American life. The report summarized "what we know about trends in private funding and earned income that contribute most of the financial support" for cultural institutions, as well as "the role of the federal government in the arts and the humanities." It also contained recommendations for "strengthening support for the arts and the humanities in the United States."

The report quoted from Benjamin Barber, who wrote an essay commissioned by the committee in which he maintained that "The arts and humanities are civil society's driving engine, the key to its creativity, its diversity, its imagination and hence its spontaneousness and liberty." The report concluded that "A society that supports the arts and the humanities is not engaging in philanthropic activity so much as it is assuring the conditions of its own flourishing." The recommendations to promote the arts and humanities in the United States included "launching the millennium initiative," a four-year project to encourage the arts and humanities in five ways: by "educating our youth for the future," "investing in cultural capital," "renewing American philanthropy," "affirming the public role," and "expanding international cultural relations."

As I read the report, I was struck by the fact that it never once mentioned the specific system for promoting the arts that was set up by the framers of the Constitution and the first Congress—the copyright system. My student research assistant at the time, Roy Evans, suggested a title for my book in its early drafts: "Copyright: The Silent Patron of the Arts." Although the book has gone in a different direction from that early suggestion, I believe that Roy pretty much got it right. Copyright does more to support the arts and humanities than all of the federal grants, subsidies, and private philanthropies put together, and on a much more egalitarian basis. We support the arts and humanities when we pay for the entertainment and information media we desire. And the law supports the arts when it sets up a system to assure that at least a portion of what we pay goes to the people and companies that create the works.

tion. The formalities that were for so long at the heart of American copyright law have been virtually abandoned. American law, since the Berne Convention Implementation Act, is as protective as almost any of the European laws that is said to have a moral rights basis. It should therefore now be possible to ascribe to American copyright law the broad theoretical basis that until recent years may have been premature.

–Edward Samuels

I'm not sure that I'd still call the American trend "less regulatory," given the Digital Millennium Copyright Act, which is highly technical and "regulatory" (see p. 112). Nevertheless, the rights set forth in that act are in addition to traditional rights of copyright, and the other recent expansions of copyright are not consistent with a begrudging view of the purpose of copyright.

So, this book is my contribution to the Millennium Initiative. I hope it helps to make copyright a little less silent as a patron of the arts.

Notes and Sources

There are many hundreds of sources for much of the information in this book. The ones I list here are either the ones I considered best, or, more often, the ones I serendipitously found, or found useful.

For quickly locating cases and other information, I usually use law school casebooks. My major sources are Ralph Brown and Robert Denicola, *Copyright* (7th ed., 1998); Robert Gorman and Jane Ginsberg, *Copyright: Cases and Materials* (5th ed., 1999); Melville Nimmer, Paul Marcus, David Myers, and David Nimmer, *Cases and Materials on Copyright* (5th ed., 1998); and Craig Joyce, William Patry, Marshall Leaffer, and Peter Jaszi, *Copyright Law* (4th ed., 1998). There are numerous treatises and outlines for law professionals and students who want to learn more about copyright. I recommend Paul Goldstein, *Copyright: Principles, Law and Practice* (2d ed., 1996, with updates). Any Internet research should start with the Copyright Office Web site, www.loc.gov/copyright, or the Copyright Society of the U.S.A., www.csusa.org.

Citations to court cases list the volume number first, then the abbreviation for the official volume where the case appears, then the page number. U.S. identifies the Supreme Court reporter; Fed. or F.2d or F.3d contains generally federal circuit court opinions; and F. Supp. contains federal district court opinions. *U.S.P.Q.* is the *United States Patent Quarterly*. The parenthetical details following the case identify the court and the year of decision. It is customary in district court cases to list the plaintiff first; but in appellate court cases, the appealing party, not necessarily the plaintiff, usually is listed first.

The current Copyright Act is codified in 17 U.S.C. (that is, title 17 of the United States Code). Textual references to the "Act" with a capital "A" refer to the current statute. The most recent complete overhaul was Public Law 94-553, 90 Stat. 2541 (that is, vol. 90, p. 2541 of the Statutes at Large). Passed in 1976 (with some provisions first effective Jan. 1, 1978), it has been much amended since then. References to the House Report are to the comprehensive H.R. Rep. No. 94-1476, 94th Cong., 2d Sess. (1976); references to the Conference Report are to H.R. Rep. No. 94-1733, 94th Cong., 2d Sess. (1976).

Citations to law review articles list the volume number before the name or abbreviation of the law review.

Introduction

For the phrase "The Machine in the Parlor," I am indebted to Leo Marx for his book, *The Machine in the Garden: Technology and the Pastoral Ideal in America* (1967, republished 1999). Marx identifies a major historical trend at the turn from the eighteenth to the nineteenth century. The pastoral world of Thoreau gave way to the world of technology, epitomized by the graphic image of a train intruding upon the quiet in Thoreau's garden. Increasingly throughout the twentieth century, the technology has not been mechanical but digital; and it has represented an intrusion into our "parlors" every bit as vivid as the intrusion upon Thoreau's garden.

Part One
Chapter 1

The Printing Press. An excellent source of information on the early production of books is Michael Olmert, *The Smithsonian Book of Books* (1992). For the history of books, their early effect on the law, and especially the history of the Stationers' Company, see Philip Wittenberg, *The Protection of Literary Property* (1978), and Bruce Bugbee, *Genesis of American Patent and Copyright Law* (1967). The Boorstin quote about the age of authorship is from Daniel J. Boorstin, *The Discoverers: A History of Man's Search to Know His World and Himself* (1983), pp. 492–93. The quote from Carl Sagan is from *Cosmos* (1980), p. 281.

The Statute of Anne. Daniel J. Boorstin, in *The Creators: A History of Heroes of the Imagination* (1992), cites many examples of authors who received specific grants of monopoly prior to the development of copyright, including Cervantes. Boorstin, who has served as senior historian of the Smithsonian Institution, director of the National Museum of History and Technology, and Librarian of Congress, is generally sensitive to the copyright issues and the social and business contexts in which creators do their work. Another major source that is sensitive to the copyright and business context is Robert E. Spiller, et al., eds., *Literary History of the United States*. I used the third revised edition (1963). Probably the most complete catalogue of plagiarism and other literary indiscretions through the ages is H. M. Paull's *Literary Ethics* (1928). Paull documents hundreds of cases of pirated works, from copies of Shakespeare (who was himself "a notorious pirate," consistent with the pre-copyright law and ethics of his day) to copies of Voltaire, Dickens, and Wordsworth. The misattribution of a 1909 draft of the English copyright act (pp. 16–17) is described in Harry Ransom, *The First Copyright Statute: An Essay on an Act for the Encouragement of Learning, 1710* (1956).

The U.S. Constitution, 1787. The copyright section of the Constitution is Article 1, section 8, clause 8. The text of the state statutes under the Articles of Confederation (p. 18) is from Library of Congress, Copyright Office Bulletin No. 3, *Copyright Enactments of the United States, 1783–1906* (1906). (Thanks to Everett Frohlich, who gave me this book as part of a set when I first went into teaching years ago.) The quote from *The Federalist Papers* is from *The Federalist*, No. 43.

The First U.S. Copyright Law, 1790. The first U.S. copyright act was Act of May 31, 1790, 1 Stat. 124. The quotes from President Washington's speech and Congress's response are from Thorvald Solberg, Copyright Office Bulletin No. 8, *Copyright in Congress, 1789–1904* (1905, reprinted 1976), pp. 115–18. You can review Noah Webster's letters to many politicians of the day in *Letters of Noah Webster*, ed. Harry Warfel (1953). Information on the life of Webster is from Harlow Giles Unger, *Noah Webster: The Life and Times of an American Patriot* (1998).

The Photocopying Machine. A description of Chester Carlson's invention and development of the photocopying process can be found in John Diebold, *The Innovators: The Discoveries, Inventions, and Breakthroughs of Our Times* (1990), p. 88.

Library Photocopying. A detailed account of the Williams & Wilkins case, as well as many of the other major turning points of modern copyright law, is contained in Paul Goldstein, *Copyright's Highway: The Law and Lore of Copyright from Gutenberg to the Celestial Jukebox* (1994). The Williams & Wilkins case is *Williams & Wilkins Co. v. The United States*, 487 F.2d 1345 (Ct. Cl. 1973), aff'd by an equally divided court, 420 U.S. 376 (1975).

Scholarly and Classroom Educational Photocopying. The NYU case was settled, so there was no court decision. The case was *Addison-Wesley Publishing Co., Inc. v. New York University* (82 Civ. 8333, S.D.N.Y.). The settlement is reported in *New York Law Journal*, vol. 189 (1983), pp. 1, 3 and in Ben Weil and Barabara Friedman Polansky, eds., *Modern Copyright Fundamentals: Key Writings on Technological and Other Issues* (1989), p. 107.

Photocopying in the Commercial Setting. The photocopy cases are *Basic Books, Inc. v. Kinko's Graphics Corp.*, 758 F. Supp. 1522 (S.D.N.Y. 1991) and

Princeton University Press v. Michigan Document Services, Inc., 99 F.3d 1381 (6th Cir. 1966) (en banc). The quotes from the Texaco case are from the district court opinion in *American Geophysical Union v. Texaco, Inc.*, 802 F. Supp. 1 (S.D.N.Y. 1992). The case was affirmed on appeal, 60 F.3d 913 (2d Cir. 1995).

Chapter 2

General treatments that were invaluable on the inventions in the entertainment and information industries generally (sound recording, radio, movies, television, telegraph, telephone, and computers) are Steven Lubar, *InfoCulture: The Smithsonian Book of Information Age Inventions* (1993); National Geographic Society, *Inventors and Discoverers: Changing Our World* (1988); and Mitchell Wilson, *American Science and Invention: A Pictorial History* (1954).

The Music Business. There are many excellent books on the music business. My favorite is Sidney Shemel and M. William Krasilovsky, *This Business of Music,* issued in new editions every few years. On early American songs, see Lynn Wenzel and Carol J. Binkowski, *I Hear American Singing* (1989), and Vera Brodsky Lawrence, *Music for Patriots, Politicians, and Presidents* (1975). The quotes are from Richard French, "The Dilemma of the Music Publishing Industry," in Paul Henry Lang, ed., *One Hundred Years of Music in America* (1961), p. 173; Deems Taylor, Foreword, *A Treasury of Stephen Foster* (1946); and Neil Baldwin, *Edison: Inventing the Century* (1995), p. 98. The reference to Stephen Foster's music as "so essentially American" is from *World Book Encyclopedia* (1957).

Piano Rolls and Records. The White-Smith case is *White-Smith Pub'g Co. v. Apollo Co.,* 209 U.S. 1 (1908). The Francis Robinson quote is from his book *Caruso: His Life in Pictures* (1957), p. 99. The 1909 recodification of copyright, containing the first music compulsory license, was Public Law 60-349, 35 Stat. 1075; the relevant hearings were Hearings on S. 6330 and H.R. 19853, 59th Cong., 1st Sess. (1906), as reported in H. R. Rep. No. 2222, 60th Cong., 2d Sess. (1909). The compulsory license is continued in the present 1976 Act, primarily in 17 U.S.C. §115, *Scope of exclusive rights in nondramatic musical works: Compulsory license for making and distributing phonorecords.* The sound recordings pictured on pp. 37–39 are the *types* that might be covered by a compulsory license; I have no idea whether the producers of these works gave the appropriate notice or paid the appropriate fees. The PBS special *Rock and Roll* (pp. 40–41) was produced by WGBH (Boston) and the BBC (1995).

Radio and Performing Rights. Details about industry reactions to records and radio (as well as the quote "vocal bellowers and booming brass" from p. 33) are contained in Joseph and June Bundy Csida, *American Entertainment: A Unique History of Popular Show Business* (1978). That book reproduces articles, photographs, and advertisements from *Billboard,* one of the leading entertainment trade magazines. Another great retrospective is B. Eric Rhoads's *Blast* *from the Past: A Pictorial History of Radio's First 75 Years* (1996). The cases discussed in the text are *Herbert v. Shanley*, 242 U.S. 591 (1917) and *M. Witmark & Sons v. L. Bamberger & Co.*, 291 F. 776 (D.N.J. 1923). (ASCAP cannot sue in its own name, since it owns only nonexclusive rights in music. The nominal plaintiffs are therefore the copyright owners of particular songs that have been performed.)

Sound Recordings: The New Industry. Each amendment to the 1976 Copyright Act can be found as it is codified in title 17 of the United States Code. The major affected sections are 17 U.S.C. §114, *Scope of exclusive rights in sound recordings;* §109, *Limitations on exclusive rights: Effect of transfer of particular copy or phonorecord;* and 17 U.S.C., Chapter 10, *Digital Audio Recording Devices and Media.* The charts in this chapter are my own.

Why Can't I Make Copies from Copies of My CDs? The Rio case is *Recording Indus. Ass'n of Am. v. Diamond Multimedia Sys., Inc.*, 180 F. 3d 1072 (9th Cir., 1999).

Chapter 3

Motion Pictures. A good, all-around history of the movies is Richard Griffith and Arthur Mayer, *The Movies* (I used the 2d ed., 1970). Joel W. Finler's *The Hollywood Story* (1988) is an encyclopedic history of the business of movies.

Ben-Hur. The *Ben-Hur* case is *Kalem Co. v. Harper Bros.*, 222 U.S. 55 (1911), and the railroad scene case is *Daly v. Palmer*, 6 Fed. Cas. 1132 (C.C.S.D.N.Y. 1868) (No. 3552). The quotes from Iris Newsom, ed., *Wonderful Inventions: Motion Pictures, Broadcasting, and Recorded Sound at the Library of Congress* (1985), are at pp. 280 and 259. The quote from Charles Musser is from his book *Thomas A. Edison and His Kinetographic Motion Pictures* (1995), p. 35.

Television. There are many fine books on the history of television. I found particularly useful Irving Settel and William Laas, *A Pictorial History of Television* (1969); Jeff Greenfield, *Television: The First Fifty Years* (1977); Curtis Mitchell, *Cavalcade of Broadcasting: Radio and Television—And How They Grew* (1970); and the textbook by Sydney W. Head, Christopher H. Sterling, and Lemuel B. Schofield, *Broadcasting in America* (7th ed., 1994). The reference to National Geographic Society, *We Americans* (1975), is to pp. 416–17.

Cable Television. For the early history of Paragould cable television, I'm indebted to Professor Willis Emmons's 1993 case study 9-794-030, *Paragould City Cable*, Harvard Business School (rev. 1996). The cable cases are *Fortnightly Corp. v. United Artists T.V., Inc.*, 392 U.S. 390 (1968) and *Teleprompter Corp. v. Columbia Broadcasting Sys.*, 415 U.S. 394 (1974). The cable compulsory license is contained in 17 U.S.C. §111.

The Videocassette Market. The Betamax line of cases is *Sony Corp. of America v. Universal City Studios, Inc.*, reported at 480 F. Supp. 429 (C.D.Cal. 1979), 659 F.2d 963 (9th Cir. 1981), and 464 U.S. 417 (1984). The quote from

Steven Lubar is from his book, *InfoCulture: The Smithsonian Book of Information Age Inventions* (1993); and quotes from James Lardner are from his fascinating book *Fast Forward: Hollywood, The Japanese, and the VCR Wars* copyright ©1987 by James Lardner. Used by permission of W. W. Norton & Company, Inc., at pp. 204 and 302–3.

Chapter 4

The Workings of the Computer. The description of computers is from my own general knowledge, acquired over the years by using computers and by reading computer magazines, most particularly *Rainbow* magazine (a now defunct magazine devoted to the now defunct Radio Shack Color Computer) and *Macworld,* with occasional references to *PC Magazine, Byte,* and *Wired.* The diagrams on the function of the computer and the look inside the computer's memory are by Anita Costello, based upon my rough sketches.

How Do We Protect the Investment? The first Supreme Court computer patent case was *Gottschalk v. Benson,* 409 U.S. 63 (1972). The CONTU report was the *Final Report of the National Commission on New Technological Uses of Copyrighted Works* (1978). The Office of Technology Assessment quote (p. 85) is from its report *Intellectual Property Rights in an Age of Electronics and Information* (1986).

The Computer Copyright Cases. The quote is from Les Freed, *The History of Computers* (1995), p. 99. The cases are *Apple Computer, Inc. v. Franklin Computer Corp.,* 714 F.2d 1240 (3rd Cir. 1983); *Apple Computer, Inc. v. Microsoft Corp.,* one portion of which is reported at 779 F. Supp. 133 (N.D. Cal. 1991); and *Computer Associates International, Inc. v. Altai, Inc.,* 982 F.2d 693 (2d Cir. 1992).

The Computer Copyright Amendments. The archival/adaptive amendment of 1980 is codified at 17 U.S.C. §117; the Semiconductor Chip Protection Act of 1984 added 17 U.S.C., chapter 9; and the Computer Software Rental Amendment of 1990 amended 17 U.S.C. §109.

Chapter 5

The Telegraph and the Telephone. The information and quotes about Joseph Henry are from Albert E. Moyer, *Joseph Henry: The Rise of an American Scientist* (1997), pp. 212–13. The Isaac Asimov quote is from *Asimov's Biographical Encyclopedia of Science and Technology* (1964), p. 244. Asimov puts Morse in his place by listing him in a subsidiary entry (211a) under the primary entry for Henry (211). Shortly after feeling smug for seeing the link between the telegraph and the Internet, I discovered Tom Standage, *The Victorian Internet* (1998), which documents the connection in great detail. The Mark Twain quote is from Charles Neider, ed., *The Autobiography of Mark Twain* (1959, Perennial Library, 1975), p. 254.

Internet—The Technology. Particularly helpful are Tim Berners-Lee, *Weaving the Web: The Original Design and Ultimate Destiny of the World Wide Web by Its Inventor* (1999); SmartComputing's *The Computing Dictionary: The Illustrated Book of Terms and Technologies* (3d ed., 1998) (the quotes are from pp. 23 and 52); and Preston Gralla's *How the Internet Works* (4th ed., 1998).

How Do We Protect the Investment? The *Wired* quote is from the March 1994 issue. The quotes from the white paper are from the *Report of the Working Group on Intellectual Property Rights*, pp. 10–11, 17, 122, 183 (n. 507), 212. There are different versions of the Edward R. Murrow quote (p. 113); this one is from Curtis Mitchell, *Cavalcade of Broadcasting* (1970), p. 254.

The Digital Millennium Copyright Act. The 1998 Act rewrote many of the sections of the Copyright Act. Most significantly, it changed 17 U.S.C. §114, and it added a new chapter 12. I'm not sure that the Digimarc in the sample photo will survive multiple scannings. If it does, you should be able to scan the image of the dog and open it in a recent version of Photoshop, which will detect the watermark (choose Filter: Digimarc: Read Watermark). If not, first try applying the blur filter (Filter: Blur: Blur).

Part Two
Chapter 6

Originality. The cases are *Sheldon v. Metro-Goldwyn Pictures Corp.*, 81 F.2d 49 (2d Cir. 1936) (Judge Learned Hand); *Bleistein v. Donaldson Lithographing Co.*, 188 U.S. 239 (1903) (Justice Oliver Wendell Holmes); *Feist Publications, Inc. v. Rural Telephone Service Co.*, 499 U.S. 340 (1991) (Justice Sandra Day O'Connor on telephone books). The quote from Benjamin Kaplan is from his book, *An Unhurried View of Copyright* (1967).

What Kinds of Works Are Protected? For the most part, the works protected by copyright are listed in 17 U.S.C. §102, as supplemented by the definitions in §101.

Maps and Charts, 1790. The quote by Charles Goodrum is from his book, *Treasures of the Library of Congress* (1980), pp. 22–23.

Prints, 1802. The description of Morse's *The Gallery of the Louvre* is from *19th Century America: Paintings and Sculpture, An Exhibition in Celebration of the Hundredth Anniversary of The Metropolitan Museum of Art* (1970) (text accompanying plate 30). The cases are *Alfred Bell & Co. v. Catalda Fine Arts, Inc.*, 191 F.2d 99 (2d Cir. 1951) and *Bridgeman Art, Inc. v. Corel, Inc.*, 36 F. Supp. 2d 191 (S.D.N.Y. 1999). Carol Wax's book is *The Mezzotint: History and Technique* (1990).

Photographs, 1865. The principal case is *Burrow-Giles Lithographic Co. v. Sarony*, 111 U.S. 53 (1884). The information about Mathew Brady is from Roy Meredith, *The World of Mathew Brady: Portraits of the Civil War Period* (1970). The Ansel Adams quote is from Ansel Adams, *An Autobiography* (Little, Brown & Co., 1985; 1996 ed.), p. 60.

Drama, 1870. The quote from John Anderson is from his book *The American Theatre* (1938), pp. 49–50. The quote from Alexander Cowie is from his entry in Robert Spiller, et al., *Literary History of the United States* (3d ed.), p. 191. The description of the dramatization of *Uncle Tom's Cabin* is from Joseph and June Bundy Csida, *American Entertainment: A Unique History of Popular Show Business* (1978), p. 22.

Paintings, Drawings, and Sculpture, 1870. The cases are *Bleistein v. Donaldson Lithographing Co.,* 188 U.S. 239 (1903) (circus poster); *Alva Studios, Inc. v. Winninger,* 177 F. Supp. 265 (S.D.N.Y. 1959) (Rodin's *Hand of God*); and *L. Batlin & Son v. Snyder,* 536 F.2d 486 (2d Cir., *en banc* 1976) (Uncle Sam bank).

Movies, 1912. The Zapruder case is *Time, Inc. v. Bernard Geis Associates,* 293 F. Supp. 130 (S.D.N.Y. 1968).

Architecture, 1990. The architecture case is *Demetriades v. Kaufmann,* 680 F. Supp. 658 (S.D.N.Y. 1988).

Boat Hull Designs, 1998. The Supreme Court case is *Bonito Boats, Inc. v. Thunder Craft Boats, Inc.,* 489 U.S. 141 (1989). The boat hull provisions are incorporated in 17 U.S.C., chapter 13.

Characters. The major cases are *Warner Bros., Inc. v. Columbia Broadcasting System,* 216 F.2d 945 (9th Cir. 1954) (*Maltese Falcon*); *King Features Syndicates v. Fleischer,* 299 F.2d 533 (2d Cir. 1924) (Spark Plug); *Detective Comics, Inc. v. Bruns Publishing, Inc.,* 111 F.2d 432 (2d Cir. 1940) (Superman); *Atari v. North American Philips Consumer Electronics Corp.,* 672 F.2d 607 (7th Cir. 1982) (PAC-MAN); *Burroughs v. Metro-Goldwyn-Mayer, Inc.,* 519 F. Supp. 388 (S.D.N.Y. 1981), *aff'd on other grounds,* 683 F.2d 610 (2d Cir. 1982) (Tarzan); *Filmvideo Releasing Corp. v. Hastings,* 668 F.2d 91 (2d Cir. 1981) (Hopalong Cassidy).

Chapter 7

Substantial Similarity. The Steven Spielberg cases are *Litchfield v. Spielberg,* 736 F.2d 1352 (9th Cir. 1984); *Zambito v. Paramount Pictures Corp.,* 613 F. Supp. 1107 (E.D.N.Y.), *aff'd,* 788 F.2d 2 (2d Cir. 1985); *Williams v. Crichton,* 84 F.3d 581 (2d Cir. 1996); and *Chase-Riboud v. DreamWorks, Inc.,* 987 F. Supp. 1222 (C.D. Cal. 1997). Schrader's unsuccessful appeal to the Writers Guild is recounted in Douglas Brode, *The Films of Steven Spielberg* (1995), p. 64.

The Story Lines of Books, Plays, and Motion Pictures. The Learned Hand cases are *Nichols v. Universal Pictures Corp.,* 45 F.2d 119 (2d Cir. 1930) (*Abie's Irish Rose*); *Sheldon v. Metro-Goldwyn Pictures Corp.,* 81 F.2d 49 (2d Cir., 1936) (*Letty Lynton*); and *Peter Pan Fabrics, Inc. v. Martin Weiner Corp.,* 274 F.2d 487 (2d Cir. 1960). The quotes from Brooks Atkinson are from his book *Broadway* (1970), pp. 249 and 75–76. The Ford memoirs case is *Harper & Row Publishers, Inc. v. Nation Enterprises,* 471 U.S. 539 (1985).

Visual Works. The cases are *Peter Pan Fabrics, Inc. v. Martin Weiner Corp.,* 274 F.2d 487 (2d Cir. 1960); *Steinberg v. Columbia Pictures Industries,* 663 F. Supp.

706 (S.D.N.Y. 1987); *Sid & Marty Krofft Television Productions, Inc. v. McDonald's Corp.,* 562 F.2d 1157 (9th cir.1977).

Photographs. The Ansel Adams quote is from *An Autobiography* (Little, Brown & Co., 1985; paperback ed., 1996), p. 305. The cases are *Kisch v. Ammirati & Puris, Inc.,* 657 F. Supp. 380 (S.D.N.Y. 1987) and *Alt v. Morello,* 227 U.S.P.Q. 49 (S.D.N.Y. 1985).

Music. An exhaustive treatment of the subject is Alfred Shafter, *Musical Copyright* (1932; 2d. ed., 1939). The book was written when the effects of radio were just being felt. What Shafter says about the difficulty of predicting how copyright and the music industry would adapt to radio in many ways parallels what current authors say about the Internet. The cases are *Bright Tunes Music Corp. v. Harrisongs Music, Ltd.,* 420 F. Supp. 177 (S.D.N.Y. 1976) ("My Sweet Lord"); *ABKCO Music, Inc. v. Harrisongs Music, Ltd.,* 722 F.2d 988 (2d Cir. 1983) (remedies stage of the "My Sweet Lord" case); and *Fred Fisher, Inc. v. Dillingham,* 298 Fed. 145 (S.D.N.Y. 1924) ("Kalua"). The quote by Robert Palmer (p. 166) is from his book *Rock & Roll: an unruly history* (1995), p. 75.

Access. The Bee Gees case is *Selle v. Gibb,* 741 F.2d 896 (7th Cir. 1984).

What Are the Exclusive Rights of Copyright? The exclusive rights are enumerated primarily in 17 U.S.C. §106. The limited "moral rights" are covered in §106A; the exclusive rights in live musical performances in §1101; and the rights in technological protection measures and copyright management information in 17 U.S.C., chapter 12. The quote from Clinton Heylin (p. 171) is from *Bootleg: The Secret History of the Other Recording Industry* (1994), pp. 205–6.

Remedies. For the most part, the remedies are provided in 17 U.S.C., chapter 5. The discussion of and quote from the Sheldon case are from the remedies portion of the case, *Sheldon v. Metro-Goldwyn Pictures Corp.,* 309 U.S. 390 (1940). The remedies portion of the Fogerty case is *Fogerty v. Fantasy, Inc.,* 510 U.S. 517 (1994).

Chapter 8

Nonprofit Musical Performances. Many of the nonprofit exceptions to the public performance right, including the new exemption for certain radio musical performances in restaurants and small businesses, are contained in 17 U.S.C. §110. The organ music case was *M. Witmark & Sons v. Pastime Amusement Co.,* 298 F. 2d 479 (E.D.S.C.), *aff'd,* 2 F.2d 1020 (4th Cir. 1924). The movie soundtrack case was *Alden-Rochelle Inc. v. ASCAP,* 80 F. Supp. 888 (S.D.N.Y. 1948). ASCAP's attempt to license camps is described in Bumiller, *ASCAP Asks Royalties from Girl Scouts, and Regrets It, New York Times,* Dec. 17, 1996, p. B1.

Compulsory Licenses. The various compulsory licenses are codified in 17 U.S.C. §115 (phonorecord compulsory license); §111 (cable); §118 (noncommercial broadcasting); §119 (satellite systems); §§1003–7 (digital audio recordings); and §114 (digital audio transmissions). The jukebox compulsory license used to be 17 U.S.C. §116, but it has been replaced by a new provision §116 that provides for negotiated licenses.

Works of Utility. The definition of a pictorial, graphic, or sculptural work is from 17 U.S.C. §101. The provision that pictures of works of utility don't extend protection to the making of such works is cryptically provided in 17 U.S.C. §113, which states that the new law does not change the old law in this respect.

The Fact-Expression Distinction. The quote from the Feist case is from *Feist Publications, Inc. v. Rural Telephone Service Co.,* 499 U.S. 340 (1991). The European Directive was issued by the European Parliament and the Council of the European Union as Directive 96/9/EC, O.J.E.C. No. L 777/20 (23.3.96).

The Idea-Expression Distinction. The cited section is 17 U.S.C. §102(b). The cases are *Nichols v. Universal Pictures Corp.,* 45 F.2d 119 (2d Cir. 1930) (*Abie's Irish Rose*); *Hoehling v. Universal City Studios, Inc.,* 618 F.2d 972 (2d Cir. 1980) (Hindenburg); and *Nash v. CBS,* 899 F.2d 1537 (7th Cir. 1990) (John Dillinger).

Fair Use. The fair use section is 17 U.S.C. §107.

Parody. The parody cases are *Columbia Pictures Corp. v. National Broadcasting Co.,* 137 F. Supp. 348 (S.D. Cal. 1955) (Sid Caesar); *Berlin v. E.C. Publications, Inc.,* 329 F.2d 541 (2d Cir. 1964) (*MAD* Magazine lyrics); *Elsmere Music, Inc. v. National Broadcasting Co.,* 482 F. Supp. 741 (S.D.N.Y. 1980) (*Saturday Night Live*); *Leibovitz v. Paramount Pictures Corp.,* 137 F.3d 109 (2d Cir. 1998) (*Naked Gun 33-1/3*); *Benny v. Loew's Inc.,* 239 F.2d 532 (9th Cir. 1956) (Jack Benny); *Walt Disney Productions v. Air Pirates,* 581 F.2d 751 (9th Cir. 1978); *Rogers v. Koons,* 960 F.2d 301 (2d Cir. 1992) (puppies); *Dr. Seuss Enters., LP v. Penguin Books USA, Inc.,* 109 F.3d 1394 (9th Cir. 1997); *Campbell v. Acuff-Rose Music, Inc.,* 510 U.S. 569 (1994) ("Pretty Woman"). I thank my daughter, Claire, for noting the similarity of the *Air Pirates* images to particular Disney frames. THE LAST TIME I SAW PARIS, words and music by Jerome Kern and Oscar Hammerstein II © Copyright 1944 Universal Polygram International Publishing, Inc., a division of Universal Studios, Inc. (ASCAP). Copyright renewed. International copyright secured. All rights reserved. *MAD* is a trademark of E.C. Publications, Inc., © 2000. All rights reserved. Lyrics used with permission. The quote from Harvey Kurtzman is contained in Maria Reidelbach, *Completely MAD* (1991), p. 29.

Compromise on Public Policy Grounds. The cases are *Sony Corp. of America v. Universal City Studios, Inc.* 464 U.S. 417 (1984) (Betamax); *Sega Enterprises Ltd. v. Accolade, Inc.,* 977 F.2d 1510 (9th Cir. 1992) (Sega Genesis); *Time, Inc. v. Bernard Geis Associates,* 293 F. Supp. 130 (S.D.N.Y. 1968) (Zapruder film); and *Harper & Row Publishers, Inc. v. Nation Enterprises,* 471 U.S. 539 (1985) (Ford memoirs). The Sobel quote is from Lionel Sobel, *Copyright and the First Amendment: A Gathering Storm?,* 19 Copyright Law Symposium 43, 78 (1971).

Chapter 9

How Long Does Copyright Last? The Mark Twain quote is from Neider, ed., *The Autobiography of Mark Twain*, pp. 304, 306. The Sonny Bono Term Extension Act extended the terms set in 17 U.S.C. §§302–4; and the Fairness in Music Licensing Act amended the provisions of 17 U.S.C. §110(5).

 The Library of Congress. The quotes from Charles Goodrum are from Charles A. Goodrum, *Treasures of the Library of Congress* (1980), pp. 21, 25–26, and 78.

 The Medium Is Not the Message! The quote from the Act is 17 U.S.C. §202.

 The Work-for-Hire Doctrine. The doctrine is set out in the statute in 17 U.S.C. §201(b), and in the definition of "work made for hire" in §101. The Third World America case is *Community for Creative Non-Violence v. Reid*, 490 U.S. 730 (1989).

 Government Works. Jefferson's instructions to Lewis are from *First Trust Co. of Saint Paul v. Minnesota Historical Society*, 116 U.S.P.Q. 191 (D.Minn. 1956). The Eleventh Amendment cases (p. 216) are *Seminole Tribe of Fla. v. Florida*, 517 U.S. 44 (1996) (Commerce Clause); *College Savings Bank v. Florida Prepaid Postsecondary Educ. Expense Bd.*, 527 U.S. 666 (1999) (Lanham Act); and *Florida Prepaid Postsecondary Educ. Expense Bd. v. College Savings Bank*, 527 U.S. 627 (1999) (Patent Act).

 Give Me Back My Copyright! The major renewal case is *Fred Fisher Music Co. v. M. Witmark & Sons*, 318 U.S. 643 (1943), holding that an author who lives to the renewal term is bound by an assignment that purports to cover that term. The cases cited in the sidebars are Oona Chaplin's settlement (never requiring a lawsuit); *Saroyan v. William Saroyan Foundation*, 675 F. Supp. 843 (S.D.N.Y. 1987), *aff'd*, 862 F.2d 304 (2d Cir. 1988); and *Stewart v. Abend*, 495 U.S. 207 (1990) (*Rear Window*). The general termination provision is 17 U.S.C. §203; the special termination rights for the extension periods of existing copyrights are set forth in §304(c).

 Patents. The Patent Act is 35 U.S.C. The novelty and nonobvious standards are set forth in 35 U.S.C. §102 and §103; the special design patent provisions are §171–73.

 Trademarks. The federal trademark law is the Lanham Act, 15 U.S.C. Groucho's letter is excerpted with permission from the publisher, Bernard Geis Associates, from *Groucho and Me* by Groucho Marx. © 1959 by Groucho Marx. Andrew Carroll's remarks are from Andrew Carroll, ed., *Letters of a Nation: A Collection of Extraordinary American Letters* (1997), p. 253. The McSleep case is *Quality Inns International, Inc. v. McDonald's Corp.*, 695 F. Supp. 198 (D. Md. 1988).

 Unfair Competition. The cases are *Gilliam v. American Broadcasting Cos.*, 538 F.2d 14 (2d Cir. 1976) (Monty Python); and *Romm Art Creations, Ltd. v. Simcha Int'l, Inc.*, 786 F. Supp. 1126 (E.D.N.Y. 1992) (Tarkay paintings).

 Contracts. The case (p. 226) is *Buchwald v. Paramount Pictures Corp.*, 13 U.S.P.Q.2d 1497 (Cal. Super. 1990). The follow-up information on the settlement can be found in Abelson, "The Shell Game of Hollywood 'Net Profits,'" *New York Times,* March 4, 1996, D1.

Defamation, Right of Privacy, and Right of Publicity. The cases are *Zacchini v. Scripps-Howard Broadcasting Co.,* 433 U.S. 562 (1977) (human cannonball); *Factors Etc., Inc. v. Pro Arts, Inc.,* 579 F.2d 215 (2d Cir. 1978) (Elvis poster); *Apple Corps. Ltd. v. Leber,* 229 U.S.P.Q. 1015 (Cal. Super. 1986) (*Beatlemania*); *Midler v. Ford Motor Co.,* 849 F.2d 460 (9th Cir. 1988); *Sinatra v. Goodyear Tire & Rubber Co.,* 435 F.2d 711 (9th Cir. 1970) (Nancy Sinatra).

Federal Preemption of State Laws. The companion Supreme Court cases are *Sears, Roebuck & Co. v. Stiffel Co.,* 376 U.S. 225 (1964) and *Compco Corp. v. Day-Brite Lighting, Inc.,* 376 U.S. 234 (1964). The DeCosta case was bounced all up and down the federal courts over a period of almost twenty years. The primary appellate opinions are *DeCosta v. Columbia Broadcasting System, Inc.,* 520 F.2d 499 (1st Cir. 1975) and *DeCosta v. Viacom International, Inc.,* 981 F.2d 602 (1st Cir. 1992).

Chapter 10

1790–1891: Copyright Outlaws. The quotes are as follows: Barbara Ringer, *The Role of the United States in International Copyright—Past, Present, and Future,* 56 Georgetown L.J. 1050, 1051 (1968); Alexis de Tocqueville, *Democracy in America,* Part II, Book One, chap. 19 (1835; 1840); *Address of the British Authors,* presented to the Senate by Henry Clay, Feb. 2, 1837, S. Rep. No. 134, 24th Cong., 2d Sess.; James J. Barnes, *Authors, Publishers and Politicians: The Quest for an Anglo-American Copyright Agreement 1815–1854* (1974), p. 53; Boorstin, *The Creators,* p. 371; Charles Dickens, reported in Hamish Sandison, *The Berne Convention and the Universal Copyright Convention: The American Experience,* 11 Columbia–V.L.A.J. Law & Arts 89 (1986); Spiller, et al., eds., *Literary History of the United States,* pp. 125–26, 129–30, and 523 (Charvat quote (p. 234)); Max Kempelman, *The United States and International Copyright,* 41 *American Journal of International Law* 413(947); and Joseph Henry, quoted in Alfred E. Mayer, *Joseph Henry: the Rise of an American Scientist* (1997), p. 238.

For Gilbert and Sullivan materials, the *Iolanthe* case is at 15 F. 439 (Cir. Ct., D. Md. 1883); the *Mikado* case is *Carte v. Duff,* 25 F. 183 (Cir. Ct., S.D.N.Y. 1885). Carte was more successful in Massachusetts, *Carte v. Evans,* 27 F. 861 (Cir. Ct., D. Mass. 1886). The Gerald Bordman quote is from his book, *American Operetta: From H.M.S. Pinafore to Sweeney Todd* (1981), pp. 60–61. The Sullivan quote in response to the *Mikado* case is from Jane W. Stedman, *W. S. Gilbert, A Classic Victorian and His Theatre* (1996), p. 234. The Sullivan speech and response are from the *New York Times,* Sept. 25, 1885, p. 5.

The Trollope quotes (pp. 238–39) are from Anthony Trollope, *An Autobiography* (1950, World's Classics, 1980), pp. 308, 309, 311, and 313. The signatures in *A Memorial of American Authors* (p. 239) are digitally cut and pasted from R. R. Bowker and Thorvald Solberg, *Copyright—Its Law and Literature* (1886, repr. 1986).

1891–1955: Copyright Outsiders. The quote from William Charvat (p. 242) is from his entry in Spiller, et al., eds., *Literary History of the United States,* p. 962.

It's a Two-Way Street! My quotes (pp. 248, 250) are from *The Public Domain in Copyright Law,* 41 *Journal of the Copyright Society* 137, 177–82 (1993).

Afterword

The earliest reference I've found to the saying "Information wants to be free" is by Stewart Brand in his book, *The Media Lab: Inventing the Future at MIT* (1987, Viking paperback edition), p. 202. He, at least, didn't intend it as a manifesto; his next sentence was, "Information also wants to be expensive." He describes the tension between the cheapness of reproducing information and its frequently immeasurable value to the recipient, leading to "endless wrenching debate about price, copyright, 'intellectual property,' and the moral rights of casual distribution."

The President's Committee on the Arts and Humanities report, *Creative America,* is available on-line at http://arts.endow.gov/pub/PCAH/First.html.

Photo Credits and Acknowledgments

The downside of copyright is that it's quite an undertaking to track down and get all the permissions that are required. It's cost me about twice my advance just to acquire the photos and pay for the permissions to use them. (Now I know why no one has ever written a book like this.) There are some people who suggested that I was getting a little fanatical about permissions, and that it would have been a lot cheaper, and not that much of a risk, to just use what I wanted under a fair use argument. Since the book is about copyright, however, I've tried to play by the rules.

Another downside is that I just wasn't able to get permission for some photos, no matter how much I was willing to pay. For example, I would have loved to have more examples of "characters" whose works are protected, but the owners of some of the most successful characters simply wouldn't license the rights. I respect that, since one right of copyright is the right to say no; but it does mean my book is not as illustrated as I would have liked.

Many of the older works are in the public domain, so no permission was required. In a few instances, I've used works even when I was unable to track down the copyright owners after several attempts. And in a few instances, particularly in the case of defendants who

Try being polite.

Just politely try asking to use a character in a book, and see what it sometimes gets you. (The following is a response to one of my requests; the emphasis is in the original.)

Thank you for submitting your proposal requesting the rights to license the above referenced property for use in conjunction with your project. While we greatly appreciate your interest in our properties, due to a variety of business and legal considerations, **we do not license the above mentioned for the purposes stated in your letter under any circumstances.**

Please be advised that all material contained in and relating to the above-referenced property is copyrighted and we control all rights. Therefore, under no circumstances are you to use any materials of any characters from the films, the titles, or make any reference to the property for any purpose whatsoever.

Warnings sometimes have to be bold in order to have any effect, but surely I'm at least allowed to refer to a character in my book, even without the permission of the copyright owner.

were found to have infringed, I've either not asked for permission, or used the defendants' works without permission, under the fair use doctrine.

For the most part, however, the authors and other copyright owners were a very cooperative lot, and I thank all of them for helping to make this a more interesting and informative book.

In a few instances, after scanning in images, I've touched them up using Adobe Photoshop. For example, I cleaned up the image of the kinetoscope parlor, even though it previously has been published with a large blotch in the lower left corner. And I've taken out some imperfections in the images of Lew Wallace, Harriet Beecher Stowe, and the cover of the sheet music to *After the Ball*. In all such cases, I consider that my efforts restored the works to their previous condition, rather than altering the intentions of the original creators.

Photo credits are to pages. Where there is more than one picture on a page, the abbreviations are as follows: T=top; B=bottom; L=left; R=right; M=middle (either horizontally or vertically).

Introduction: Thomas Jefferson Never Saw Anything like This

4L *Music at Uplawn,* 1880s, photo by Leonard Dakin, New York State Historical Association, Cooperstown, N.Y.

4R CORBIS/Bettmann-Gendreau

5L Ed Clark/*Life* magazine © Time, Inc.

5R, 6 © Edward Samuels

Chapter 1: Books and Other Literary Works

10TL Jan van der Straet's Nova reperta, Smithsonian Institution Libraries, Smithsonian Institution

10TR, 10B © Bettmann/CORBIS

13 Reprinted from Harry Ransom, *The First Copyright Statute: An Essay on an Act for the Encouragement of Learning, 1710* (1956)

15 H. B. Hall & Sons engraving of a portrait by Samuel F. B. Morse, Yale Picture Collection, Manuscript and Archives, Yale University Library

17 Collection of the New-York Historical Society, negative 277

19T, 19B Courtesy Xerox Historical Archives

21 Courtesy National Institutes of Health

23L, 23R © Bion Smalley, reprinted by permission

Chapter 2: Music and Sound Recordings

32L Culver Pictures

32R Reprinted from Lynn Wenzel & Carol Binkowski, *I Hear America Singing* (1989)

33 Courtesy U.S. Dept. of the Interior, National Park Service, Edison National Historic Site

34T © Hulton-Deutsch Collection/CORBIS

34B Photo by Clarence Thorne

36T Courtesy of Sears, Roebuck and Co.

36B Photofest

37 © Diplomat Records

38T © Palace Records

38B © Damont Records Ltd.

39L © Eurovox Music, Rozenlaan 43, Schilde, Belgium

39M © Capitol Records, Inc.

39R © Audio Fidelity

41 Reprinted from National Geographic Society, *Those Inventive Americans* (1971)

42L, 42R Collection of the New-York Historical Society, negatives 73197 and 73198

42B Courtesy of Herbert Jacoby, photographer unknown

46L © Eastman Kodak Co., Industrial Laboratory, reproduced from C. P. Gilmore, *The Scanning Electron Microscope: World of the Infinitely Small* (1972), courtesy of Eastman Kodak Company. KODAK is a trademark.

46R "Stylus" illustration from *The Way Things Work,* by David Macauley. Compilation copyright © 1988 by Dorling Kindersley, Ltd. Illustration copyright © 1988 by David Macauley. Reprinted by permission of Houghton Mifflin Co. All rights reserved.

47T Illustration by Chris Costello from *Infoculture: The Smithsonian Book of Information Age Inventions,* by Steven Lubar. Copyright © 1993 by Houghton Mifflin Co. Reprinted by permission of Houghton Mifflin Co. All rights reserved.

47B Courtesy Mark of the Unicorn

Chapter 3: Movies and Television

56T Bettmann/CORBIS

56BL, 56BR Courtesy U.S. Dept. of the Interior, National Park Service, Edison National Historic Site

58 Culver Pictures

59T, 59B Billy Rose Theater Collection, The New York Public Library for the Performing Arts. Astor, Lenox, and Tilden Foundations.

60 Library of Congress, LC-USZ62-536

61 From *The World Book Encyclopedia* © 1957, by permission of World Book, Inc.

62T, 62B Photofest

67 Illustration by Chris Costello from *Infoculture: The Smithsonian Book of Information Age Inventions,* by Steven Lubar. Copyright © 1993 by Houghton Mifflin Co. Reprinted by permission of Houghton Mifflin Co. All rights reserved.

68 Reprinted with permission. Paul Conrad. Los Angeles Times Syndicate, 1981

73L, 73R © Roger Ressmeyer/CORBIS

Chapter 4: The Computer

74 Illustration by Anita Costello

75 Cover photo by Jon Brenneis, by permission from Scientific American, Inc.

78TL Culver Pictures, by permission of Philips Electronics N.A. Corporation

78TR PAC-MAN® © 1980, 1985 Namco Ltd. All rights reserved. Courtesy of Namco Holding Corp.

78BL, 78BR Copyright 2000 Nintendo. Images courtesy of Nintendo Corp. of America, Inc.

83T, 83B, 87T Photos courtesy of Apple Computer, Inc.

87B Reprinted with permission from Microsoft Corporation

90L, 90TR, 90BR Reprinted by permission of Intel Corporation. Copyright Intel Corporation 2000

90MR © Owen Franken/CORBIS

94T Illustration by Anita Costello

94BL © CMC Research

94BM By permission of DeLorme Mapping

94BR Reprinted with permission from Microsoft Corporation

96T Photograph has been altered using Kai's Power Goo software. This image belongs to Scansoft, Inc. www.scansoft.com

96M, 96B © Claire Samuels 2000, using Ray Dream Studio

Chapter 5: The Internet

97T Detail from *Men of Progress,* by Christian Schussele, National Portrait Gallery, Smithsonian Institution

99B Collection of the New-York Historical Society, negative 28545

100L National Museum of American History, Smithsonian Institution

100R Property of AT&T Archives. Reprinted with permission of AT&T

107 By permission of MIT

109L, 109R By permission of IBM, Ogilvy & Mather, Denis Leary, and Jeremy Blake Collins

113L, 113R Photo by Dave McFarland, reprinted by permission of *Macworld* magazine

118 © The New Yorker Collection 2000 Jack Ziegler from cartoonbank.com. All rights reserved.

121L © TotalNEWS

121R © Fox News Network, L.L.C.

Chapter 6: What Does Copyright Protect?

129 © 2000 Sesame Workshop. © 2000 Jim Henson Company

132L, 132R © New York City Transit Authority, used with permission of the Metropolitan Transportation Authority

133 Reprinted from *Samuel F. B. Morse,* by William Kloss, The Vincent Price Treasury of American Art

134 Reprinted from Rockwell Kent, *World Famous Paintings* (1939)

135L, 135R By permission Bridgeman Art Library

136 Reprinted from Roy Meredith, *The World of Mathew Brady: Portraits of the Civil War Period* (1970)

137 Photo by Napoleon Sarony, reprinted from New York Metropolitan Museum postcard, Gilman Paper Co. collection

139 Reprint courtesy of Eastman Kodak Company. KODAK is a trademark.

140L Culver Pictures

140R The Harvard Theatre Collection, The Houghton Library, Harvard University

141 Library of Congress, LC-USZ62-24541

142L, 142R Photos by Clarence Thorne, banks courtesy of Robert Faber

143L The Metropolitan Museum of Art, Gift of Edward D. Adams, 1908 (08.210). All rights reserved, The Metropolitan Museum of Art.

143M, 143R Photos by Clarence Thorne, courtesy National Archives and Records Administration, New York

145TL, 145TR Courtesy Dance Notation Bureau, from Muriel Topaz, *Elementary Labanotation: A Study Guide* (1966) (illustrations by Jessica Segall)

145BL *Eventide,* choreographed by Paul Taylor (1996–97), notated by Siân Ferguson (1996–97)

145BR © Johan Elbers, 1997 from *Eventide,* by Paul Taylor; Lisa Viola and Richard Chen See, dancers

146L, 146R Suzanne DeChillo/NYT Pictures

147 Culver Pictures. *The Maltese Falcon* © 1941 Turner Entertainment Co. A Time Warner Company. All rights reserved.

148TL, 148TR, 148ML Courtesy King Features Syndicate and National Archives and Records Administration, New York, photos by Clarence Thorne

148BL Superman is a trademark of DC Comics © 2000. All rights reserved. Used with permission.

148BR *Tarzan and His Mate* © 1934 Turner Entertainment Co. A Time Warner Company. All Rights Reserved.

149L By permission of U.S. Television Office, Inc.

149R By permission of Foxrock Books, Inc.

Chapter 7: What Rights Does Copyright Grant?

153L Culver Pictures. *The Cohens and the Kellys* copyright © 2000 Universal City Studios, Inc. Courtesy of Universal Studios Publishing Rights. All Rights Reserved.

153R Billy Rose Theater Collection, New York Public Library for the Performing Arts. Astor, Lenox, and Tilden Foundations.

154T Vandamm Studio, Billy Rose Theater Collection, the New York Public Library for the Performing Arts. Astor, Lenox, and Tilden Foundations.

154B Culver Pictures

156L, 156R By permission of Henry Glass & Co., photos by Clarence Thorne, courtesy National Archives and Records Administration, New York

157T Copyright © 1976 Estate of Saul Steinberg/Artists Rights Society (ARS), New York, with permission of The New Yorker Magazine, Inc.

158TL, 158TR By permission of Sid and Marty Krofft Productions

158BL, 158BR © McDonald's Corporation

160L © Edward Samuels 2000

160R Thanks to the Ansel Adams Publishing Rights Trust

161L © John Duke Kisch—Separate Cinema Archive

162T © Howard Alt

165 From Alex Brychta, *The Legend: The Illustrated Story of the Bee Gees* (1983) (illustration by David English), by permission

176L © Fantasy Records

176R © Warner Bros.

179 All © Business Software Alliance, by permission

Chapter 8: Copyright Limitations, Exclusions, and Compromises

181L Cuesheet to *King of Kings,* Paramount Pictures, reprinted from John Baxter, *Sixty Years of Hollywood* (1973)

181R Bettmann/CORBIS

182 By permission of Girl Scouts of the USA

185 Chair by Eero Saarinen, Knoll International, photo from Robert Bishop and Patricia Coblenz, *American Decorative Arts* (1982)

186 © Spiegel Publishing Company 1999 (year of first publication). Disney characters © Disney Enterprises, Inc., used by permission

187 Martha Holmes/Life Magazine © Time, Inc.

189 Photofest

190 © Bion Smalley, reprinted by permission

193L © 1992 Annie Leibovitz/Contact Press Images, courtesy of the artist

193M Courtesy of Paramount Pictures. *Naked Gun 33⅓* Copyright © 2000 by Paramount Pictures. All rights reserved.

193R Photographed by Carolyn Jones. Paintbox photo illustration by Phillip Hefferman, Copyright Spy Magazine, L.P.

194TL © Art Rogers/Pt. Reyes, by permission

194B "Odie" © Paws, Inc. All rights reserved.

195TL *The Cat in the Hat*™ & © Dr. Seuss Enterprises, L.P. 1957. All rights reserved. Used by permission.

195BL *Green Eggs and Ham*™ & © Dr. Seuss Enterprises, L.P. 1960. All rights reserved. Used by permission.

196TL Photofest. *From Here to Eternity* © 1953, renewed 1981 Columbia Pictures Industries, Inc. All rights reserved. Courtesy of Columbia Pictures.

196BL Photofest. "Your Show of Shows" courtesy of NBC Studios, Inc.

196TR Photofest. *Gaslight* © 1944 Turner Entertainment Co. A Time Warner Company. All rights reserved.

196BR Photofest. Used by permission of CBS Photo Archive.

198TR Disney Characters © Disney Enterprises, Inc., used by permission

198B *MAD* is a trademark of E.C. Publications, Inc. © 2000. All rights reserved. Used with permission.

199L, 199R Courtesy of Lil' Joe Records, Inc./Lil' Joe Wein Music (BMI)

203T © *Sixth Floor,* c/o Jamie Silverberg

Chapter 9: Other Major Copyright Principles

207 *Tom the Dancing Bug* © 1998 Ruben Bolling. Reprinted with permission of Universal Press Syndicate. All rights reserved.

208 Culver Pictures

210 © Michael Freeman, reprinted by permission

214 By permission of Community For Creative Non-Violence, photograph by Gayle Krughoff

217 *Rear Window* copyright © 2000 by Universal City Studios, Inc. Courtesy of Universal Studios Publishing Rights. All Rights Reserved.

220 © MGM/UA

226L By permission of Hugo Zacchini, the younger, son of Edmond

226M Photo by Bud Skinner, © 1977 Pro Arts, Inc., Medina, Ohio

227R Photograph © Bob Scott, by permission

228L, 228R AP/Wide World Photos

Chapter 10: International Copyright Relations

232 Reprinted from Barry Pritzker, *Mathew Brady* (1992)

235 By permission of Philips Electronics N.A. Corporation

239 Culver Pictures

243 Photofest

247 M.C. Escher's *Drawing Hands* © 2000 Cordon Art B.V.-Baarn—Holland. All rights reserved.

INDEX

LIBRARY
ST. LOUIS COMMUNITY COLLEGE
AT FLORISSANT VALLEY